GEORGE P. KNAUFF'S

Virginia Reels

AND THE HISTORY OF AMERICAN FIDDLING

American Made Music Series

Advisory Board

David Evans, General Editor
Barry Jean Ancelet
Edward A. Berlin
Joyce J. Bolden
Rob Bowman
Susan C. Cook
Curtis Ellison
William Ferris
John Edward Hasse
Kip Lornell
Bill Malone
Eddie S. Meadows
Manuel H. Peña
Wayne D. Shirley
Robert Walser

GEORGE P. KNAUFF'S

Virginia Reels

—— AND THE ——

HISTORY OF AMERICAN FIDDLING

CHRIS GOERTZEN

UNIVERSITY PRESS OF MISSISSIPPI ✦ JACKSON

www.upress.state.ms.us

Designed by Peter D. Halverson

The University Press of Mississippi is a member of the
Association of American University Presses.

Copyright © 2017 by University Press of Mississippi
All rights reserved

First printing 2017

∞

Library of Congress Cataloging-in-Publication Data

Names: Goertzen, Chris.
Title: George P. Knauff's Virginia reels and the history of American fiddling
/ Chris Goertzen.
Description: Jackson : University Press of Mississippi, [2017] | Series:
American made music series | Includes bibliographical references and
index. |
Identifiers: LCCN 2017016688 (print) | LCCN 2017018762 (ebook) | ISBN
9781496814289 (epub single) | ISBN 9781496814296 (epub institutional) |
ISBN 9781496814302 (pdf single) | ISBN 9781496814319 (pdf institutional)
| ISBN 9781496814272 (cloth : alk. paper)
Subjects: LCSH: Fiddle tunes—Virginia—19th century—History and criticism.
| Reels (Music)—Virginia—19th century—History and criticism. | Knauff,
George P.
Classification: LCC ML3551.7.V8 (ebook) | LCC ML3551.7.V8 G64 2017 (print) |
DDC 787.2/155409755—dc23
LC record available at https://lccn.loc.gov/2017016688

British Library Cataloging-in-Publication Data available

For
Alan Jabbour
AND
Paul F. Wells

Contents

LIST OF FIGURES

IX

PREFACE AND ACKNOWLEDGMENTS

XI

- CHAPTER ONE -

George P. Knauff and the Publishing of His *Virginia Reels*, the First Collection of Southern Fiddle Tunes

3

- CHAPTER TWO -

"Speed the Plough" and "Money Musk"
Knauff and the Dance Music Component of Early American Popular Music

28

- CHAPTER THREE -

"Peter Francisco" and "Richmond Blues"
The Titles of Knauff's Virginia Reels

55

- CHAPTER FOUR -

"Lady of the Lake" and "George Booker"
Knauff Digs More Deeply into Local Oral Tradition

78

- CHAPTER FIVE -
Knauff's "Ohio River" and "Indian Whoop"
The Rhythmic and Timbral Puzzles of Blackface Minstrelsy and of Modern Old-Time Fiddling
111

- EPILOGUE -
"Forked Deer," Multivalent Nostalgia, Sustainability, and the Edge Effect
145

- APPENDIX -
The Willig Edition of Knauff's *Virginia Reels*
175

NOTES
201

REFERENCES
207

INDEX
215

List of Figures

Figure 1. Drawing of the Buckingham Female Collegiate Institute, where Knauff worked in 1839.
Figure 2. Unattributed newspaper photograph of the collapse of the EACO Theatre on February 11, 1984.
Figure 3. The EACO Theatre was partially rebuilt as a small, pedestrian analogue of a drive-in movie theater.
Figure 4. Thistles photographed in Scotland.
Figure 5a. Title page of Knauff's own collection called *Gatherings*, with a label identifying it as having been sold at his short-lived store.
Figure 5b. Detail from the title page of an anonymous and undated sheet music item, "The Old Maid," with Knauff's later label.
Figure 6. "Speed the Plough."
Figure 7a. "Monny Musk. a Strathspey. by D[aniel] D[ow]."
Figure 7b. "Money Musk," versions from early nineteenth-century music commonplace books.
Figure 7c. "Money Musk," as printed many times in the nineteenth century by Elias Howe.
Figure 7d. "Money Musk," three modern performances.
Figure 8. Detail of *Natchez Under the Hill*, painted by Louis Joseph Bahin in 1852.
Figure 9. Knauff's "Old Virginia," to which is glued an anonymous poem expressing nostalgia for older Virginia. Copy on Deposit in the Special Collections Library of the University of Alabama.
Figure 10. Knauff's places: his homes and the locales in central Virginia referenced in the tune titles in his sheet music.
Figure 11. Scottish tune titles and Knauff's own titles for several of the *Virginia Reels*.

Figure 12.   Members of Knauff's *Virginia Reels* that were published repeatedly in other American collections.

Figure 13.   Tune title roundup: titles in the *Virginia Reels*, common titles at Galax and Clifftop in 2014, and possible parallels between these.

Figure 14.   "Crockett and His Fiddle," illustration by Michael Hague.

Figure 15a. Knauff's comic song from oral tradition: "Three Farmers Went a Hunting."

Figure 15b. Knauff's comic song from oral tradition: "Three Farmers Went a Hunting," concluded.

Figure 16.   Knauff's "Blue-Bonneted Scotts" and related tunes.

Figure 17.   Some musical characteristics of the individual *Virginia Reels*.

Figure 18.   "Lady of the Lake" and its descendant "Ducks on a Pond."

Figure 19a. From "Marquis of Huntley's Farewell" to Knauff's "George Booker."

Figure 19b. "George Booker" as played by Jake Krack during an interview at Galax in 2012.

Figure 19c. "George Booker" as played by Alita Stoneking Weisgerber, Hallettsville, 2015.

Figure 20.   Knauff's "Billy in the Low Grounds" and relatives.

Figure 21.   "The Flowers of Edinburgh": the first four measures of various versions.

Figure 22.   From "Largo's Fairy Dance" to "Mississippi Sawyer," high strain only.

Figure 23.   After the first publications of "Boatman Dance," boatmen were often depicted dancing. This picture is of the title page of "Song of the Negro Boatman," written by J. W. Dadman (1862).

Figure 24.   John Hill Hewitt, *The Crow Quadrilles* (1837), title page.

Figure 25a. Versions of the tune best known as "My Love She's But a Lassie Yet."

Figure 25b. "Too Young to Marry" in fiddle and banjo heterophony.

Figure 25c. "Darling Child," played in the Galax substyle of old-time style by Eddie Bond.

Figure 26a. Cover of *Ethiopian Quadrilles*, arr. A. Nagerj Onyqjva, 1843.

Figure 26b. "Boatman Dance," from the *Ethiopian Quadrilles*.

Figure 26c. Knauff's "Ohio River" and a modern performance of "Boatman."

Figure 27.   Titles in the *Virginia Reels* that may be depicted to some extent in the music.

Figure 28.   "Indian Whoop": beginnings of three strains by three fiddlers.

Figure 29.   A "Forked Deer," successfully hunted.

Figure 30a. "Forked Deer," simple versions.

Figure 30b. "Forked Deer," played in a West Virginia style by Bobby Taylor.

Figure 30c. "Forked Deer," played in Texas style by Wes Westmoreland III.

Preface and Acknowledgments

BOOKS AND COLLECTIONS OF MUSIC CAN BE LONG-LASTING FRIENDS. Back in my graduate student years (in the late 1970s–early 1980s), I got acquainted with one such companion, *Virginia Reels*, a four-pamphlet collection of a total of thirty-five American fiddle tunes as arranged by George P. Knauff for piano circa 1839. For my version of the arcane ritual of writing a dissertation, I had been tracing a path through the history of American fiddling by hunting down and studying as many examples as I could of a pair of fiddle tunes both of which are now named "Billy in the Low Ground." That title appeared in Knauff's *Virginia Reels*, a collection that turned out to be interesting for broader reasons: it was an intriguing array of southern fiddle tunes from an era when those were rare in print.

As a pleasurable sidelight to the main thrust of the dissertation research, I studied that collection carefully, visited Farmville, Virginia, which had been Knauff's home for many years, and pored through historical records there. Later during the same trip, I did some research in the Library of Congress. While there, I met one of my heroes, fiddler and fiddle scholar Alan Jabbour, who was then director of the American Folklife Center. It turned out that Alan had researched Knauff and the *Virginia Reels* back in the 1960s and had read a short paper on that topic at the 1967 meeting of the American Folklore Society. I had been retracing Jabbour's research paths unknowingly. We chatted about Knauff, and Jabbour suggested that we write an article together. Our historical research in Farmville had revealed exactly the same facts, suggesting that more would not be readily forthcoming from there! He knew far more than I about modern fiddling in the Upper South, and so could name modern cognates of many of the *Virginia Reels*. I had spent more time poring over microforms of newspapers from in and near Knauff's

Virginia. He gave me a copy of his early paper. I wrote a draft of an article, he diplomatically rescued the prose from my epidemic-level malapropisms, and we published "George P. Knauff's *Virginia Reels* and Fiddling in the Antebellum South" in *American Music* in 1987.

As I continued to study fiddle tunes, my closest collaborator became Paul F. Wells, the founder and for decades the director of the Center for Popular Music at Middle Tennessee State University, in Murfreesboro, Tennessee. He made the library at the center a wonderful place to research fiddling and has been a fine friend and co-cogitator for decades now. I can't count the times he located a performance of a tune for me or sent a CD or file my way. He helped immeasurably in these and other ways with this book, which is dedicated to him and to Alan.

How can 1987, when that article on the *Virginia Reels* came out, be so long in the past? Since then, I've learned more about fiddling and about the history of the American South through conventional research techniques, and the Internet has helped in its own quirky ways. Also, publishing that article stimulated some helpful reactions. In particular, Carolynn Knauff Waldon, a descendant of George Knauff, read the article, got in touch, and helped me learn more about Knauff's life.

After I published *Southern Fiddlers and Fiddle Contests* (2008), I wondered what fiddle project to work on next. That book had been largely about contemporary fiddling, and focused on fiddle contests. I wanted to write more about the history of American fiddling, especially about transformations of musical style, both in terms of how tunes have been typically shaped as melodies during different periods and of how they have been performed. Knauff's *Virginia Reels* beckoned again. Presenting this additional research allows me to correct a pair of misunderstandings marring the original article, to incorporate newly available information, and, especially, to plumb the *Virginia Reels* for a widened and more nuanced series of resonances with contemporary fiddling.[1]

Some readers will notice—and perhaps lament—the absence of intensive discipline-specific theorizing in this book. This omission is deliberate. I do, however, embrace another source of complexity by including a fair number of detailed music transcriptions and discussions of those. The *Virginia Reels* are music belonging primarily to oral tradition, but reduced to the printed page; in a general way, making transcriptions is continuing in the spirit of the collection. But that is not why the transcriptions are there. What musicians assert verbally and how they express themselves through what they play (and how they play it) don't always match, and their music offers testimony at least as heartfelt and revealing as their words. And there is a practical value to transcribing: it lets an analyst and later the reader slow the music down and home in on significant details.

I decided against creating a supplemental website or CD in order to honor the imprecise but important line between what about the sound of a traditional tune being played is proprietary and what is not. The fiddlers whose performances I transcribed are all fine players, most of them active, and in most cases gaining some income from their playing. Interested readers should consider seeking out their commercial recordings (and, for some of these fiddlers, lessons and other fiddle-related services). As of this writing, that quest can start with simple searches on YouTube and on amazon.com.

I owe much to many people and organizations for their help with this book. First is, as always, Valerie Goertzen, my wife and patient sounding board. She came to numerous fiddle events with me and was the primary invitee for two summer stays in the guest quarters of the Brahmshaus Baden-Baden, where I drafted much of this book. Again, my thanks to Alan Jabbour for help with the subject matter in the mid-1980s, and to Paul F. Wells for all kinds of help regularly since. Further thanks are due to fiddlers and fiddle scholars Steve Green and Harry Bolick, to old friend Laurel Zeiss, and to innumerable librarians. The University of Southern Mississippi awarded me several modest but indispensable travel grants financing visits to festivals and research collections. Special thanks also to Jonathan McCollum and David G. Hebert, who included my article "Southern American Fiddling through the Mid-Nineteenth Century: Three Snapshots" in their edited volume *Theory and Method in Historical Ethnomusicology* in 2014. Organizing that article helped me decide how to shape the present book. And last but far from least, I am grateful to the many fiddlers who were welcoming to this project and allowed me to record their playing.

GEORGE P. KNAUFF'S

Virginia Reels

AND THE HISTORY OF AMERICAN FIDDLING

Figure 1. Drawing of the Buckingham Female Collegiate Institute, where Knauff worked in 1839. This photograph reproduces the illustration (artist not credited) in the center of a tattered copy of the title page of a sheet music item from 1857 entitled "Buckingham Grand March," by Arnaud Préot, Knauff's successor at the institute. This piece of sheet music is in the library of Farmville, Virginia's Longwood University.

- CHAPTER ONE -

George P. Knauff and the Publishing of His *Virginia Reels*, the First Collection of Southern Fiddle Tunes

HOW CAN THE *VIRGINIA REELS* HELP US UNDERSTAND THE HISTORY and essential characteristics of southern fiddling? We can begin by simply referring to repertoire: the *Virginia Reels* is the first printed collection to contain lots of tunes and tune titles known to fiddlers in the American South today. But fiddling is much more than the bare bones of melodies. It's the totality of sound. And it's the people who are involved—performers and fans and mere toleraters—their societal position(s) and their attitudes (toward music, but also toward home and toward history). So, observing that many of the tunes (and titles) in the *Virginia Reels* survive in southern fiddling is just the first and easiest part of mining the value of this gathering of melodies. This book is an attempt to *start* with those enduring fiddle tunes as such, but then find out what else about the history and essential nature of southern fiddling is anticipated in this collection.

Before turning to the main business of this book, we must confront an important fact: The sheer existence of a published collection of antebellum southern American fiddle tunes is remarkable, just as surprising as it is gratifying. A necessary first step in putting the collection into context is to trace the life and work of George P. Knauff, the man who arranged these fiddle tunes for piano. It would have been wonderful to also be able to write about the fiddler or fiddlers from whom Mr. Knauff got the tunes, but that information remains out of reach. Knauff himself was a fascinating—indeed, endearing—individual, but he did not achieve the level of celebrity that leaves bold traces in the historical record. His most notable accomplishment, publishing the *Virginia Reels*, was a modest venture for him, one among many small sources of income. He was a musician and merchant trying to support his family. His combination of an original mind with a high-powered work ethic led him to publish this unusual and important tune collection.

From Germany to America

Knauff was probably born and raised in Germany. His descendant Carolyn Knauff Waldon located the record of a birth of a George Phillip Knauff in Marburg, Germany, on September 29, 1800, "the son of Johann Friedrich Knauff and Anna Martha Zecher. This couple also had a son named Johann Conrad Knauff, born May 26, 1803. There was a John C. Knauff in Richmond, Virginia, in the mid-1800s, who on the 1850 census was 47 years old, and therefore was born in 1803" (Waldon n.d., 1). The brothers probably arrived in the United States during the 1820s, likely disembarking in Baltimore circa 1826.[1] This was just before the bulk of nineteenth-century German immigration to the young United States. Nearly all immigrants to the United States during the first half of the nineteenth century came from Great Britain, Ireland, or German-speaking areas (Ferrie 1999, 35). The first massive wave of non-British European immigration would materialize during the two decades immediately before the Civil War; the arrival of the Knauffs just preceded that influx. Luebke's reading of appropriate census records has some 5,753 Germans arriving during 1820–1829 (some 14.5 percent of total immigration), then 124,726 coming in 1830–1839 (rising to 23.2 percent of the total) (1990, 95).

Most of these immigrants came from the southern or western portions of what is now Germany; Knauff's birthplace of Marburg lies in the west, about sixty miles north of Frankfurt. Why did so many of these Germans leave home? Shortly *after* this period, political and religious considerations would convince large numbers of Germans to emigrate. But at this time, it was instead a confluence of straightforward economic forces that inspired many enterprising young men to seek their fortunes elsewhere (Luebke 1990, 97). On the land, primogeniture left many second and subsequent sons without good prospects, and crop failures, while not as dramatic as in Ireland, were another significant factor. Cottage industries suffered from competition from rapidly industrializing England (Martin 2011, 87). It comes as no surprise that many German immigrants were single men (Ferrie 1999, 17), as were the Knauff brothers, and that this group of men was especially rich in farmers and in other skilled labor ranging from a flood of carpenters to a smaller but important trickle of musicians. As part of a general evaluation of striking contributions of Germans to American culture, Totten neatly summarized how Germans like Knauff were of broad importance to American musical activity over the centuries: "From the popular appeal of the blue-capped 'little German band' on the street corner to the most ambitious symphony orchestra, both lowbrow and highbrow tastes were satisfied" (1983, 20).

Why does it matter that Knauff came from Germany, and, since his parents did not emigrate, seems to have done so as an adult? German men were more likely to have formal musical educations than were their American contemporaries. If we assume that Knauff's training in music and initial acquaintance with tunes in oral tradition took place while he grew up in Germany, it becomes highly unlikely that he would have encountered the tunes that make up the *Virginia Reels* before coming to America. Also, he would not have been in as good a position to form concrete opinions concerning which types of music would be commercially viable in his new home as would American- or British-trained musicians. He must have been relatively open-minded about how to make a living from music—perhaps partly through originality, but certainly partly through ignorance.

Marriage and the Good Life in Farmville, Virginia

George P. Knauff married a planter's daughter, Ann S. C. Bondurant of Farmville, Prince Edward County, Virginia, on November 21, 1832. She was a decade younger than he. Although such a disparity in age was then quite common, it's moderately puzzling that this immigrant in his twenties came to travel in the same circles as the teenaged daughter of an affluent landowner; young women of her age and station were carefully shielded. In the most plausible scenario, they met when he gave her piano lessons, likely in the context of a "female seminary" (finishing school) in Richmond. The marriage was not rushed: Knauff bought a lot in downtown Farmville well beforehand (exact purchase date unknown) and hired a contractor to renovate an apparently dilapidated house already present on the lot. The contract, dated September 13, 1832, required one John P. Hawkins to do some brick underpinning, to erect three brick chimneys and to plaster the interior (*Prince Edward County Deed Book* 20, 597). There probably was already one chimney in place, and many typical good-sized rectangular houses in Farmville had four chimneys (see Burke 1998). This improvement brought the building in line with many of the better local houses and marked young George and Ann Knauff as belonging to the affluent class.

The marriage bond was executed by Knauff and Ann's father, James Bondurant (Waldon, 1). But did the bride's parents truly welcome this alliance? Her father was among the very wealthiest of Prince Edward County's planters. Many marriages involving members of the county's upper crust were announced in the *Richmond Enquirer* (then the principal newspaper serving this part of Virginia), but this ceremony was not. Perhaps the omission was accidental, but more possibly it indicates that the match was not a cause for celebration in the view of the bride's parents (his own parents were, of course, an ocean away). This would fit with my guess that Knauff had been Ann's teacher, since teaching was a profession at a relatively low social level at that time in the South. (In related speculation: if Knauff was employed in a female seminary in 1830 — perhaps meeting Ann there — and resided on the premises, that would account for an omission in the historical record, that is, his not being listed as a head of household in the 1830 census.)

Farmville was still a small town at the time Knauff and his bride took up residence. The land had long been rich in both vegetation and animal life. Indians had been living there for at least eight thousand years when colonists arrived. The Native American populations had included the Weyanoke, an Algonquian-speaking group belonging to the Powhatan confederacy (Bogen-Garrett et al. 1999, 7), plus several populations speaking languages in the Siouan language group: the Tutelo, Saponi, Catawba, and Manacan, who were enemies of the Powhatan tribes (Dwight 1935, 135). English who traveled up the Appomattox River colonized the area, supplemented with some Huguenots and more Scots-Irish, who are noted for having headed west swiftly as a group, but who left many members behind at each stage in their journey (Bradshaw 1935, 137). Prince Edward County was founded in 1753. By 1820, the county had some 12,000 citizens; Appomattox County would later be carved out of it (Bogen-Garrett et al., 1999, 8).

Farmville was laid out in 1798 and incorporated in 1832, shortly after Knauff had arrived. The town's location was quite desirable, in lovely, slightly hilly land near the inward extent of the navigable portion of the Appomattox River. Mapmakers of the day marked all waterways very boldly, much more conspicuously than is done today. That is because rivers and lakes and of course the ocean were much more important as transportation arteries then than now. Farmville's function as mercantile center for the surrounding rich agricultural area resulted from its being reachable by waterway from Petersburg (for these riverine connections, see fig. 10). A batteau—a flat-bottomed boat up to sixty feet long and just six feet wide, with a draft of no more than two feet when loaded (Ely 2004, 150), propelled by poling—could carry a dozen hogsheads of tobacco downstream, then deliver construction materials and domestic goods on its return trip.

By Knauff's day, Farmville had become the fourth-largest tobacco market in Virginia, although a town of only around eight hundred even by the mid-1830s (Ely 2004, 345). This crop could be shipped out by road to Richmond, but it was far cheaper to send it by batteau downriver to Petersburg, by one estimate, a third of the cost (Bogen-Garrett 1999, 11). It was about 70 miles by road to either city, and about 120 miles by boat to Petersburg, but the bateaux could carry much heavier loads than could any wheeled conveyance. True, there could be problems when moving merchandise by boat through "sandy shoals and rock-strewn rapids" (Bogen-Garrett 1999, 11), especially when dry spells slackened the flow of the river, leaving bateaux stranded for weeks. Nevertheless, the Appomattox remained the main freight route to and from Farmville until the railroad arrived decades later.

Knauff's home also housed his business on the main floor. This was the Farmville Fancy Store, through which he offered higher-end, *not* homemade domestic ("fancy") goods and musical merchandise to his largely rural clientele. By mid-1834 the focus of his advertising had shifted from domestic to musical goods, and he had acquired a business partner. His advertisements in the *Richmond Enquirer* tell a story of ever-evolving emphases in both merchandise and sales techniques. A detailed ad appeared in the *Enquirer* on May 24, 1834:

FARMVILLE MUSIC & FANCY STORE. George P. Knauff keeps constantly for sale, an assortment of superior Piano Fortes (with grand actions and metallic plates) from the celebrated manufactory of Messrs. Dubois & Stodart. The advantages of buying from me will be, that the buyer runs no risks of injury or loss, which often happen during the voyage from New York, or even from Richmond in this neighborhood; and they will be warranted and kept in tune for 12 months. Also, second-hand Pianos, at low prices, keyed and plain Flutes, Guitars, Violins, Clarionets, and other musical instruments, a large assortment of newest and standard MUSIC for the Piano, Guitar, Flute, &c. Instruction Books, best Roman strings, Mantlepiece Looking Glasses, Sofas, Settees, Rocking and Fancy Chairs of all kinds, &c., &c., &c., some of which are at and some below the Richmond price. Farmville, May 21.

Knauff supplemented his earnings at the store by teaching piano. We don't know when he turned to this source of added income, or how many students he taught. Fortuitously, receipts of lessons given to a Miss M. J. Jeter from September 15, 1835, through May 11, 1837, are included in the Jeter family papers, which are on deposit in the library of the Virginia Historical Society. We learn from this evidence that Knauff charged the going rate of seventy-five cents per lesson. These family papers make clear that the Jeter family was prominent in Amelia County. They sponsored small female "seminaries" (finishing schools) in their home on several occasions. Amelia County is due west of Farmville; the entire county was within Knauff's free delivery range for all merchandise he marketed (see below). His piano sales were coupled with offers to do regular tunings (initially included in the sales price), sell sheet music, and, of course, to give piano lessons.

Knauff was the first music merchant in his part of the country to advertise in the fulsome manner that would characterize nearly all advertising within a few years. His longest and most extravagant ad first appeared in the *Richmond Enquirer* of October 13, 1835, and was reprinted an average of three times a month for nine months:

TO THE LADIES AND GENTLEMEN.—Farmville Music and Fancy Store.—I have in store, am constantly receiving, and will be very glad to sell, the most splendid assortment of PIANOS; and all other kinds of musical instruments, strings, music, furniture, and many fancy substantives. As puffing is odious, I will merely state that my Pianos are more beautiful, their tone sweeter and more powerful, that they remain in tune longer, and are better built than all inferior ones; and lastly, that they can be learnt to play on in half the time as some other instruments; in short, they are as much superior to many sold at other places, as a church organ is to a jew's harp, with the tongue broke out. As to other musical instruments, furniture and fancy goods, they are far above any comparison. I will sell lower than any other person in the state—indeed, so low, that you will be astonished. All new Pianos, after sold, I will deliver gratis, any distance under 40 miles. I also warrant and keep them in tune 12 months. I hire out Pianos, repair old ones, and take them in exchange. I will sell Chairs lower than any other person, and be very polite, particularly to Ladies.

GEO.P. KNAUFF

Rural music merchants invariably sold nonmusical goods, too, such as the "fancy goods" Knauff stocked, or books and related items. They purchased their merchandise from larger retail stores in major cities. Knauff sold several brands of pianos, some probably obtained from agents in Richmond and especially in Baltimore, where his music would later be published. His professional versatility—his combining piano performance and teaching with a retail business and, eventually, piano construction (plus, in a sad coda, as debt collector)—was not unusual in terms of breadth. Several planters in Prince Edward County doubled as physicians, lawyers, or land surveyors, while more humble farmers were often qualified as blacksmiths or carpenters (Ely 2004, 107).

Knauff's publishing of a "puff" ad so early on was an innovative and therefore risky move, perhaps inspired by the financial straits in which his business was apparently often mired. However, he was far from alone in frequently having business difficulties. It was a cash-poor economy; it seems that every property owner was both creditor and debtor. Finances in the young United States were quite tumultuous. In conjunction with considering the effects of the general business climate on Knauff's store, we will turn to his personal life, which took positive and demoralizing turns in rapid order.

Tragedies and Professional Changes: Knauff at the Buckingham Female Collegiate Institute

Carolynn Waldon's typescript timeline of the Knauffs' fortunes notes that their daughter, S. A. Irene Knauff, was born circa 1834. A son followed soon: John Wellington Knauff was born on March 20, 1836. Sadly, Ann Knauff did not outlive the event by long; she died a month later, on April 20 (n.d., 1–2). And between the two births, George Knauff suffered financial reverses. Knauff and other American businessmen faced a severe credit shortage in 1833, a massive crop failure in 1835, and a progressively less stable monetary situation culminating in the panic of 1837, which was followed by a depression lasting about six years. The crop failure closed many shopkeepers' doors, especially in agricultural areas like Farmville. Late in 1835, Knauff attempted to auction off most or all of his inventory and much of his family's household goods for ready cash (*Richmond Enquirer*, May 6). We do not know if this auction met with success. A year later fire consumed his house and store. The account of this in the *Richmond Enquirer* indicated that "two small families" in addition to the Knauffs lived in the building at the time, and that Knauff lost "every thing; his dwelling house, kitchen, smoke-house full of bacon, a number of very valuable Pianos and musical instruments, new furniture, music, and all his papers and books. Nothing was insured" (June 3, 1836).

In a remarkable show of resilience (and probably support from the Bondurants, the parents of his late wife and grandparents of his children), Knauff reentered the business world as a piano builder less than a year later. An ad in the *Richmond Enquirer* of May 13, 1837 reads:

> PIANO FORTE MANUFACTORY, at Farmville, the only one south of Baltimore.—I have opened a manufactory of Piano Fortes at this place, and am prepared to supply the country on the most reasonable terms. Having procured first rate workmen and materials, I can assure the public that the Pianos made at my manufactory are at least, equal in tone and workmanship to any made in the North. It will be apparent that my expenses here are much less than those of manufacturers in larger cities, and in consequence of which I am enabled to sell my Pianos lower than any other maker. In addition to the above, I keep constantly in store an assortment of Pianos of the most celebrated manufacturers in the North, which I will sell

lower than the Richmond prices. Also, all other kinds of musical instruments, strings, every kind of music, instruction books, &c. &c. I will send all new pianos, bought at my store, free of expense and at my own risk, any distance not exceeding 30 miles, keep them in tune and repair for 12 months. I repair, tune, hire out Pianos on the most reasonable terms.

This vigorous response to a succession of hammering blows of fate was doomed too. The times were far from propitious for any such bold move, and, as bad luck would have it, Knauff also faced skillful competition. The lower end of the piano market that he intended to exploit was dominated within the year by the flamboyant and well-financed E. P. Nash of nearby Petersburg. Nash introduced ads based on customer testimonials to piano sales in Virginia; he was the first Virginia music merchant to employ this and other mass-marketing techniques successfully (see *Richmond Enquirer,* April 18, 1837, for decades). Also, William Knabe—like Knauff, a recent German immigrant—would open a piano factory in Baltimore in 1838.

Knauff managed to keep a hand in the business world for some time, but posted no more advertisements. On July 16, 1838, he mortgaged what appear to have been most of his remaining belongings. These included a parcel of land in Farmville (likely the one on which the piano factory stood), "a negro woman named Susan, a negro child Maria, and a negro boy named George," two horses, a sulky (a light-weight two-wheeled cart), ten used pianos, two new pianos, an unspecified amount of music, a gold watch, and "all debts due unto me, the said George P. Knauff" (as listed in the Prince Edward County Deed Book 22, 264–65). The stage was set for yet another major change in his life.

The 1839 catalogue of the Buckingham Female Collegiate Institute lists Knauff as "Professor of Instrumental" (West 1990, 18). Taking on a teaching job was a step down socially. It is no coincidence that this was also the year during which he was most prolific as a composer and arranger of sheet music, indeed, probably the year of the first printing of three of the four pamphlets making up the *Virginia Reels.*

The "female seminary"—and the Buckingham Female Collegiate Institute was an especially ambitious entry into this broad field—was the environment in which daughters of prosperous citizens received a more advanced education than was possible in their homes. True, small schools often were held at plantations, with a live-in tutor serving the owner's several children (a half dozen or so in instances in which I have seen a roster) plus perhaps the children of affluent neighbors. The female seminary, parallel to the preparatory schools young men attended, was a step up. Typical faculties included at least a few specialists, and most young women resided at the "seminary" during academic terms. The 1830s was an especially rich time for the founding of these schools. Both Prince Edward County and Buckingham County had long been dotted with "various small private schools of a temporary nature," often staffed by teachers from the North, since teaching was not considered "an especially 'high calling' in the South" (Shepard 1940, 168 and 365). Immediately preceding the Buckingham Female Collegiate Institute, and remaining as less-ambitious competition during the first years of the institute's lifespan, was a nearby Buckingham High School for Young Ladies, run by a family named Fairchild, who had indeed come from New England. The school was built in 1825 and burned in 1846. Course offerings included English, other languages, "instrumental music for [an extra] $30, and vocal music for [an extra] $10" per term, taught by Miss O. A. Bigelow (Shepard 1940, 168). There were similar girls' schools in Farmville, including one that would develop over time into Longwood University.

Young women's and young men's schools shared considerable subject matter. But while young men studied advanced mathematics, Latin, and Greek at the height of their precollege training, young women instead took "ornamental" courses that were generally not available to young men.[2] These included music (voice, piano, or perhaps guitar), visual arts (drawing, oil painting, and watercolors), and modern romance languages. Neither of these gender-segregated arrays of special courses was extraordinarily practical for future agriculturalists or their future wives, though the courses for males were more useful overall. Future ministers profited from learning classical languages, as did future doctors and lawyers to some extent, and higher mathematics would be useful to those who became architects and surveyors, for example. However, on both sides of the emphatic gender divide, the main goals of these non-shared courses were not directly practical, but rather intellectual and social.

Christine Farnham, in her rigorous and persuasive study "The Education of the Southern Belle: Higher Education and Student Socialization in the Antebellum South" (1994), wrote that "the ideal of the Southern lady and its adolescent counterpart, the Southern belle, do not exemplify a new set of roles resulting from the growth of industrialization and urbanization, for the South remained tied to commercial agriculture. Instead, they represent a romanticization of white domination in a slave society" (2). I would add here that class differences likely were at least as important to demarcate as were racial ones, since class affiliations were less apparent to the eye and were more easily permeable. Farnham continued as follows: "Southern schools [for young women] used the formal curriculum of the liberal arts and the informal curriculum of instructing in ladylike values and etiquette acquired from the North to inculcate the Southern version of femininity.... The South evidenced the greatest interest in female colleges of any region." Northerners feared that advanced education for women would incite an attack on sex segregation of professions, but in the South, the "desire for a classical education [served] as a marker of gentility" (1994, 2). No one seems to have worried that this education might incite young women to seek employment outside of the home. In general, female education in the South—for that matter, all higher education—was not meant to effect change, but rather to maintain the status quo. For parents, educating girls asserted "their daughters' value in the marriage market, as insurance against downward mobility" (31). William Shepard, referring specifically to the Buckingham Female Collegiate Institute, summarized that "a thoroughly intellectual education, attended by suitable moral restraints, is the first object in view" (1940, 177).

Music was indispensable in the curricula of this and all such schools. Indeed, music courses were the most popular of the pedagogical offerings classified as "extras," even though separate fees for lessons and for the use of instruments added up. Farnham asserted that "the purpose of a musical education was home entertainment. Consequently, instruction was organized with a view toward developing a repertoire of pieces that might be enjoyed by family and friends," these focusing on sentimental numbers cast in easy keys (1994, 87). This matches my own impressions gained through thumbing through many dozens of binders' volumes. Young ladies learning the piano accumulated many individual pieces of sheet music. Many of those players—almost all were young ladies—eventually took their collections to a book maker and had them bound into thick volumes. An average binder's volume included many current songs, at first almost all sentimental ones, then later, by the mid-1840s, a few comic songs coming out of minstrelsy. The last third or so of a typical collection included easy dances and marches, perhaps capped by a few variation sets or other relatively challenging selections.

Playing such an assortment of pieces may have afforded the girls chances for self-expression that were otherwise in short supply. I will quote just three of my personal favorites among the draconian rules that were printed in the 1839 catalogue of the Buckingham Female Collegiate Institute (retaining the numbering from the original list). The students: "6. Could not sit in the window or talk out the window or throw anything out the window." "7. Could not read novels or stories or tell stories which would excite the imagination or call forth feelings of fear and apprehension." "9. Could not ride, walk, or hold conversation with any gentleman other than father or brother except in the presence of a faculty member. Neither shall she visit in the neighborhood unless in the company with a teacher" (West 1990, 23). In short, self-expression through behavior was out of the question. Self-expression through writing or the visual arts would have been easy to monitor, but, luckily, the emotional qualities conveyed by music are less explicit and thus harder to assess or censor. Sarah Knight Malloy, valedictorian of the Buckingham Female Institute sometime in the early 1840s, delivered a doubtless learned and decorous address on Christianity at her graduation, then played a very ambitious and expressive concert including a pair of sentimental songs, a Beethoven sonata, and two battle pieces (Shepard 1940, 183). One of the songs, Henry Russell's exuberant "I'm Afloat, I'm Afloat," includes in its lyrics (by Eliza Cook) such phrases as "I fear not the monarch, I heed not the law," and "Let her sheets [sails] kiss the wind, and I warrant we'll soon leave the seagulls behind" ([1841?³]), sentiments that would seem to exceed the boundaries suggested by institute rule number 7 above, that is, to "excite the imagination." In addition, one of the battle pieces Miss Malloy played, Franticek Koczwara's then ubiquitous "Battle of Prague," is extraordinarily flashy: How could sections such as "Attack," "Cries of the Wounded," and "Turkish Music" not arouse the emotions of both performer and listener?[4]

Two publications by local historians tell the story of that school, the serial journal article by William Shepard referenced above (1940, parts 1 and 2), and a small book by Sue Roberson West, the title of which summarizes the narrative: *Buckingham Female Collegiate Institute: First Chartered College for Women in Virginia, 1837–1843, 1848–1863* (1990).

Both histories draw largely on letters written by the students and other family papers, as most official antebellum records for the county were lost because they were housed in the Buckingham County Court House, which burned. West located a copy of the 1839 school catalogue. Plenty of prominent citizens were involved in its governance: the "Committee of Supervision" included one doctor, one colonel, and three "Esquires" (lawyers), while the larger "Committee of Examination" included six ministers, a colonel and a lawyer, plus one man with the A.M. degree (the master's degree with the initials directly following the Latin "atrium magister," as has long been done at William and Mary and at Harvard). The institute's total faculty in early 1839 consisted of these teachers:

- Rev. Perlee B. Wilbur, A. M., President and Professor of Natural Moral Sciences, and Belles Lettres.
- Robert G. Loving, A. M., Professor of Mathematics and Ancient Languages and Literature.
- Mr. George P. Knauff, Professor of Instrumental.
- Mrs. Mary C. Wilbur, Governess and Preseptress [sic] in the Ornamental Branches.
- Miss Sarah A. Heustis, Assistant Governess and Teacher in the English Department.

Was it remarkable to have a piano teacher be one among a faculty of merely five? Judging from the lists of employees at female seminaries that I have seen, no. Faculty rosters almost never exceeded a half dozen, and always included a music teacher. But Knauff's tenure was brief. There seems to have been considerable turnover of faculty, including of the leadership of the institute. I have seen references to some five different people teaching music there. A student—one Mary Catherine Malloy, sister of the recitalist mentioned above—referred in several letters to receiving instruction in music, French, and Spanish from Mr. [Arnaud] Préot. A letter dated December 14, 1839, refers to his lessons in Spanish, and added that Mrs. Préot helped her "to make tapestry" (Shepard 1940, 184). Perhaps the key to Knauff's being supplanted lay in Mr. Préot's pedagogical versatility, and because he was married—Préot's wife and daughters helped out at the institute over the next years.[5] Knauff had sold pianos to the institute and been otherwise involved in advance planning. But Préot was diplomatically adept. For instance, a piece of his sheet music a copy of which reposes in the library of Farmville's Longwood University courts the favor of the institute's directors energetically. The title page offers a picture of the institute, along with this inscription: "Buckingham Grand March. Composed and Respectfully Dedicated to the Directors of the Female Collegiate Institute of Buckingham, Va. By Arnaud Préot. Published by Miller and Beachem, Baltimore, Suc[cessors] to F.D. Benteen" (1857; this is the publisher's plate 3117). The picture of the institute given at the beginning of this chapter reproduces part of the title page of a copy of this piece that remains near the institute, in the library of Longwood University, in Farmville.

All of the few known letters written home by students at the institute that refer to musical experiences mention Mr. Préot, who worked at the institute during parts of both stretches during which it was open. Mary Catherine Malloy noted in a letter probably dating from 1840, the year that she graduated (aged sixteen), that "I work very hard at my music. Mr. Préot gives me hopes that I may be a good musician. I have learned a long composition for the piano which you will like. It is very martial and astonishing. It made the Institute hounds howl, and the girls applaud" (Shepard 1940, 183).

One student at this school wrote home after the Panic of 1837: "'Hard Times' is a great enemy to Female Institutions." The letter was quoted by Christine Farnham, who went on to generalize that "although female education was becoming more widely accepted in the South, it was still a luxury, and one of the first items to be eliminated when families had cash problems (1994, 58). In the case of the Buckingham Female Collegiate Institute, an impractical excess of pride in the elegance of the furnishings in general and of the pianos in particular also contributed to the fragility of school finances. Shepard noted that "On the left of the [main lecture] hall was the music room. In this room, furnished with a stage on which were placed four pianos made by Ernest Rosenkranz of Dresden, all of rosewood and short of one octave by the modern piano, were several panels set between the windows and representing the Greek muses. The painting was done by Juan Padilla, who came down from Baltimore at the suggestion of George P. Knauff" (1940, 173). None of this was cheap! Further, in a letter written shortly before the first closing of the institute, the music tutor at the time, Mr. Préot, suggested replacing a defective piano with one made by Knauff. Actually, Knauff offered to repair the problem instrument, but Préot stated that "they must have a new one" (191).

Publishing Sheet Music, Including a Surprise: The *Virginia Reels*

The two anecdotes just cited, which illustrate a cavalier attitude toward expenses that probably contributed to the demise of the Buckingham Female Collegiate Institute as a business, also show that Knauff, although no longer teaching there, continued to be connected with the institute in various ways. A substantial link was through his publishing sheet music that the students could be persuaded to buy. His output divides rather neatly into two batches, from 1839—his year of employment at the institute—and 1851–1853. Indeed, the main batches of printings of the *Virginia Reels* are from those two periods. The array of genres, parade of titles, and patterns of dedications offer a generous mosaic of musical life in this time and place, and also a snapshot of those of Mr. Knauff's professional activities and aspirations that most immediately surround his arranging of the *Virginia Reels*. Here are George P. Knauff's publications other than the *Virginia Reels*, listed alphabetically:

Afton Grove Waltz. Composed for and Dedicated to Miss Mary S. Burke of Prince Edward Co., Va., [by] Mrs. J.E.C. of L. Co., Va. Arranged by Geo P. Knauff." Baltimore: Benteen [1851–1852], no plate number cited.

"Allegheny Waltz. Arranged for the Piano Forte by G.P. Knauff." Richmond: W. L. Montague, 1849 (no plate number).

"Amelia Springs Cottillion, by Geo. P. Knauff." Baltimore: Geo. Willig Jr., 1839 (above Blue-Bonneted Scotts on a broadside).

"Awake My Love and Come with Me. Written, Composed and Dedicated to Miss S.A. Irene Knauff by Geo. P. Knauff." Baltimore: F. D. Benteen and Co., [ca. 1852] (plate 2397; for voice and piano).

"Blue Bonnetted Scotts: A Cottllion [sic] Arranged by Geo. P. Knauff" [see above].

"Colonel Hubard's March & Quick Step, Composed for & Dedicated to Col. Edmund W. Hubard of Buckingham Va by His Friend G.P. Knauff." Baltimore: Geo. Willig, Jr., 1839.

Gatherings: A Collection of Choice Pieces of Music for the Piano Forte, Arranged by Geo. P. Knauff. Baltimore: Geo. Willig, Jr. [n.d.]. This collection contains "Bonaparte's Quick Step," "Quick Step by G.P. Knauff," "Polonaise," "Beautiful Waltz by Beethoven," "Napoleans Grand March," "Fishers Waltz," "Eccosaise," and "Ladies Waltz."

"General Pierce's Presidential Inauguration March and Quick Step. Composed and Dedicated to President Frank[!] Pierce by Geo. P. Knauff." Baltimore: Miller and Beachem, 1853 (plate 2447).

"Irene Waltz, Composed for & Dedicated to Miss S.A. Irene Knauff, by Geo. P. Knauff." Baltimore: Miller and Beachem, 1853 (plate 2449).

"Jackson's Cotillion. George P. Knauff." Baltimore: Willig, 1839 (no plate number).

"Ladies Quick Step, Arranged by Geo. P. Knauff." Baltimore: F. D. Benteen and Co., [ca. 1852] (plate 2339).

"Louisa & Mohegan Waltzes, Composed by Geo. P. Knauff." Baltimore: Geo. Willig Jr., 1839.

"Love and Pastry. For the Piano Forte by Geo. P. Knauff." Baltimore: Miller and Beachem, 1854 (plate 2571).

"The Metamora Waltz." Geo. Willig (at Duke).

"Mount Elba Waltz, Composed & Dedicated to Miss Virginia A.B. Shields by Geo. P. Knauff." Baltimore: F. D. Benteen, [ca. 1852] (plate 2400).

"Three Farmers Went a Hunting, Comic Song Arranged by Geo. P. Knauff." Baltimore: F. D. Benteen; New Orleans: W. T. Mayo, 1851 (plate 2162). For voice and piano.

"The Toothache or the Quilting, a Comic Song Written & Composed by George P. Knauff." Baltimore: F. D. Benteen; New Orleans: W. T. Mayo, 1852 (plate 2259). For voice and piano.

"Trumpet March, Arranged and Partly Composed by Geo. P. Knauff." Baltimore: Geo. Willig, Jr., 1839.

"Turkish March, Composed & Dedicated to the Ladies of Oldenplace Seminary (Dinwiddie Co. Va.) by Geo. P. Knauff." Baltimore: F. D. Benteen; New Orleans: W. T. Mayo, [ca. 1852] (plate 2398).

"Virginia Cotillion by Geo. P. Knauff." Baltimore: Geo. Willig, Jr., 1839. This piece is not included in any of the following collections.

Virginia Cotillions, Composed for the Piano Forte and Dedicated to the Ladies of Virginia by Geo. P. Knauff, No. 1. Baltimore: F. D. Benteen; New Orleans: W. T. Mayo, [ca. 1851–1852] (plate 2199). This collection contains "The Richmond Ladies," "The Belle of America," "Roberta," "Oldenplace," "Sweet Sally," and "Virginia."

"Virginia Quick March, by Geo. P. Knauff." Baltimore: Geo. Willig, Jr., 1839.

"Wait for the Wagon, Ethiopian Song for the Piano Forte. Arranged by Geo. P. Knauff." Baltimore: F. D. Benteen, 1851 (plate 2169). For voice and piano.

The *Virginia Reels* themselves present a complicated picture due to their having been issued several times, and by two publishers. I will summarize this story, then flesh it out through giving full annotated citations of the individual editions. The broad outline is this: Knauff issued pamphlet 1, then also pamphlet 2 through George Willig Jr. of Baltimore, during or shortly before 1839, without plate numbers. Then, apparently emboldened by interest evinced in the music, Willig reissued those two pamphlets and added a third (all now bearing consecutive plate numbers) in 1839. Willig's Baltimore competitor F. D. Benteen put out his own editions of pamphlets 1–3 in the early 1840s, omitting any reference to Knauff and adding a few pieces to pamphlets 1 and 3.

Knauff's later flurry of publication—both of the *Virginia Reels* and of his sheet music in general—started in 1851 or 1852, and seemed to respond to the popularity of blackface minstrelsy, and thus to a part of fiddlers' repertoires not openly celebrated in pamphlets 1–3 of the

Virginia Reels. Willig published pamphlet 4, which contains minstrel tunes. However, on the title page, he retained the elegant decoration common to the title pages of the first three pamphlets, apparently seeking sales of pamphlet 4 to the people who had bought numbers 1–3, and for the same reasons. Even the minstrel tunes in volume 4 were to be interpreted as decorous dances for girls being channeled toward elegant domesticity in a customary way. Benteen followed the opposite visual and thus sales strategy. He reprinted number 4—now with Knauff's name attached—with a new kind of decoration, one featuring the bold black lines more characteristic of minstrel sheet music covers. He also reissued his versions of numbers 1–3 with new covers to match that of number 4; his goal was to capitalize on the explicit and known minstrel associations of tunes in pamphlet 4 to increase the sales of pamphlets 1–3. The main market would still be upper-class young women, but Benteen was more aggressively exploiting the bizarre but very real overlap between rough-edged minstrelsy and refined parlor music that I will look at carefully near the beginning of chapter 5 of this book.

Next comes the detailed consideration of the various editions of the *Virginia Reels,* starting with the Willig editions. The tune titles may or may not match those in use today; this will be discussed in the following chapters.

Virginia Reels, Selected and Arranged for the Piano Forte by G.P. Knauff. No. 1. Baltimore: Geo. Willig, Jr. [n.d., and no plate numbers]. Contents: "Killie Krankie," "Republican Spirit," "Natchez on the Hill," "The Two Sisters," "Speed the Plough," "Slighted Jenny," "Mississippi Sawyer," "Forked Deer," "Whiskey Barrel," and "Love in a Village." This is the edition chosen for reproduction in this book.

Virginia Reels, Selected and Arranged for the Piano Forte by G.P. Knauff, No. 2. Baltimore: Geo. Willig, Jr. [n.d. and no plate numbers]. Contents: "Old Virginia," "Richmond Hill," "Villalave," "Petersburg Ladies," "The Hero," "Peter Francisco," "The 22nd of February," "The Island," and "Richmond Blues." I have seen just one copy of this printing of this number. While it lacks plate numbers, the pages are numbered 8 through 13 (the only numbering of pages in any edition of the *Virginia Reels*). That suggests that the purchaser might buy Number 1, which consists of 7 plates including the title page, then discard the title page of this Number 2 and append the music-bearing sheets to the end of No. 1.

Virginia Reels, Selected and Arranged for the Piano Forte by G.P. Knauff, Nos. 1–3. Baltimore: Geo. Willig, Jr., [1839], [1839], and 1839, plates 1535, 1536, and 1537, respectively. The contents of the first two volumes match those of the two editions listed above; only the title page has been changed to include tables of contents, and the subsequent pages now have the plate numbers added. Contents of pamphlet 3: "George Booker," "Oh Where Did You Come From," "Colonel Crocket," "Rose on the Mountain," "Billy in the Low Grounds," "Lockwell," "Lady of the Lake," and "Scotts Favorite." My duplication is of Nos. 2 and 3 of this edition; the title page of No. 1 is like that of No. 2 in many cases (that is, listing the contents of No. 1 and No. 2, with the applicable number underlined or otherwise marked by hand). But a few copies of No. 1 just have the table of contents for that volume. No. 3 is the only one of the eventual four volumes that has the publisher listed on every page. It seems that this number was conceived as divisible, that is, with the option of printing and selling each page of music separately, with the back left blank. I have not seen any such individual pages, but on occasion they were indeed advertised as such.

Virginia Reels, Selected and Arranged for the Piano Forte by G.P. Knauff. No. 4. Baltimore: Geo. Willig, Jr., [probably 1852], plate 2459. Contents: "Sich a Gittin Up Stairs," "Gaston," "Indian Whoop," "Love from the Heart," "Ohio River," "The Flying Indian," "Nancy Anderson," and "Midnight Serenade." Willig kept the plate for the title page of No. 3 and simply made additions to it for No. 4.

Virginia Reels, a Collection of the Most Admired Reels, Dances, &c., Selected and Arranged for the Piano Forte, No. [1, penciled in]. Baltimore: F.D. Benteen, [ca. 1842], plates 45–50. This edition of volume 1 is from Benteen's own reengraved plates. Knauff's name appears nowhere on the edition. Two pieces are added to those Willig had printed, "Virginia Reel. Mrs. McLeod's Reel" as the newly inserted fourth piece and "The Ridge" as an added last piece. Otherwise, the contents match those of the Willig edition of No. 1 note-for-note; the only change being that the titles are in bolder fonts. There is no evidence that Knauff had anything to do with the additions or the publication in general, which is therefore not considered in this book.

Virginia Reels, a Collection of the Most Admired Reels, Dances, &c., Selected and Arranged for the Piano Forte, No. [2, penciled in]. Baltimore:

F.D. Benteen, [ca. 1842], plates 51–56. Again, printed from Benteen's own plates, again without Knauff being mentioned. No new contents; matches the Willig edition.

Virginia Reels, a Collection of the Most Admired Reels, Dances, &c., Selected and Arranged for the Piano Forte, No. [3, penciled in]. Baltimore: F.D. Benteen, [ca. 1844], plates 369, 370, 371, 372, 373, and 374. The title page matches that shared by the first two numbers of the Benteen edition, just with a different number written in. The volume adds several pieces to the uncharacteristically skimpy Willig edition, including "Colonel Crocket: A Virginia Reel" (a different piece from the one given this title in the Willig edition; the earlier incarnation is deleted); "Billy in the Woods"; "Juniper Hall"; "Miss Clark's Hornpipe"; "Old Dominion Reel"; "The Fox Hunt"; and "James River Reel."

No. 4 of Virginia Reels, Dedicated to Thomas Ritchie Esq. of Washington City by Geo. P. Knauff. Baltimore: F.D. Benteen [ca. 1851–1852], plates 2196 and 2198. This edition has the same contents as the Willig edition; the big differences are the restoration of Knauff's name—he was now printing music with Benteen—and dark swirls in the decoration of the title page, which now associate this array of tunes with minstrelsy. The first three numbers in the Benteen edition were also reprinted at this time, with the music from the original Benteen plates, but title pages identical to that of number 4, just with different volume numbers penciled in.

Just as the *Virginia Reels* had many more editions printed than the rest of Knauff's compositions (with the exception of Knauff's one truly popular song, the "Ethiopian" hit "Wait for the Wagon," which was, like the *Virginia Reels*, an arrangement), it is these publications that survive in far and away the most copies. Many more copies of the Willig editions remain extant than their Benteen counterparts. Of the Willig numbers, the first survives in the most copies.

It seems that the *Virginia Reels* defined its own niche for decades. Many binder's volumes dominated by songs and dances published in the 1850s or early 1860s include one to three of the first three numbers of the Willig edition of the *Virginia Reels*, from 1839, but contain nothing else that early. Let me reiterate: every category of sheet music in these mid-century binder's volumes was represented by recent publications except one, the dances that were done to the *Virginia Reels*.

What was a "Virginia reel?" Reels were line dances, done throughout the British Isles and defined as much by the music to which they were done (duple time, rhythmic texture basically of eighth notes in cut time) as by the precise steps, which could vary. The lines of men and women couldn't be too close, because much of the dancing was of the outer couples, and took place on diagonals within the lines. Elias Howe printed a "Virginia Reel" in his *Quadruple Musician's Omnibus* within a section devoted to line dances. The tune, called there simply "Virginia Reel," was the common one then called "Lord MacDonald's Reel," and now still called that in the North, but known as "Leather Britches" in the South. This page of the *Musician's Omnibus* is crammed full of dance tunes and their figures, the nine dances including this "Virginia Reel," and several of the tunes Knauff gathered into his *Virginia Reels*, "Money Musk" (which he called "Killie Krankie"), "Speed the Plough," "Miss Brown's Reel" (his "The Hero"), and some others (1869, 41). The lengthy but not really elaborate dance directions for Howe's "Virginia Reel" are as follows:

> First lady down the centre half way (foot gentleman up at the same time to meet lady), balance there and return to places, 1st gent. and foot lady the same, 1st lady and foot gent meet and swing with left hand and back to places. 1st gent and foot lady the same, 1st lady and foot gent meet and swing with right hand and back to places, 1st gent and foot lady the same, 1st lady and foot gent meet and swing with both hands and back to places, 1st gent and foot lady the same, 1st couple give right hands and swing one and a half round, swing 2nd with right hand, partner with left, 3rd with right, partner with left, 4th with right, pt. with left, 5th with right, pt. with left, 6th with right, pt. left, centre with pt. and swing, all lead round (ladies to right, gents to left), all up centre, 1st couple down centre to stop.

Knauff after the Collegiate Institute, and the Collegiate Institute after Knauff

In mid-1842, Knauff stated in his last newspaper advertisement that he was available to tune pianos in a four-county area, and that he would be willing to collect debts for others during his rounds (*Richmond Enquirer*, June 24, 1842). In letters dated 1843 and 1844, he dunned a planter of Halifax County, one Captain Thomas Spraggins, at some length, closing one missive with the pathetic appeal that "you are rich and I am Poor."[6]

(It is not clear whether the debt in question was owed to Knauff or to someone else, with Knauff working on a percentage basis.) He himself was pressed for the payment of assorted debts in numerous lawsuits during those years, but too much should not be made of that. It seems that most property owners in this area were debtors (and creditors) most of the time.

Knauff last appeared in the Personal Property Tax Lists of Prince Edward County in 1847 (volume for 1830–1850). Perhaps he then moved again to Buckingham County; the loss of county records in a courthouse fire allows this conjecture. Two bits of evidence might at first glance seem to suggest that he might have relocated to Dinwiddie County; he dedicated his "Turkish March" of circa 1852 to "the Ladies of Oldenplace Seminary (Dinwiddie Co. Va.)" and the first set of the "Virginia Cotillions" (from the same time) includes a number entitled "Oldenplace." Unfortunately, Dinwiddie County's Oldenplace female seminary did not attract local historians as well as did the Buckingham Female Collegiate Institute. But what looks like the solution to the question of Knauff's possible association with that school is available in the 1850 census records for the county, which have his daughter "S.A.I. Knauff, age 16, born Virginia" in residence (472, household #31). Perhaps Knauff was angling for employment at Oldenplace; perhaps he was simply courting sheet music sales. In any case, Irene Knauff's attending school may well have sparked his second and final flurry of composing and arranging. Also, the sheer fact of her attending a female seminary tells us that Knauff was doing adequately in financial terms toward the end of his life.

Apart from the importance of the *Virginia Reels* (and of the one song that became quite popular, "Wait for the Wagon"), Knauff's immediate legacy was the same that most of us can hope for, children who make us proud. Both Irene and John Wellington Knauff were well educated, she as explained above, he at Farmville's Hampden Sydney College (though he had to take a break and earn money teaching for two years, because George Knauff died after John Wellington's junior year). Both Knauff children became teachers for the long term, she in Virginia, he first in Virginia, and then in Arkansas (coupling teaching with farming there). A remark in a biographical sketch of John Wellington Knauff, printed in *Biographical and Historical Memoirs of Eastern Arkansas* closes George Knauff's story laconically: "The father of the subject of this sketch died in 1855" (1890, 712).

Two characterizations of Knauff remained in local oral tradition, and were transferred to print by local historians. Shepard noted that he was "a man of various learning and an exceptionally quick wit" (1940, 186). A longer description appeared in a reprint of a 1935 edition of the *Farmville Herald* entitled *Today and Yesterday in the Heart of Virginia*. Scott Hart wrote that: "Among [Farmville's] citizenship was one interesting, but little-known-of personage—George Knauff, proprietor of the only music store in the entire region and an importer of musical instruments from the famous house of Ernest Rosenkranz of Dresden. It appears that Mr. Knauff was also a builder of pianos, but it is impossible to know the extent of this enterprise. It is known that he was a gentleman of high sensibilities and culture and a musician of some renown in his time. He had moments with the cup, but even so could handle his instruments with such power and authority that ladies would sit enraptured as he musically dreamed and aspired over masterly compositions in concert" (1935, 163–64).

The site of Knauff's home and store in Farmville—the corner of Main and Fourth Streets—bears a historical marker, but this refers only to a later use of the property. Knauff had sold the land on which his house (and store) had stood to Dr. William Henry Robertson, who had graduated from the University of Virginia School of Medicine in 1851. Robertson rebuilt on the spot of Knauff's burned-out building. The site later housed the Educational Amusement Company (EACO) Theater, built in 1922, and renamed State Theatre in 1940. After many decades of entertaining the citizens of Farmville, the theater collapsed during an ice storm on February 11, 1994. Figure 2 reproduces a scan of a picture of the ruined building given in a *Farmville Herald* article the following Friday. The scene immediately became a Longwood University Archaeological Site, under the direction of Dr. James Jordan, who was kind enough to share his files concerning the dig. He and his students uncovered the foundations of the Robertson House, finding along the way buttons, marbles, parts of light fixtures, pottery shards, a doll's leg, and an 1854 half-dime that had been inserted in Robertson's Foundation Wall. After the study was complete, the city partially restored the theater in a charming way. Just the screen and its wall remain, with some support from bits of the side wall. Today, this is used in a way I expect Knauff would have liked. It has become a pedestrian analogue of a drive-in theater. Locals bring lawn chairs and watch evening movies.

Ice collapsed the roof of the State Theatre in Farmville on Friday afternoon. The middle of the building came crashing down upon itself but miraculously, nobody was hurt, including one man who was inside the building at the time.

Figure 2. *Farmville Herald* photograph of the collapse of the EACO Theatre on February 11, 1984 (collection of Dr. James Jordan, Longwood College). This theater was built on the site of Knauff's house in Farmville.

I will close this chapter with an anecdote from the last days of the Buckingham Female Collegiate Institute. Local repercussions of the Civil War sent most students packing by 1862. The main building was employed to house refugees from the fighting late in the war; that building would decay over subsequent decades, and the bricks and other materials would be plundered for other construction. It is now just a spot in a pleasant cow pasture; only the President's Cottage still stands, according to the author of a historic marker commemorating the school placed on a country road two miles away.

What little instruction that continued to take place in 1863 was done by the last president of the institute, Dr. Blackwell, or by members of his family, in the President's Cottage. Payment was made in flour or bacon. An incident during the time that refugees occupied the main building was told by local historian William Shepard:

> Dr. Blackwell went to Lunenburg on a visit during the winter and the refugees decided to have a dance to relieve their taut minds of the thoughts of war and memories of wrecked homes. They ob-

Figure 3. The EACO Theatre was partially rebuilt as a small, pedestrian analogue of a drive-in theater. Local residents bring their own folding chairs.

tained some local fiddlers and a pianist, Mr. Mahr, and began [to dance] the Virginia reel in the hall and side rooms to music composed by Mr. Knauff. Dr. Blackwell unexpectedly returned and in his astonishment at the scene within when he opened the door he dropped his hat. As he stood in the door a gentleman then turning past the vestibule left his partner and approached him. "I am afraid you never expected to see a dance here, Sir." "Nor a war in Virginia," said Dr. Blackwell. "We could not prevent the war, I will not prevent your dancing." Drawing the other aside he said quietly, "Let no others hear I have returned. I am tired of long faces. I hope you and the ladies will feel better for the night. Go back and dance. I will go to my house and pray to God to forgive us for our sins and mostly for my own sin and weakness." He made a gesture of silence and stepped into the snowy lane which led to the cottage near at hand. (1940, 364)

- Chapter Two -

"Speed the Plough" and "Money Musk"

Knauff and the Dance Music Component of Early American Popular Music

WHEN KNAUFF MOVED TO FARMVILLE, HE JOINED THAT VERY SMALL town's upper crust. All of these affluent citizens' social events apart from church services and funerals included dancing, and he and his well-born wife would have enjoyed being among the dancers. Most or all the melodies would have been new to him. Although he doubtless arrived with broad musical training, he would have had plenty to learn about pan-British popular music.

Sometime in the late 1830s, Knauff took advantage of an opportunity that may have dawned on him gradually, that there was a body of music in regular use in his part of Virginia that included many tunes that were not yet published. As a musician trained in Germany, he may have reflected on the histories of the waltz and the Ländler—that is, that these were folk dances first, and then fashionable, popular genres that enterprising composers exploited to make some money. When versatile musician and entrepreneur Knauff heard a fiddler (and perhaps a pianist) playing the *Virginia Reels* melodies for dancing at social events held at the home of his wife's parents, he sensed a similar chance to enhance his income. Exactly when he launched into composing and arranging music for profit remains up in the air, because a few—I believe the earliest—of his publications lack dates and plate numbers; this includes the first printing of the first two volumes (at least) of the *Virginia Reels*. This suggests an alternative scenario: that his activity as a composer and arranger started after his home and business burned, and

Figure 4. I attended the 2010 North Atlantic Fiddle convention in Aberdeen, Scotland. While visiting a botanical garden there, I asked several employees what flower would best represent the tune "The Flowers of Edinburgh." An easy consensus emerged: the thistle, species of which also flourish in Virginia. The thistles pictured here grew in a private garden in Aberdeen.

piggybacked on his next focus for earning a living, which was teaching. As explained in the previous chapter, his first dated music is from 1839, the same year as his brief tenure at the Buckingham Female Collegiate Institute, where his students constituted a literally captive audience and market.

Knauff and the Music Business

Knauff's choosing to compose, arrange, and publish music was nothing startling, whether initially part of his brick-and-mortar business or coupled with his subsequent stint teaching. Writing and arranging music was a natural ingredient of any music career at that time. Men who were primarily music merchants also performed and gave lessons, and few men who were primarily performers did not also welcome a chance to boost their incomes by selling physical embodiments of the music they

Figure 5a. Title page of Knauff's own collection called *Gatherings*, with a label identifying it as having been sold at his short-lived store.

played, much like many minor pop musicians of today hawk their own recordings at their concerts.

I have seen just one piece with the pasted-in "Sold at George P. Knauff & Co's Music and Fancy Store, Farmville, Va." This was a copy of his own collection called *Gatherings*. And I've seen just a few pieces of sheet music that he evidently sold after he lost the store, these bearing labels that merely state "Bought of Geo. P. Knauff, Farmville, Va." My favorite

Figure 5b. Detail from the title page of an anonymous and undated sheet music item, "The Old Maid," with Knauff's later label.

of these is a two-page comic piece that imparted a social lesson: young women ought not to be too choosy when selecting a husband. "The Old Maid, or When I Was a Girl Eighteen Years Old" was published by George Willig of Philadelphia, the German immigrant father of George Willig Jr., through whose Baltimore house Knauff would do most of his own publishing. The anonymous piece is not dated and lacks a plate number.[1] Knauff could have sold this at any time after his home and store burned.

Since the total time during which Knauff devoted substantial energy to creating sheet music was brief—just during 1839 and 1851–1852—his output remained modest. Of course, with so many of his pieces surviving in just one or two copies, and with the indexing of sheet music collections in the United States still in its infancy, we can't know what percentage of his work has been located. Fortunately for the current purpose, the *Virginia Reels* was his most successful publication, and enough copies of each version of each of its parts remain that we can be confident that few surprises remain in terms of the physical sheet music.

This chapter will focus on the first pamphlet of the *Virginia Reels*. Of the four pamphlets, just two have obvious themes, the second and fourth numbers. The second volume consists of pieces the titles of which have associations with localities or individuals from around Knauff's part of Virginia; I discuss the broad topic of tune names in connection with a general appraisal of the contents of that volume in chapter 3. The fourth pamphlet is the easiest to characterize due to its association with blackface minstrelsy. Modern old-time music of the Upper South derives directly from blackface minstrel performance; I will talk about how tunes from the *Virginia Reels* and tunes like those are played in chapter 5.

Pamphlet 3 is somewhat harder to analyze. Just one of the tunes in it had been published previously in an instrumental anthology, that being in Scotland, and just that one (Knauff's "Old Virginia," nearly always printed as "Flowers of Edinburgh") had reached print in any setting in the United States before Knauff arranged it. On the other hand, the tunes in this set have the best survival rate when compared with those in the other three volumes; most are played today. I will discuss this volume as representing the stream of tunes that flourished fully in oral tradition, with emphasis on a hypothetical continuity of in-your-face personal virtuosity that may well have been routine on the moving frontier, where dances were relatively rare. Several of these tunes (and a few from elsewhere in the *Virginia Reels*) are played today in American fiddle styles where variation is the rule rather than an exception, including the fancier fraction of West Virginia performance and especially Texas style, which has given rise to a near-nationwide matrix of contest styles; I will talk about modern performances of several members of the *Virginia Reels* in those styles in chapter 4.

The first volume of the *Virginia Reels*, the subject of this chapter, remains the hardest to characterize. When it came out, Knauff may not have planned beyond it: this probably would have been the only volume of the *Virginia Reels* that appeared had it not garnered a promising measure of commercial success. It contains tunes that might have been placed instead in later pamphlets if Knauff's intention from the start had been for each volume to have a somewhat different emphasis.[2] For instance, "Forked Deer," although Knauff placed it right in the middle of volume 1, belongs in my scheme to volume 3, since it had not been previously published, and incidentally flourishes well today, in fact more healthily in more styles than any other member of the *Virginia Reels*. In addition, the first pamphlet's "Natchez on the Hill" might have been anthologized instead in volume 4, since its relative "Old Zip Coon" became a minstrel standard. And both "Natchez on the Hill" and the title "Mississippi Sawyer" have specific geographic associations and thus might have come out in volume 2, although those associations are not with locations in Virginia.

The factor that comes closest to unifying the first number of the *Virginia Reels* is not musical, but rather biographical: this volume represents the beginning of Knauff's realizing his quest to make money by publishing arrangements of tunes from his local oral tradition. He wanted for this traditional music also to be marketable, to be "popular" music too, as were a few items in volume 1 already. These hits were "Speed the Plough" and "Killie Krankie" (under its usual name, "Money Musk"), plus the first tune in volume 2, "Old Virginia" (very similar to the widely distributed "Flowers of Edinburgh"). Out of respect for this laudable ambition, I am linking my discussion of the contents of this volume with the overlap of oral tradition "folk" and potentially marketable "popular" that he was seeking to exploit. That is the common ground inhabited by what we now recognize as early nineteenth-century American fiddle tunes, melodies that were published alongside other popular music in instrumental anthologies, but at the same time were fiddled at dances with *or without* printed music being present.

Fiddling and the Broad Concept of Popular Music in the Young United States

By the time that Knauff decided to create an anthology of local fiddle tunes, fiddling had been going on for centuries in America. Instruments may not have arrived along with the first British settlers in the colonies that would become the United States and Canada, but there would have been some present as soon as dancing became common. Unfortunately, the first evidence of the nature of fiddling in British North America remains tantalizingly vague. We can expect that fiddlers in the British colonies in North America were composing tunes at the same time that other British fiddlers were doing so, but they didn't have connections with a music industry dominated by British individuals and repertoires. Finally, in the early nineteenth century, specific fiddle tunes entered the historical record in the United States. Many tunes that were already played and that were already danced to in England (or Scotland, but especially England) appeared in the earliest sizable group of substantial American published popular music compilations—collections that differ little from their English models—and in personal manuscripts that drew on those publications. This stream of tunes, which reflected the English popular music mainstream in America, is what Knauff attempted to supplement.

Of course, "popular music" is a constantly evolving concept. The best broad characterization of popular *song* as it flourished in early nineteenth-century America remains that given in the preface of Charles Hamm's groundbreaking and still unmatched *Yesterdays: Popular Song in America* (1979). Hamm defined popular song as (1) "written for, and most often performed by, a single voice or a small group of singers, accompanied by either a single chord-playing instrument or some sort of band, ensemble, or small orchestra"; (2) "usually first performed and popularized in some form of secular stage entertainment, and afterward consumed (performed or listened to) in the home"; (3) "composed and marketed with the goal of financial gain"; (4) "designed to be performed by and listened to by persons of limited musical training and ability"; and (5) "produced and disseminated in physical form—as sheet music in its early history, and in various forms of mechanical reproduction in the twentieth century" (xvii).

Hamm's definition has the virtue of resulting from the analysis of plenty of commercial song; it is a concept derived from data. Hamm excluded from his definition several categories of short pieces of music that did share the commercial life of popular song, including instrumental genres such as ragtime and band music (xviii). But, just as we witness considerable overlap between band music and pop song today—for instance, in the programs juxtaposing marches with arrangements of movie themes and popular songs that are performed at football game halftimes by high school bands—early nineteenth-century dance tunes might have had texts earlier in their lives, that is, have been songs before they were fiddle tunes. Also, other fiddle tunes that seem to have been instrumental numbers from the start nevertheless often traveled with songs in social situations and as a consequence commercially.

A Slice of English Culture in America: Fiddle Tunes in Early Published Anthologies

The contents of instructional books for instruments printed in early nineteenth-century America illustrate the place of oral tradition fiddle tunes within commercial music. As a sample of this stream of publications, I selected *Blake's New and Complete Preceptor for the Violin. With a Favorite Selection of Airs, Marches &c. Fourth Edition* [1810s?]. The title page includes the information that this book was assembled and published by one G[eorge] E. Blake in Philadelphia, and that Blake sold it at his store at No. 13 South Fifth Street (where one could also purchase flutes, clarinets, and "Violins of all Kinds from One Dollar to One Hundred Dollars"). Blake claimed that one could procure all the paraphernalia one needed to become a musician in his store (instruments, accessories, published music with instructional content, and even live music lessons). In a similar claim of comprehensiveness, each anthology of instrumental music was advertised as being able to stand alone, to teach the basics of music and of performing on one or several instruments (in the absence of a teacher, which was a common condition away from major cities), and to offer a satisfactory sample of melodies from all genres of secular popular music.

Roughly three-fifths of Blake's forty-four tunes were song airs (many of which had been premiered on stage, following Hamm's definition of popular song), a fifth were marches or other patriotic tunes, and the remaining fifth were dance tunes representing various dance genres, including a few venerable fiddle tunes. The three recognizable fiddle tunes (preexisting as such and surviving today) were "Speed the Plough," "White Cockade," and "The Rose Tree," which was a song melody that was also played as a dance tune. Blake arranged these as bare-bones melodies. Two of these tunes find echoes in the *Virginia Reels*, "Speed the Plough" in a conventional version of this common and stable tune, and "The Rose Tree" as the ancestor of both the minstrel standard "Old Zip Coon" and Knauff's "Natchez on the Hill."

Blake's *New and Complete Preceptor*, like many instrumental collections of the day, was marketed as a stand-alone tutor: a beginner on a given instrument was told that if he or she owned an instrument and such a publication, they could learn to play and would have a repertoire to draw on. Each such preceptor started with a pedagogical section.

In this one, the first twelve pages introduce the topics of—the reader should take a deep breath before continuing—holding the violin and the bow (one sentence each), tuning, accidentals, left-hand positions, the act of bowing, note lengths, marks such as repeat signs (and triplets and staccato wedges), various types of trills and other ornaments ("shakes"), transposition, keys, and meters, closing with a one-page "Short [!] Dictionary of Musical Terms." Following the parade of tunes, the last page of the volume features scales, arpeggios, and preludes in G, D, and C Major.

Blake reproduced most of this pedagogical sequence verbatim in his various anthologies (with tiny adjustments for each instrument), and countless similar collections put out by his English and American contemporaries were similarly introduced. How much of this cursory instruction did the instrumentalist playing from such an anthology actually employ? In the *New and Complete Preceptor*, although most tunes remain fairly simple in appearance, five melodies venture into the violinist's third position (moving the left hand up the neck so that the first finger is where the third finger usually sits, and so adding a span of a third to the available range), ten employ grace notes, four each feature trills or staccato markings, and three each include triplets or tempo designations. But the three fiddle tunes take part in absolutely none of this. Indeed, in this book and in most similar publications, editors were accustomed to adding niceties to some of their printed song melodies and marches, but left the fiddle tunes plain. This was not a matter of articulated or completely consistent policy, but rather a cumulative array of parallel independent decisions: these professional musicians believed that fiddle tunes were to be played simply, without shifts and without ornaments, precisely as they appeared on the page.

Roughly the same proportions of song airs, marches, and dance tunes hold in the few significantly larger collections of instrumental melodies. The most readily available of these is English immigrant Edward Riley's *Riley's Flute Melodies*, published by him in New York in four volumes (1814, 1817, 1820, and 1827; the first two books are widely circulated conjoined in a one-volume Da Capo reprint). Why would a collection for flute be pertinent? Editors of anthologies for a given instrument usually made allowances for the capabilities of the other popular instruments in order to maximize sales. In Blake's *New and Complete Preceptor for the Violin*, he never carries a melody below the violin's open *d* string—there might as well not be a *g* string—in order to make the melodies playable on the flute and fife as then constructed. At the same time, flutist Riley rarely takes a melody over the *b* reachable by a violinist's fourth finger playing on the *e* string in first position. And when Riley lets a melody rise further, the *d* stopped by the violinist's fourth finger in relatively easy third position forms a barrier.

Riley printed nearly all of the fiddle tunes that were frequently published in his day and that remain in broad use in the United States now. These include common-time tunes: "College Hornpipe" (usually "Sailor's Hornpipe" now; I, 2), "Durang's Hornpipe" (I, 91), "Fisher's Hornpipe" (I, 52), "Flowers of Edinburgh" (I, 5), "Lord MacDonald's Reel" (still played under that title on occasion in New England, but now called "Leather Britches" in most of the United States; I, 32), "Mason's Apron" (today, "Jack of Diamonds"; II, 91), "Money Musk" (II, 72), "Rose Tree" (I, 9), "Speed the Plough" (III, 94), and "White Cockade" (I, 35). Riley also anthologized a few jigs (dances in a brisk 6/8) that have survived: "Irish Washerwoman" (I, 52), "The Priest in His Boots" (I, 6), and "St. Patrick's Day in the Morning" (II, 62 and IV, 9). Just two fiddle tunes common both in the raft of similar early nineteenth-century American publications and now are lacking: "Soldier's Joy" and "Rickett's Hornpipe." One can also find a few fiddle tunes that flourished in the early 1800s but not today, such as "Madam Parisott's Hornpipe" (II, 73), which is essentially the same tune as Knauff's "Whiskey Barrel"; I would guess that this would add about two dozen more fiddle tunes to the mix. This may at first seem like a substantial repertoire of fiddle tunes. But compared to the thousands printed in the heyday of Scottish fiddling late in the eighteenth century through the early nineteenth century and the thousands that flourish today in British and American oral tradition, it is a small number. If we assume that the total repertoire did not thin dramatically at this time, the meagerness of this offering means that only the hits reached print.

Most of these musicians who were also businessmen, including Blake and Riley, came from England, and had been educated in music and commerce there (the British were joined by Germans like the elder Willig during this generation, then other Germans including Knauff and piano maker Knabe during the next generation). Might there have been elements of American taste or practice that the publishers didn't fully understand? Did conditions in the young United States cause fiddlers, flutists, and fifers to lack interest in some genres or specific tunes that sold well in Britain, and/or to prefer certain genres or tunes more than did their British counterparts? In any case, publications like Blake's *New and Complete Preceptor* were expensive enough (in this case, 75 cents!) that buying one was a serious decision, and many an aspiring musician instead copied out his or her favorite parts in music commonplace books, thus offering a window on local and personal taste.

Music Commonplace Books: Young Americans Illustrate Personal Taste

"Commonplace books" are individuals' compilations of memorabilia (proverbs, poems, recipes, or on occasion pieces of music) recorded by hand in previously bound blank books. Many instrumentalists in English- and German-speaking areas maintained melody-filled commonplace books during the late eighteenth and early nineteenth centuries; this was the heyday of the practice, the era when published collections of tunes were available but neither ubiquitous nor cheap, so that laboriously copying melodies out of them was a reasonable thing to do. The resultant manuscripts included song airs, marches, and dances, entered in no particular order (though examples in given genres sometimes appeared in clusters). The tunes are usually notated in unhesitant hands in instrumental (beamed) notation, reflecting the fact that the compilers were almost always working directly from their friends' or neighbors' printed collections of instrumental music, collections such as the one by Blake discussed above.

One such music commonplace book reposes in the music library of the University of Illinois, where I was finishing my degree requirements around 1980. On one opening, the compiler wrote out a proposed title several times: *Philander Seward's Musical Deposit.* The name Philander Seward is distinctive; I found its owner just once in appropriate census records. Once I knew who Seward was and where he lived, it was easy to learn more about him from county records (see Goertzen 1982). I will discuss this manuscript and its owner in some detail, as background for the first of two sample explorations of music commonplace books.

Philander Seward was born in 1791 in Fishkill, New York, to affluent and educated parents owning a farm and a mill. His handwritten book contains seventy-seven items: sixty-two titled but not texted tunes notated in treble clef, ten bass lines notated in bass clef, plus a few song texts and an epigram. Several of the tunes were first published in 1807, so Seward could not have completed the manuscript before then. Tune ranges and a few fingering indications suggest that Seward played at least the violin and some bass instrument. The tunes as he wrote them down lack idiomatic character and appeared commonly in collections for various instruments. The proportions of airs, marches, and dances are roughly as in Blake; Seward was a teenager making his own version of a collection like Blake's, though minimizing the pedagogical materials (he included just one prelude, and one exercise aptly named "Major Minor"). How should I go about discovering what was most interesting about this collection of melodies? I borrowed a technique common to historical musicology and folklore: finding and examining multiple concordances of the collection's individual items.

I compared the tunes penned in the *Musical Deposit* with matching or similar melodies, titles, or both found in thirty-four music commonplace books (penned from the 1780s to the 1820s in the cases in which I could establish dates), 179 printed collections (published from the 1780s through the 1950s; most of these collections housed in the Library of Congress or the New York Public Library), and lists of tune titles and/or melodic incipits found in various bibliographies (in particular Sonneck and Upton 1945 and Wolfe 1964). In the decades since, I have taken note of those titles and tunes when I've been poring over likely sources for any reason. My conclusions from the early 1980s hold: First, Seward compiled a wide range of tunes, neither just hits nor just rarities, and did not grant particular genres of pieces any more preference than had publishers like Blake; the manuscript contains an average sampling of the secular music of his day. Second, when a piece appeared in plenty of these collections, the fact that it was then common didn't mean that it would last longer: most pieces, common or not, vanished quickly. This was indeed mostly *popular* music, entering and leaving the scene like clockwork, though at a markedly slower pace than that at which today's pop music travels.

Most interesting for the purposes of this chapter is that, although most concordances matched the versions found in the *Musical Deposit* or differed from them only in their keys, a few differed from Seward's versions and from one another repeatedly in minor matters of detail. These include those of Seward's tunes that had been common fiddle tunes before his time, and which remain in the American folk fiddle repertory today: "Money Musk," "Rickett's Hornpipe," "Devil's Dream," "Fisher's Hornpipe," "Flowers of Edinburgh," and "The Irish Washerwoman" (remember: Knauff placed both "Money Musk" and "Flowers of Edinburgh" in the *Virginia Reels*, though renamed respectively "Killie Krankie" and "Old Virginia"). In Seward's time, printed (and manuscript) versions of these tunes varied in certain ways. General contours, diagnostic tones (notes that are metrically and harmonically prominent), and a few catchy melodic motives remained stable, but exact rhythms, passing tones, and other metrically weak notes were apt to vary.

Differences among these versions correspond to differences in how versions of these tunes contrast in modern playing in New England, the part of the United States where these six tunes are most at home today (see Wells 1978). This suggests that these tunes were already in oral tradition early in the nineteenth century—that is, in the remembered repertoires of the English immigrants who were the main performer/teacher/publishers of the instrument compilations on which the American compilers of music commonplace books drew. Those American keepers of manuscript collections were—in the cases where their identities can be established with reasonable certainty—like Seward, teenagers in affluent (and literate, and even music literate) families. Since the commonplace books of Seward and his cohorts are inventories of pieces that American individuals wished to learn, they illustrate personal taste and, taken together, at least a slice of American taste.

The publishers of the books from which these teenagers copied, although British in training and preferences, did seek out American content in marches and patriotic songs, which they arranged from American sheet music. Teenager Philander Seward endorsed that nationally associated trend when he wrote down the tunes for "General Green's March," "Philadelphia March," and the very common "President's March," which later acquired the text and title "Hail Columbia." Also, Seward notated two rarer fiddle tunes with Americanized titles: his versions of the common British tunes "Gary Owen" and "Whistle O'er the Lave O't" (or "Johnny in the Nether Mains") were retitled respectively as "Washington's Ode" and "New Haven Green." That last transformation of title was both local and personal: Seward's father had attended Yale University.

How representative were Seward's manuscript and the early American publications on which it drew? Fiddlers in settled areas were relatively likely to have parents who were sufficiently monied to support their teenagers' desires to learn to play an instrument and to value music literacy. Settlers on the ever-moving frontier had less time and opportunity to perform music and certainly to learn to read and write music. At any rate, fewer music books—whether publications or manuscripts—would have been in evidence. But most of the economy, rich or poor, was still based on agriculture. There remained something of a rural feel to what are now big cities, and, at the same time, any settled clump of farms would probably witness its citizens trying to have a civilized good time. Survivals of music publications in sparsely settled areas would be good evidence for a vigorous outreach of city life, but such evidence is slim. Nevertheless, the occasional music commonplace book illustrating practice in surprising regions does turn up.

Since I work in Mississippi, I am always on the lookout for evidence of musical activities in that state's early years. The first substantial documentation of any Mississippi fiddler's activity as early as the beginning of the nineteenth century reached public view recently. The featured item in the April 2012 "Recent Acquisitions" catalog of J & J Lubrano Music Antiquarians was a Mississippi music commonplace book. The third page of the Lubrano Catalog includes the following paragraph (the quotation marks and brackets are present in the catalog):

> Versos of a number of pages consist of a printed Army enlistment form, including one on the verso of the final page of musical notation completed in manuscript with the name "Samuel W. Watkins" born in "the Mississippi Territory" aged "nineteen" years, "five" feet "ten" inches high, of "dark" complexion, "dark" eyes, "dark" hair, and by profession a "Schoolmaster" [stating that he does] hereby acknowledge to have this day voluntarily enlisted as a soldier in the Volunteer Military Corps in the Army of the United States of America . . ." dated March 12, 1813 in manuscript, and another partially completed with the name "John Watkins" born in "the Mississippi" in manuscript.

The "Mississippi Territory," an administrative unit beginning in 1798, then consisted of a Tennessee-shaped rectangle including parts of today's southern Mississippi and southern Alabama, until 1817, when it expanded northward to encompass all of the land now constituting those states. The "Territory" was split in mid-1817, and Mississippi became the twentieth state later that year. Population remained sparse at the turn of the nineteenth century, but mushroomed soon thereafter, as immigrants from the East came to exploit the fertile land in the Delta area. Members of the Watkins family were part of this population explosion.

Watkins's music commonplace book contains handwritten dates ranging from 1805 through 1813, thus beginning when he was a boy of nine and concluding when he was seventeen. The collection of melodies he copied shows remarkable parallels to that which Philander Seward was noting at about the same time. In addition to a handful of tunes falling into the central reel/hornpipe/breakdown genre of American fiddling, Watkins wrote down examples of other dances (minuets and cotillions), lots of song melodies, and some religious tunes (e.g., "93rd Psalm" and "Zion's Hill"). Watkins also noted directions on how to perform certain ornaments and effects (sample ornaments: "A turn'd shake," "A superior apogiatura," [sic], sample effects: "Staccato," "Swelling"). This suggests that Watkins, even more than Seward, did not anticipate having regular access to an appropriate teacher, but expected instead to learn to play on his own.

Last, Watkins notated quite a few marches (e.g., the ubiquitous "Washington's March"), and several tunes borrowed from art music, including "Geminiani's Minuet" and "Minuet in [Handel's oratorio] Samson." Since both Watkins and Seward were learning to fiddle in an age when vernacular fiddling overlapped considerably with pop and art music, fiddlers could and would play almost anything they heard. And this was an age when bellicose facts or intentions inspired the writing of marches that then would be played on whatever instrument(s) were available. (Today, our new war songs are country-western songs rather than fiddle tunes, and actual marches are performed primarily by wind bands.)

The degree of overlap between the music commonplace books kept by Philander Seward and Samuel Watkins illustrates how shared purposes resulted in similar creations; indeed, most coeval American music commonplace books resemble theirs. Some have significant religious components, like that of Watkins, and some do not, like Seward's *Musical Deposit*. Seward went to church; his family had a box at their church in Fishkill, New York. But he, like many teenagers, didn't incorporate religious music into their personal ambitions for performance. Also, some of these commonplace books contain as much instructional material as

Watkins wrote out, and some as little as Seward chose to inscribe. But the broad categories of secular tunes are in generally consistent in both identity and approximate proportion from manuscript to manuscript. These teenagers copied out popular music items from a printed total repertoire of thousands of pieces, though each person was limited in his or her choices by which published sources they encountered. These two manuscripts illustrate how different personal repertoires could be. Each young man had just one piece with clear local associations; just as Seward wrote out "New Haven Green," Watkins anthologized a "Guest March in ye Battle of Orleans" (yes, the composer could have been referring to Orleans, France, but Watkins was unlikely to have known that). And each young man collected both widely distributed tunes and obscure ones. The only melodies that both wrote out were the fiddle tune "The Flowers of Edinburgh," the very common song "How Imperfect Is Expression," the military-connected "President's March," "The Duke of Holstein's March" (Watkins shortened the title to "Holstein's March"), "Port Gordon," and "Roslin Castle," altogether an assembly of hits.

The main lesson learned from studying these music commonplace books as sources of fiddle tunes is this: The reason that we have notations (both published and manuscript) of a number of fiddle tunes in oral tradition in the young United States is that those particular tunes were simultaneously traveling in the realm of popular music. The simplicity of the notations does seem to reflect a performance practice much less elaborate than in Scottish drawing rooms, but this does not surprise, since the ideological associations of Scottish fiddle tunes that invited content-rich versions mattered little in England or New England. Straightforward notations would have been fine for dance accompaniment, just as straightforward melodizing still is.

Two Fiddle Tunes Common in New England

Three fiddle tunes that Knauff arranged in the first three numbers of the *Virginia Reels* would have been extremely familiar to amateur fiddlers like Seward and Watkins: "Speed the Plough," "Money Musk" (called "Killie Krankie" by Knauff), and "The Flowers of Edinburgh" (closely related to "Old Virginia" in the *Virginia Reels*). All three of these ubiquitous dance tunes varied in small ways from version to version both in published collections of instrumental music and in the music commonplace books that drew on those published collections. But they flourished somewhat differently in the early nineteenth century and have had contrasting fates since. In this chapter, I will look at "Speed the Plough" and "Money Musk." "The Flowers of Edinburgh" is discussed at the end of chapter 4.

"Speed the Plough" came originally from England (Kuntz 2012; in contrast, "Money Musk" and "The Flowers of Edinburgh" were first written down in Scotland). All three of these common tunes that Knauff found in his part of Virginia have had and still lead healthy lives in Scotland, Ireland, England, the United States, and other English-speaking areas. "Speed the Plough" as notated in the young United States can stand for most fiddle tunes of the day in many ways (see fig. 6). It has two strains that begin in contrasting ranges, with one strain more emphatically hammering on the tonic chord than the other (that emphasis generally being in the low strain, as is the case here). Each strain is eight measures long. But this does not add up to total of a full sixteen measures of musical material. Each strain is broken up into two 4-bar phrases (as is the case in a majority of fiddle tunes), and the two phrases comprise an antecedent plus a consequent expression of the same idea. In addition, the low and high strains share cadential material. In the end, what seems initially like a short musical expression is even shorter, verging on the epigrammatic. So why is this tune pleasing and memorable; why is even the most straightforward performance of it satisfying?

Good fiddle tunes contain some sort of "hook," that is, a distinctive, attractive, memorable gesture, and are assembled with verve and balance. "Speed the Plough" starts with a half-measure march up from the tonic—not very distinctive yet!—then the signature gesture of the tune, a certain turn: a given pitch, a note a step or leap higher, the initial pitch, then the one a third lower. This figure finishes the first measure, then fills the second measure, then is replicated a step lower, then another step lower to make up the third measure, followed by a cadence (circling the tonic once, then marching through or to the tonic, depending on whether we are in the antecedent or consequent phrase). The high strain hammers on the high a in the first half of the first measure, checks a downward loop, then saw-tooths down rapidly in the second measure. Thus, after an emphasis on the tonic twice as long as in the low strain, the downward contour is twice as fast . . . and then the third and fourth measure replicate those of the low strain.

Figure 6. Early versions of "Speed the Plough."

That general description fits all of the versions of "Speed the Plough" given in figure 6. Nevertheless, these versions differ in the small ways cited in my discussion above of fiddle tunes in antebellum America, while clearly being considered the same tune then and now. The matters of continuity that qualify these versions manifestly different takes on a single tune rather than distinct tunes center on the "hook," which I consider consists of both the shape of the characteristic turn and how it is repeated and modified. The broader contours of the other parts of the tune matter, too—the initial march up and the cadential gestures—but the melodic turn is the real center of the tune's identity. The non-hook contours varied more than the hook-dominated measures in antebellum fiddling, and vary more today, though no variation ever implies a change in the underlying harmony—that stays rock solid.

What part of a tune can vary most easily without the tune's identity being compromised? Again, broad contours like the opening swoop up are less concrete in intimate detail and more apt to vary than intimate contours like the characteristic turn of "Speed the Plough." However, in that turn's three iterations before it starts the march downward—that is, the turn's precise shape in the second half of the first measure through the end of the second measure—has two forms, the dominant one the high note of which is *f#*, and the accent-producing main alternative, in which the highest note is the *a* above that *f#*. The commonest sequence in Knauff's day was as in the first and second versions given in figure 6. The last version was reprinted endlessly in the publications of Elias Howe (1850, I, 41; 1851, 29; 1863, 41; the 1850 version is slightly different, the other two standard).

The most unusual aspect of Knauff's version is not really very striking. This concerns leaps up within the melodic hook. In printed and handwritten versions of "Speed the Plough" in the antebellum United States, that hook fills the second half of the first measure and both halves of the second measure based at the same level. If the three iterations of the hook there are not identical, it is generally the middle one that reaches up to the note *a*, as in the two versions in figure 6 taken from music commonplace books. Knauff does exactly the opposite: his first and third iterations reach *a*, while the inner one has its highest note as *f#*. Might that represent the only way his source fiddler played it? Or was it just Knauff's favorite way among several ways that the fiddler played it? We can't know. But this is not a dramatic departure from how the tune was usually shaped, and may simply be taken as one of the many tiny variations that demonstrate that the tunes took part in oral tradition. There are no other surprises. The tune remains in its usual key, the rhythmic density seems appropriate, and so on.

Boston publisher Elias Howe Jr. soon standardized how this and many hundreds of tunes would be printed for decades. He reprinted hundreds of tunes to swell the thicknesses of each of his very large collections, which dominated the American market for instrumental anthologies for much of the remainder of the nineteenth century.[3] The full bibliographic citations tell much of the story (see, e.g., 1850, 1851, and 1863). His activity probably helped the melodies remain in circulation, and it is valuable to modern scholars to see that the tunes continued to reach print, but we can't tell much about how they sounded or even if they were actually played. Oral tradition went its own way in the South; when hillbilly recordings showed what fiddle tunes sounded like in the 1920s, Howe's versions were a distant memory. Nevertheless, "Speed the Plough," primarily a northern tune, still often sounds much like it looked on paper in the nineteenth century. In the churning of the hook, the high form of that melodic turn may or may not appear; the point now seems to be the rapid motion, with no need for the accent. The tune flourishes in the Ozarks and especially New England, and here and there throughout the country in older fiddlers' repertoires that are both retrospective and notation-connected. In New England, this melody is generally played as one entry in a sequence of tunes constituting the musical accompaniment of a contradance—that is, as one member in a medley of a handful of tunes.

The first tune of the *Virginia Reels*, which Knauff gave the title "Killie Krankie," is a typical version of the common tune nearly always named "Money Musk." (The melody more usually called "Killie Krankie" is primarily a song that is also sometimes fiddled; this tune bears no resemblance to "Money Musk.") The most likely reason for Knauff renaming his version of "Money Musk" is that a form of the danced Virginia reel was called "Killie Krankie." The tune "Money Musk" must have been played for that dance in the Farmville area, and Knauff witnessed this.

"Money Musk" was among the most popular tunes in antebellum America, but it has a more complicated history than has "Speed the Plough." "Money Musk" has a very tight construction. In many versions from the young United States, both of the eight-measure strains break cleanly into identical four-measure phrases. That is, this melody doesn't even contain contrasting simple antecedent and consequent phrases, just the latter. This is almost always the case for the lower, main strain. Almost always presented in the key of A Major, the tune begins with an arpeggio hammering on the tonic chord: the open *e* string, the open *a*, *c#* on that string, then the open *a*. Each of the first three measures starts with that figure. The action is in the second half of the measure, which offers a little more drama in each measure until the story has accumulated enough power to pull the first half of the measure free of the tonic for a cadence.

The original Scottish form was both more and less powerful. Fiddler and composer Daniel Dow was routinely credited for the tune (1776); I give a more widely distributed version published in a collection by the famous Gow family at the top of figure 7a (from [ca. 1802], 10–11). The Gow version is almost identical to the Dow original; there are small differences between these two and other late eighteenth-century Scottish versions that, as in the slightly later American prints and commonplace books, show individual opinions about a tune's details. The way that these Scottish versions are relatively powerful is in their distinctive and carefully rationed rhythms. Especially notable are the uses of Scotch snap: here, a sixteenth note followed by a dotted eighth note, creating an aggressive moment of syncopation to start measures one and two (and five and six) of the first strain, then, in a complementary placement, in the cadential measures of the second strain. The weaker side of the Scottish versions is in their key. In the original key of G Major, the motion between the first two notes is awkward. The fiddler is asked to go from the *d* that is stopped by the third finger of the left hand on the *a* string to the *g* that is fingered identically on the *d* string. This requires that the fiddler either make a quick move from one string to the other (likely shortening one or the other note), or to straddle the two strings with the left-hand third finger. This is not a challenge for a skilled violinist—and the published Scottish fiddlers were skilled violinists, too—but it is not easy for student or amateur players. The key of A Major is a much better home for the initial figure, and that is the key swiftly adopted in England and the antebellum United States. (I have seen a few early American versions that retain the key of G, but most are in A.) The opening figure that is awkward in G is very natural in A, as the first, second, and fourth notes in the opening figure are all open strings. This makes the figure easier for the left hand and allows more resonance—more continuous total sound—and more ringing from strings not being stopped for the next note and from sympathetic vibration.

Three versions from antebellum American music commonplace books follow the Dow/Gow version in figure 7a. The first version was penned in 1806 by one Arthur McArthur, a Maine teenager attending Fryeburg Academy. In his commonplace book, now on deposit at the

New York Public Library, McArthur not only noted when he started at this preparatory school—1805—and when he matriculated at Bowdoin College—1808—but precisely when he notated many of pieces in his book. McArthur's version shows the influence of Scottish fiddling in its thorough permeation with dotted rhythms. However, it is in A Major, there is no Scotch snap, and there are no trills, though a few simple turns remain. Thus, this is a transitional version.

The commonplace book versions penned by Philander Seward and by Samuel Watkins simplify the original considerably. The implied harmonies remain constant, the contrast in range between low and high strain is stable, and the general contours still fit the broad conception of the tune. But the essence of this tune is not in general contours, but highly specific ones; these two versions seem like student-oriented oversimplifications. Knauff's version is more in line with the main printed version of the mid- to late nineteenth century, that of Elias Howe Jr., given at the bottom of the figure.

The main home for "Money Musk" in the modern United States is New England. See figure 7b, top, for a version typical of the tune as it is used for contemporary contradancing. The first two strains offer no surprises, but there is a third strain in this version, a strain heard in many modern versions. Why is it there? As mentioned above, such tunes are often gathered into medleys today. That's one way for a simple two-strain fiddle tune to become more interesting in response to audiences listening increasingly more closely: they become part of a suite. Alternatively, a simple way for a tune to grow in aesthetic weight without combining with others (as in such medleys) is for it to grow in length!

Here is a question to be asked repeatedly in this book: how do performances of short tunes become "bigger?" When audiences listen more and more closely to performances, how can content be added to reward that increased attention? The answers will vary according to the style of performance, and given tunes will be well suited for one or two styles, and fit not so naturally elsewhere. The last few paragraphs of this chapter follow "Money Musk" into the main categories of contemporary southern fiddling, and find it not doing as well as in New England. That is, while surviving healthily in the contradance environment of New England and also found occasionally in the living museum of older Ozark playing, "Money Musk," like "Speed the Plough," does not have a stable home in either Texas fiddling (including related contest styles) or in

Figure 7a. "Monny Musk. a Strathspey. by D[aniel] D[ow]."

southeastern old-time performance. I have heard the tune played just once each in those two styles in contests during the last twenty years. Each of these instances was obviously an exception to normal practice and had features that demonstrated that exceptions can indeed prove rules.

The climax of the Texas State Championship, held annually in Hallettsville, is a so-called round robin. The top three contestants ascend the stage, and must stay there for five rounds of competition defined by genre. A contest administrator who is also a domino champion turns over a domino the value of which is linked to a fiddle genre (waltz, hornpipe, etc.). Then each contestant plays one tune in the genre. In the 2013 contest, one of the finalists in the Gone to Texas bracket, Tom Weisgerber of Minnesota, took his turn playing a reel. His choice was "Money Musk." I asked him later how he had encountered the tune. His wife's family lives in Missouri, where fiddle tunes and repertoires have changed relatively slowly (she is Alita Stoneking Weisgerber). Some older melodies still flourish in the Ozarks, and some Texas-style fiddlers with Ozark roots have adapted some of the tunes their parents played to Texas style. But this particular recasting of "Money Musk" showed that this is not an easy task.

Tom Weisgerber's "Money Musk" is transcribed in the middle of figure 7b. He played with a modest amount of swing, and the guitar accompanists used a typical march-through-jazz-changes approach. In terms of these factors, this version has been adjusted to Texas style. But the normal low and high strains (the A and B strains in the transcription) were not adjusted. Weisgerber's performance of both venerable strains incorporated no specific stylistic traits in terms of pitch choices or variation technique. Through that part of his version, the audience

Figure 7b. "Money Musk," versions from early nineteenth-century music commonplace books.

heard the tune as it has passed through history, still amazingly stable, probably due to the circumstance that the identity of the tune focuses on intimate contours.

Only in the third, C strain did Weisgerber's version translate into Texas style in terms of freedom of pitch choices. This strain still fits the tune, since it consists of arpeggios on appropriate chords, and falls into the same four-measure divisions ending on the tonic as the original two strains. However, three factors illustrate that we have entered Texas style in terms of notes chosen. First, it is especially in Texas and related contest styles that American fiddlers regularly venture into third position; indeed, they are informally obliged to do so to demonstrate their virtuosity. This strain is not merely in third position, but calls for the fourth finger to be extended to catch the high *e* atop the arpeggiated A Major chord. Second, the shape of the arpeggio creates a sort of syncopation shared by bluegrass arranging and many moments in contest fiddling; typically, in a rhythmic texture of constant eighth-note motion, those are parceled into groupings defined by intervallic direction into two sets of three and one set of two notes in any combination. Here, in the first through third measures (and thus also the fifth through seventh measures, since these repeat the first through third measures), the eighth notes are in

Figure 7c. "Money Musk," as printed many times in the nineteenth century by Elias Howe.

a repeated pattern of 2+3+3. Third, in the repetition of the C strain, we finally encounter a taste of the variation technique typical of Texas fiddling: in a repetition of a strain, implied harmonies do not change, and both broad contours and a few signature licks are also retained, but the intimate course of the tune meanders away from the initial version here and there. Strain C' illustrates such departures very nicely. Weisgerber's total performance was quite beautiful, and helped him win his division that year. But at the same time, the somewhat jarring aural effect of alternating New England and Texas approaches to choosing pitches was only partly papered over by the Texas rhythmic swing and the Texas-style accompaniments. This was a skilled and inventive fiddler contributing a delightful change of pace to the contest. But I doubt that "Money Musk" has much of a future in Texas-style fiddling.

In a series of interviews that I conducted during the summer of 2000 with fiddlers in the area where North Carolina, Virginia, and Tennessee meet, I asked a dozen top old-time fiddlers if they played tunes from the *Virginia Reels*, including "Money Musk." I hadn't heard this melody during dozens of weekends spent at festivals in the area in the 1990s. Among fiddlers I interviewed, the only one who knew the tune was Brian Grim, of mountainous Independence, Virginia. He said he had learned it from French-Canadian and English friends, and had little opportunity to perform it. His "Money Musk" was an imaginative take on the tune. His first two strains reminded me of the traditional strains of "Money Musk" if I listened carefully and a bit willfully, but only when the performance reached the C strain—the one adopted for New England versions during the twentieth century—was the piece clearly recognizable. Old-time style, with its near-constant drones when those are readily available, is not very hospitable to arpeggios, since the melody notes and those

Figure 7d. "Money Musk," three modern performances.

produced by the drone can be confused. The regional performance style and the details of the intricate tune simply weren't very compatible in this fiddle milieu, only about two hundred miles from Knauff's home in Farmville.

Folklorist and fiddler Alan Jabbour recorded master fiddler Henry Reed playing "Money Musk" in 1966–1967; that performance and Jabbour's transcription appear on the wonderful website resulting from their interaction, *Fiddle Tunes of the Old Frontier: The Henry Reed Collection*. But fiddlers unacquainted with Reed didn't have to wait for this website to be created to hear his tunes: Jabbour played them frequently all over the Upper South soon after collecting them. Reed's repertoire included quite a few of the tunes anthologized by Knauff long before. Reed's home of Glen Lyn, Virginia, is about 175 miles west of Farmville on a logical route through the Allegheny Mountains. It's easy to imagine Knauff's source fiddler or fiddlers (or other local fiddlers who knew the same Prince Edward County tunes) stopping in Glen Lyn, perhaps to stay, perhaps on the way west. In any case, Jabbour's championing of Reed's repertoire brought a number of the *Virginia Reels* back into regular usage, especially in West Virginia (Glen Lyn is right on the border) and among revivalists. But some of Reed's tunes were adopted (or readopted) more readily than others; "George Booker" and "Ducks on a Pond" ("Lady of the Lake" in the *Virginia Reels*) suited contemporary old-time style, and can be heard today in southern old-time circles, while "Money Musk" didn't catch on.

The first pamphlet of the *Virginia Reels* was an all-purpose effort in 1839, but seems transitional now: some of the tunes do indeed survive in modern southern fiddling, and some remain more closely allied to what was the published mainstream in Knauff's day, tunes surviving best today in New England. But we must keep in mind that fiddling has always been dynamic in terms of performance practice and repertoire. That Henry Reed played "Money Musk" not so many generations ago, but that the tune was in the process of losing its spot in southern fiddling, illustrates the continued differentiation of regional fiddle repertoires. In this first pamphlet, Knauff was trying to build a bridge between the world of American pop music printing—a world centered to the north—and the music of Virginia fiddling, the music that he wanted to profit from publishing. The next chapters will explore how he ventured more deeply into specifically southern repertoires and practices.

- Chapter Three -

"Peter Francisco" and "Richmond Blues"

The Titles of Knauff's Virginia Reels

JUST A FEW OF THE MELODIES MAKING UP THE *VIRGINIA REELS* BEAR their customary modern names or similar ones in that publication, few enough that they can be listed quickly: "Speed the Plough" is the same tune printed and performed under that name from the late eighteenth century forward. "Forked Deer" survives today under that name; this was its first appearance in print. The melody "George Booker" survives under that name in the United States, though that title is newly associated with its tune in the *Virginia Reels*. And several titles are close to their usual ones: "Natchez on the Hill" is a version of the rare tune now generally entitled "Natchez Under the Hill"; "Billy in the Low Grounds"— a new title for the tune with which it is linked in the *Virginia Reels*—is still played under that name in the United States, though a much more common tune has largely usurped the title. "Sich a Gittin Up Stairs," a recognizable version of the minstrel tune "Getting Up Stairs," is not quite defunct in oral tradition, and retains its name. Last, the title "Ohio River" makes sense as an alternative title of "Boatman Dance," and "Midnight Serenade" makes similar sense as a temporary title for the tune usually called "Buffalo Gals." In both cases, the title in the *Virginia Reels* issues from the text of the song. There's a tune called "Mississippi Sawyer" in the first pamphlet of the *Virginia Reels*; the melody linked with that title in contemporary oral tradition appears in volume 4, under the name "Love from the Heart."[1] That completes the roster of surviving tunes among the *Virginia Reels* that bear unsurprising titles in that collection, just nine of thirty-five.

Figure 8. Detail of "Natchez Under the Hill," painted by Louis Joseph Bahin, 1852. This painting is owned by the Morris Museum of Art (in Augusta, Georgia; accession number 2000.045) and used by permission. For this illustration, I asked museum personnel to crop their digital image of the painting to include a specified part of the lower left of the composition, and also to change the original muted brown tones to black and white. Bahin (1813–1857) lived in Natchez. He was primarily a portraitist; this scene is his only surviving landscape.

The Basic Conventions of Fiddle Tune Titles

Fiddle tune titles serve as handy identifiers and can add value to these short tunes by being piquant, intriguing (or, conversely, reassuringly familiar), by asserting an alliance between music and social values or local identity, or by combining several virtues. In an unpublished article written in 1990 entitled "Title, Text and Tune Interrelationships in American Fiddle Music," Steve Green eloquently argued for a holistic approach to the study of fiddle tunes. He noted that titles of tunes had been undervalued by earlier scholars, who characterized them as of little interest since they were impermanently linked to the tunes. The titles' most intriguing feature in the consensus scholarly opinion was simply that they constituted attractive representations of folk imagery. Green found instead that "titles can be—and often are—useful signifiers pointing the way toward potential melodic, textual, and conceptual connections between pieces. . . . With a great many fiddle tunes, the title is related in some way to some text that at some time was sung to some part of the tune." In looking at changes in titles, he noted that similarities of many kinds could symptomize relationships between titles and often between tunes, including patterns of syntax, rhythmic patterns of versification where tunes are texted, conceptual relatedness, and retention of morphemes and phonemes (9–14).

Green illustrated his hypotheses with a case study of one group of contemporary fiddle tunes whose contours, titles, and associated scraps of occasionally sung text worked together to demonstrate relationships of long standing. My intent in this chapter is to accomplish a complementary but broader task, to employ Knauff's titles as a springboard for a discussion of patterns of syntax and significance of fiddle tune titles. Since not even one of the tunes in the second pamphlet of the *Virginia Reels* bears its current usual name, this is a good point at which to begin to consider these linked topics. I will then broaden the discussion to include the titles in the other three pamphlets and, more briefly, the titles Knauff employed in his other music.

There are thousands of fiddle tunes, and the total repertoire has always been in flux. Tunes evaporate when neglected (especially if never published), and other tunes enter the repertoire, some through self-conscious composition, and some through quiet, perhaps gradual transformations of existing fiddle tunes. Yet others enter the repertoire as melodies borrowed from elsewhere in American musical life, particularly from genres of dance music that have outlasted fashion or from down-home songs in popular music or in oral tradition. In short, the music of American fiddling has never been a stable or conservative or even bounded body of music. On the other hand, the formal conventions of fiddling immediately envelope adopted tunes. That is, whatever shapes the melodies originally have, they normally become pairs of eight-measure strains which contrast in initial range and often overlap in content. At the same time, titles of adopted tunes may change to fit their new cultural and musical environments.

Just as the musical elements of each tune are compact, titles are short and fit their own conventions. Some titles cling to tunes as they enter the fiddled repertoire from elsewhere, particularly when pop songs become fiddle tunes; these titles may retain their original shapes as part of recalling their associations with song texts (as in "Such a Getting Up Stairs"). But most contemporary American fiddle tune titles are short and arresting. At least nine out of ten of these titles consist of a noun preceded by a significant modifier (an adjective, or second noun narrowing the meaning of the final one, or a verb): "Mississippi Sawyer"; "Indian Whoop." Melodies named after people or places generally follow that shape, too: "Peter Francisco," "Old Virginia." Many of the remainder also have two main ingredients, but the modifier follows the main noun. In such cases, the titles accrue conjunctions, articles, or prepositions: "Twenty-Second of February," "Rose on the Mountain."

Nearly all of Knauff's titles follow these syntactic patterns. In addition, the topics of titles that Knauff employed anticipate those in use now. Each theme appears already in the first pamphlet of the *Virginia Reels*. These include the most popular type of fiddle title: salty—pungent, multivalent within a framework of nostalgia—rural images (e.g., "Forked Deer" and "Speed the Plough"), plus general or quite specific references to people ("The Two Sisters," "Slighted Jenny") or to places ("Killie Krankie," "Natchez on the Hill"). There are also titles that mix types. A "Mississippi Sawyer" is a sunken tree whose occasionally surfacing limbs present a navigational hazard to passing steamships, but the title also includes a geographical reference. In modern times, most fiddle tune titles, whether salty ("Leather Britches") or referring to people ("Smith's Reel") or to places ("Tennessee Waltz") can be gathered under the umbrella feeling of nostalgia for rural life of earlier times. Knauff's titles evoked relatively contemporary images, though often already imbued with nostalgia.

I will first consider the titles in pamphlet 2, the only one of the four short volumes for which tunes seem to have been assembled *because* of their titles. These nine tune names all refer to places and people, almost all in Knauff's Virginia (the only possible exceptions being the two titles the meaning of which remain elusive). Some of these titles also bear salty associations.

Local Geography, Local Fighters, and Tune Titles in the *Virginia Reels*

Pamphlet 2 of the *Virginia Reels* begins with the title that is the broadest geographically: "Old Virginia." While we should keep in mind that antebellum Virginia included today's West Virginia, (and, until 1792, today's Kentucky), "old" Virginia referred to the state as first substantially

Figure 9. Knauff's "Old Virginia," to which is glued an anonymous poem expressing nostalgia for older Virginia. Copy on Deposit in the Special Collections Library of the University of Alabama.

populated. This is roughly the same as the state as now bounded, which has Buckingham County—where Knauff did his stint of finishing school piano teaching—as its geographic center. The word "old" resonates on several levels. Fiddling had become less fashionable than flute-playing decades earlier, and the genre of the reel paled in novelty when compared to the younger waltz and polka. But continuity and trustworthiness had their own appeal. "Old" Virginia, already the subject for widespread nostalgia in the antebellum South, would be celebrated in numerous poems, some of which became songs. A copy of this second pamphlet now housed in the library of the University of Alabama has a poem attached to the upper left-hand corner of the "Old Virginia" page. It's one of several poems in which the narrator asks to be "carried back" to older Virginia, though it's neither the lyrics of the James Bland megahit of much later in the nineteenth century nor the words of the earlier, also very popular "Floating Scow of Old Virginia," a song popular with Confederate soldiers.

Both the second and the last titles in this pamphlet include the word "Richmond," naming Virginia's largest city (a count of 16,060 in the census of 1830), while the fourth tune bears the title "Petersburg

Ladies" (Petersburg, then Virginia's third-largest city, received a count of 8,300 in that census; Joseph Martin 1835, 23). The last title in this set, "Richmond Blues," refers to a volunteer militia unit, thus men balancing the "Ladies" of Petersburg. These were the most important big cities to Knauff both in personal and business terms. He may have lived in Richmond and may have met his bride there. Much of what we know about him comes through the advertisements he placed in the *Richmond Enquirer.* However, Petersburg became more important to his business. Just as Richmond is located at the fall line of the James River—that is, the point limiting passage of sizable ships—Petersburg marks the fall line of the Appomattox. Ocean-going ships stopped in Petersburg, but systematic dredging between Petersburg and Farmville during the late eighteenth and early nineteenth centuries made it possible for the long, slender boats called bateaux to reach Farmville; a bateau drew less than two feet of water fully loaded. Batteaux going from Farmville to Petersburg transported tobacco, and Farmville became the fourth-largest processing and shipping point for tobacco in Virginia during the 1830s. It was also cheaper to ship all supplies (including pianos and materials to make pianos) by ship to Petersburg and then by bateau to Farmville than to transport anything by road; trains were not yet an option.

The title "Richmond Hill" and the tune it names probably entered this particular pamphlet because Knauff, as a recent immigrant, was not aware that Richmond Hill did not name a location in Richmond or elsewhere in Virginia, although the Virginia town of Richmond was indeed named for England's Richmond Hill. The older English city named Richmond, which was then near London and is now surrounded by it, includes Richmond Hill. That gentle slope offers a lovely view of the River Thames, a view so special that it is actually protected by an Act of Parliament, the Richmond, Ham, and Petersham Open Spaces Act of 1902. Virginia's Richmond got its name due to a perceived similarity between that view of the Thames and the view of the James River from the site of the future Richmond.

"Villalave," the third title in this pamphlet, proved untraceable. The word must be a crunching together of Villa la Vé or Villa la Vie (in the same way that Delaware is named for a Baron de la Warr). But I could not find a "Villa la Vé" (or "Vie") in Knauff's Virginia, though there are plenty of hotels by one or the other name dotting the modern world. There must have been such a hotel in antebellum Virginia, but it did not leave a mark in the historical record. The main point here is that Knauff gathered up tunes the titles of which referred to different levels of geographic specificity, from the state level through cities to minor locations such as the hypothetical Villa la Vé/Vie.[2]

The remaining titles in the second number of the *Virginia Reels* have military links, all again specific to Knauff's part of Virginia. "The Hero" probably refers to the same person whose name is spelled out in the next title, "Peter Francisco" (1760–1831), the most famous enlisted man in the Revolutionary War. His bizarre story begins with a kidnapping: five-year-old Pedro Francisco (born July 9, 1760) was abducted in the Azores, then abandoned in 1765 on a wharf near present-day Hopewell, Virginia. Rather than being placed in the Poor House of Prince George County, he was taken home by Judge Winston of Buckingham County. But he was neither adopted nor educated to his sponsor's level. Instead, he was trained as a blacksmith. He grew to what was then considered quite a size, over six feet tall and weighing some 260 pounds. At the age of sixteen, Francisco enlisted in a Virginia militia regiment that was soon absorbed into the Continental Army. The story becomes episodic and repetitive: Francisco was in a battle, was wounded, but in an act of remarkable heroism and astonishing strength, killed many British soldiers. He was demustered and went home. He joined another branch of the American army, was in a battle, was wounded, and so on. During the course of his picaresque and repetitive Odyssey, he convalesced with Lafayette, was given an out-sized sword by Washington, and was offered but declined a captaincy; he was said to have insisted that officers ought to be literate, which he was not (Ward 2011, 39–44).

After the war, Francisco returned to Buckingham County and ran a tavern in New Store, about fifteen miles from Farmville, and half that distance to the Buckingham Female Collegiate Institute; he was certainly a *local* hero for Knauff! He was not successful—debts always loomed—but his legend kept growing, now focusing on feats of strength. For instance, when a strong young man came from "Kaintuck" to challenge him, he threw the visitor and then his horse (!) over a fence. In his old age, Francisco was granted an appropriate sinecure: he was sergeant-at-arms at the Virginia House of Delegates from 1825 until his death. This "Hercules of the Revolution" became the subject of several amateur histories (e.g., Racer n.d.) and of a short epic poem, on deposit along with an out-sized desk and other personal artifacts in the Buckingham County Historic

Museum (the same as the Housewright House; see http://www.historic-buckingham.org/Museum.html).

The following title in the second pamphlet of the *Virginia Reels*, "Twenty-Second of February," marks the birthdate of Virginia's favorite son, George Washington. Although a national figure, he was local, too, and his birthday was already enthusiastically celebrated in Knauff's time. Just as the tune titles naming places within this number of the *Virginia Reels* reach from the intimate to statewide, so do the titles that refer to people. Of course, this particular title refers as much to the holiday's festivities as to Washington the man.

The next title, "Island," presents a puzzle. Many islands ornament the coast of Virginia, and a handful of pleasant ones punctuate the major rivers. But most Virginia islands interesting enough to be celebrated in the title of a tune have more specific names. However, the placement of this melody within the collection offers us a clue. It sits between "Twenty-Second of February" and "Richmond Blues," the name of a fashionable militia unit. What generically named "island" was most important in defending Virginia? In Joseph Martin's *Gazetteer* of 1835 he discussed just one Virginia island devoted solely to a military purpose. Military engineers designed a new island to house a fort to complement Fort Monroe (located on one side of the entrance to Chesapeake Bay), and thus to keep the British from a further attack on the capitol, which they had burned during the War of 1812. Fort Wool was built on the new land. This island didn't have a more specific name because it was young, in fact still being built during the 1830s. Here is some of Martin's effusive prose:

> The area of the structure as originally staked off includes 5 acres [15 eventually], a great part of which was 22 feet below the surface of the sea . . . To get a foundation above water for the Fort or Castle, an Island has been raised, by throwing rocks into the water, until, by gradual accumulation, it has emerged above the tides . . .
>
> The present aspect of the place is rough and savage, and when the surge rushes in among the hollow piles of granite, and the wind whistles among the naked spars, which are planted round the walls for the support of the scaffolding, the music of the surrounding elements of sea and air, is quite in keeping with the dreary, desolate spot, which, at a distance, looks like Gibraltar, beaten down by cannonade, and fallen prostrate in the sea . . .

The ancients tell us that Venus rose from the sea, but it would seem a much fitter element, to give birth to the god of war; and never was there a nobler scene, or nobler temple, than that appropriated for his cradle. . . . He will appear here, not like the goddess of love, borne in a shell upon a summer's sea, but upon a tower of strength amidst the noise of restless surges,—a fit emblem of the American people, whose martial strength belongs alike to the land and to the ocean.

It is a circumstance worth notice, that the material for the structure . . . is drawn from most of the commercial states of the Union. In walking over the piles you behold the dark grey granite of Maine—the whitish blue and black speckled granite of Connecticut—the red free stone of the same state—the deep blue of the Little Falls of Potomac—and the ash colored of the James River.

It is this edifice, which is to form a strong hold in a central position—defend our great naval depot, and to protect our naval power over the ocean; and especially to afford a place of refuge to the commerce of the nation, each commercial state may point to a portion of the blended strength which it has contributed to the common structure.

If this is the "Island" of the tune title, naming a Virginia reel "Island" was timely and patriotic, touching two themes for these titles, that of a place nearby in Virginia and that of the military. The same holds for the last title in this pamphlet, "Richmond Blues," a renaming and re-purposing of the common Scottish tune usually called "My Love She's But a Lassie Yet." The Richmond Light Infantry Blues was a volunteer militia company organized in 1789. The company struggled to maintain enthusiasm and enrollment at first, because the uniforms were initially red, leading to disapproval due to the potential for confusion with British uniforms. Once they became blue, enlistment stabilized (Cutchins, 4–5). The new color became part of the organization's official title, which then was abbreviated in regular use as "Richmond Blues." Quite a few militia units were named informally this way: On May 10, 1843, the Richmond Blues hosted the Petersburg Greys at a local festival (Cutchins, 51).

The Richmond Blues would eventually participate in the Civil War, and then in all subsequent American wars through World War II. But in Knauff's day, the unit remained primarily a gentlemen's social club celebrating chivalry, a mixture of a parading unit and a modern chamber of commerce or a benevolent society like a Lion's Club.[3] Emphasis remained focused on the gaudy uniforms:

> The regimental coat was the same worn by the old Continental officer. The cap was a sugar-loafed fur hat, with a gray fox tail front to rear, over the top, a leopard skin around the brim over the fox tail, tied with a blue ribbon behind, and an oval tin plate in front, having an eagle and stars painted upon it and the name and date of the Company, with a large plume of black feathers, tipped with white, a cockade of leather on the left side in the form of a half circle with rays. (Cutchins, 8)

The group had no active duty before John Brown's Raid on Harpers Ferry in 1859; instead, they participated in four annual celebrations—their own anniversary on May 10, the Fourth of July, the 19th of October (the anniversary of the battle of Yorktown), and the 22nd of February. Cutchins reported that "On Washington's Birthday, the Blues, together with the other militia companies of the city, paraded the streets in the afternoon. A salute was fired by the artillery and a patriotic address was made by some prominent citizen. The ceremonies generally concluded with a military ball in the evening, given by the Blues. This annual ball was one of the most brilliant social events in the life of the city" (46). This celebration seems to have been especially flashy and large in 1821: "250 Ladies honored the Ball with their presence and pronounced it the most splendid they had ever seen" (10). In short, this tune title was the perfect finale for the pamphlet, quoting the name of the city as part of the title of its most important social club—which happened to be explicitly patriotic—a club that nurtured the city's future leaders and gave them opportunities to both march and dance.[4]

Tune Titles in Pamphlets 1, 3, and 4 of the *Virginia Reels*

Several other *Virginia Reels* bore titles that refer to people or places from the South, and often specifically from Virginia, though not as systematically as in pamphlet 2. The titles "Nancy Anderson," "Gaston," "Slighted Jenny," and "Two Sisters" remain of unknown provenance and significance.⁵ But the actual "George Booker" must have belonged to the large clan of Bookers living in and around Farmville. One member of the local Bookers named George served as a militia lieutenant in the Revolutionary War, probably the same George Booker who was a local lawyer by 1809 (Bradshaw n.d., 118 and 223); the family name is common in the little cemeteries that dot Prince Edward County's farms. "Colonel Crocket" refers to Davy Crocket, who, while not a Virginian, was celebrated throughout the South; his death at the Alamo predated the publication of Knauff's "Colonel Crocket" by just three years.

The tune title "Lady of the Lake" must refer to the long poem by that name by Sir Walter Scott. First published in 1810, it was wildly popular in the antebellum South.⁶ That would tempt us to associate the immediately following title "Scotts Favorite" with that author; the proximity of the titles suggests that Knauff made that mental connection. But it is at least as likely that this title refers to General Charles Scott (1739–1813), who was born in Goochland County (now Powhatan County), Virginia, and active primarily in Kentucky. In either case, this was a young reference.

Among places mentioned outside of the second number of the *Virginia Reels* is Killie Krankie, a Scottish village, naming a battle that took place in that village in 1689, a well-known nostalgic song, a dance . . . and perhaps partly because of that last association, this retitling of the ubiquitous Scottish and then American tune "Money Musk." "Lockwell" may refer to a place, or perhaps to a person: I could not trace the title.

The remaining two references to places in titles of the individual *Virginia Reels* refer to a watercourse and to a city on one. "Ohio River" borrows its title from within the lyrics of the song whose melody it employs, "Boatman Dance." The last is "Natchez on the Hill." Natchez, situated on the hilly Mississippi side of the Mississippi River, consisted then of two sections, the "good" part of town sitting high above the river, then several houses of entertainment in a small patch of land down by the river. This tune is normally named for that disreputable little waterfront area, "Natchez Under the Hill." That had long been the nickname of that unsavory few acres, but I can imagine either the fiddler from whom Knauff learned the tune or Knauff himself thinking that "Natchez Under the Hill" sounded geographically improbable, and revising the title to "Natchez on the Hill."⁷ The notoriety of the dockside patch of land led to its being painted many times, including by Louis Joseph Bahin in 1852. In that rendering, the river and sky loom large, overshadowing the buildings and people as if proportioned by Caspar David Friedrich. I extracted a small section and increased the contrast for figure 8, at the beginning of this chapter.

Knauff's Cotillions, Waltzes, Marches, and Songs

All of Knauff's sheet music publications were meant to earn him money. Most were his own compositions, though a few, like each of the *Virginia Reels,* were instead "arranged" by him. A full half of his pieces were arrangements of the dances that regularly took place locally, in those new incarnations shifting to piano pedagogy and to drawing-room performances.

A few of the cotillions were individual dances: "Virginia Cottillion," "Jackson's Cottillion," and "Blue Bonnetted Scotts: A Cottllion [*sic*] Arranged by Geo. P. Knauff," which is of special interest because he specified that he had merely "arranged" it. These were all from 1839. He also composed a set of cotillions during his second spate of publishing, in the early 1850s, "Virginia Cotillions, Composed for the Piano Forte and Dedicated to the Ladies of Virginia by Geo. P. Knauff." This is the collection containing "The Richmond Ladies," "The Belle of America," "Roberta," "Oldenplace," "Sweet Sally," and "Virginia." The girls' school that his daughter Irene attended was named Oldenplace.

Knauff's cotillion title "Amelia Springs" referred to a sulphur spring and recreational establishment located about twenty miles east of Farmville. Medicinal springs were important institutions, benefiting physical health but even more in social terms for their affluent patrons. The Amelia Springs were the closest medicinal springs to Knauff's Farmville.[8] There were many sulphur springs in use in antebellum Virginia, so many that fashion could afford to turn away from some of them. Joseph Martin, in the over six hundred pages of his *Comprehensive* [!] *Gazetteer of Virginia and the District of Columbia* of 1835, mentioned dozens of resorts built around one or another type of sulphur springs; he specified in his descriptions of about half of the establishments that they were no longer kept up.

Women and children living in the major cities came inland to such resorts to escape heat and insects, and working men joined them on many a weekend. The buildings at Amelia Springs allowed for both lodging and entertainment; several hundred guests could be seated for dining. The men were served by a racetrack and gaming tables, and all adults enjoyed a large ballroom (Hadfield and McConnaughey 1982, 72). In a recurring "Tournament of Knights," the men donned colorful costumes and "rode their chargers at a series of ring posts. The honor of crowning his favorite lady as queen was given to the Knight who secured the most rings. The next nearest winner chose the maid of honor, and so on until four selections had been made. During the 'tournament' days, Tom Booker, known as 'Marse Tom,' and his banjo, and Dr. Junius Seay, with his violin, helped the Miller boys make music for balls" (Hadfield and McConnaughey 1982, 73).

I haven't encountered the names of those particular musicians elsewhere, though "Marse Tom" Booker was probably related to the George Booker for whom one of the *Virginia Reels* was named. By naming a cotillion for the springs, Knauff was inviting his own potential customers to associate him with the glamour of the site (and he would have been delighted to work there or at any similar place). The violin and banjo played during "Tournament Days" suggest that blackface minstrel tunes were part of the entertainment fare, tunes like those Knauff anthologized in the final pamphlet of the *Virginia Reels*.

Knauff also composed waltzes and marches. A few of his waltzes are named after people, including "Beethoven's Favorite Waltz" and "Fisher's Waltz" appearing in his collection *Gatherings*—both preexisting pieces that came to him already named for famous individuals he never met— and, of course, the "Irene Waltz" he wrote for his daughter. But more of his waltzes bear names of places, often ones located in "Old Virginia." "Mt. Elba Waltz" referred to a sizable farm about thirty miles northeast of the Buckingham Female Collegiate Institute. I would not be surprised if the dedicatee, a Miss Virginia A. B. Shields, was a student at the institute, or if her family had purchased a piano from Knauff. The "Afton Grove Waltz" probably presents a similar case of a geographically—and professionally—intimate association. It may also have been named for a farm, perhaps the home of a student or customer; it is dedicated to "Miss Mary S. Burke," and there is an Afton Grove Road about fifty miles south of the institute, in today's Kenbridge.[9] The "Allegheny" and "Mohegan" waltzes probably point to locations in the eastern part of today's West Virginia. "Allegheny" could have referred to the mountain chain dividing current Virginia and West Virginia, or the county then bearing that name located due west of Prince Edward County. "Mohegan" is now a tiny town in West Virginia, about twenty miles from the Virginia border. Students at the Buckingham Collegiate Institute certainly could have come from just across the mountains. "Louisa" is a Virginia county north of Knauff's immediate environs. "The Metamora Waltz" probably also refers to a location in Virginia, but one that did not survive under that name in gazetteers. There are several villages in the Midwest called Metamora: could they have been named after an older settlement in Virginia, one that has faded from the historical record? At any rate, the titles of Knauff's waltzes emphasize geography (as remains true today for a substantial fraction of fiddled waltzes), and often name very local locations.

Most of Knauff's many marches also bear titles referring to places or to people, but with the proportions reversed: now associations with people dominate, ones ranging from famous persons to local citizens. Starting at the most general level, there is a "Ladies Quick Step" (ca. 1852) and a "Trumpet March" (1839; notable not just for a few melodic flourishes reminding us of the title, but because Knauff characterized the piece as being "arranged and partly composed by him," a careful calibrating of responsibility). Two pieces in the collection *Gatherings* ([n.d.]; probably ca. 1839) refer to the most famous international military figure: "Bonaparte's Quick Step" and "Napoleon's Grand March." Then we edge closer to home with Knauff's own "Virginia Quick March" (1839) and "General Pierce's Presidential Inauguration March and Quick Step" (1853). The most intimate reference is in the title "Colonel Hubard's March & Quick Step, Composed for & Dedicated to Col Edmund W. Hubard of Buckingham Va by His Friend G.P. Knauff" (1839). Finally, the piece "Turkish March" ([ca. 1852]) has both international and local resonance. Knauff was partaking in the Europe-wide vogue for Janissary music—that is, referring to the Turkish military wind bands, as did Mozart, Beethoven, and many others, often by incorporating cymbal and triangle into the orchestration of individual variations in variation sets. But his dedication to "the Ladies of Oldenplace Seminary," which his daughter Irene attended, adds an intimate personal aspect to the title page.

Most among Knauff's handful of songs survive as single copies, the notable exception being his one big hit, "Wait for the Wagon." Just one of the songs has a serious text, an ardent pastoral idyll dedicated to his

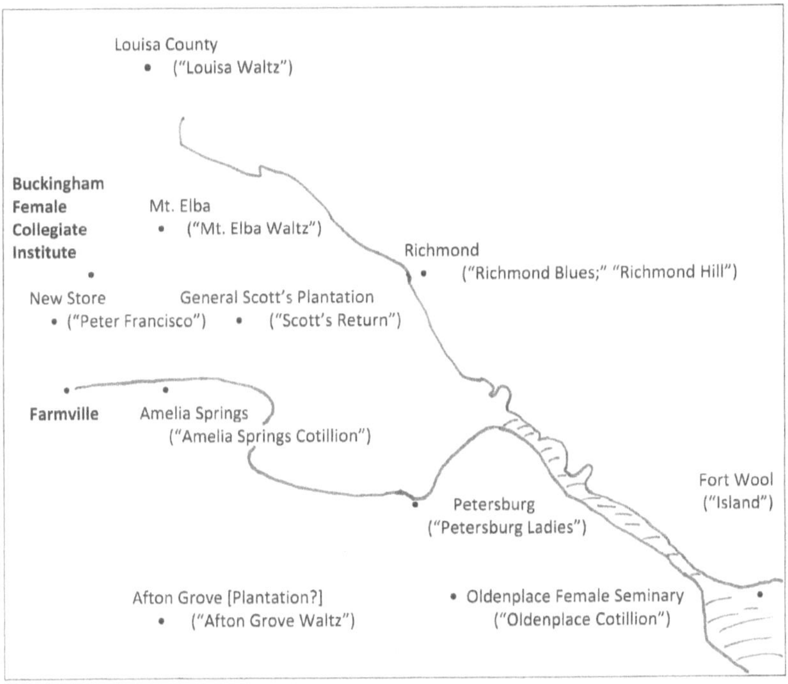

Figure 10. Knauff's places: his homes and the locales in central Virginia referenced in the tune titles in his sheet music.

daughter, Irene: "Awake My Love, and Come with Me" (1852). "Love & Pastry" (1854, thus Knauff's last surviving work) is a setting of a poem in which a suitor fails to gain the hand of a pastry cook because he is poor. This could have been classified as a "comic song." The other songs I will mention were called that on their title pages. "The Tooth-Ache or the Quilting" narrates a social event during which a young couple was caught kissing, and claimed the young lady had fainted due to pain associated with a toothache; the young man gallantly kept her from falling. During the course of this narrative, many young women were named; this item must have been aimed at the pocketbooks of their parents and friends. The "Comic Song" "Three Farmers Went a Hunting" (1851), which Knauff "arranged," is indeed the formulaic English and American children's folk song known under that title. "Wait for the Wagon," often referred to as an "Ethiopian Song" (1851), was again "arranged" by Knauff. Verse 3 of that first edition reads: "Do you believe my Phillis, dear, old Mike with all his wealth, Can make you half so happy, as I with youth and health?

We'll have a little farm, a horse, a pig and cow; And you will mind the dairy, while I will guide the plow." This Jacksonian message must have pleased Knauff, a man whose wife came from a higher social station.

Knauff's Tune Titles in Historical Contexts

Were Knauff's *types* of titles new, or have the numbers of given types of titles shifted over time in interesting ways? Did his titles illustrate or even establish (or reinforce) later conventions for naming fiddle tunes? To answer these questions, we must compare the titles of the *Virginia Reels* to earlier, contemporary, and present-day arrays of fiddle tune titles.

The first body of fiddle tunes published in large numbers and whose titles can be profitably compared to those of the individual *Virginia Reels* were from mid- to late-eighteenth-century Scotland. The environment in which these fiddle tunes flourished mixed informal dances with more cultivated occasions, and fiddling offered an opportunity to proceed in a specifically Scottish way. These books of tunes contained both inherited tunes—some with what I have been calling "salty" titles, and some with associations to people and places—and new tunes, which emphasized the people-and-places type of title. Most of the people named in those tune titles were patrons of fiddling, and most of the places referenced were their homes. Several ancestors of tunes in the *Virginia Reels* bore titles in Scotland conforming to that formula: "Madam Parisott's Hornpipe" (in the *Virginia Reels*, "Whiskey Barrel"), "Perthshire Hunt" ("Richmond Hill"), "Marquis of Huntley's Farewell" ("George Booker"), and "Duke of Gordon's Rant" ("Scott's Favorite"). These Scottish titles thus reinforced social order by referencing well-known and powerful Scottish citizens; the collective message was nationalistic.

Other Scottish titles of tunes that would later appear in the *Virginia Reels*, titles in the "salty" category, include "Johnny in the Nether Mains," the direct ancestor of Knauff's "Billy in the Low Grounds," and "Flowers of Edinburgh," the tune very similar to "Old Virginia." "Money Musk" (Knauff's "Killie Krankie") presents a mixed picture. Both tune names are Scottish. "Money Musk" started its published life in 1773 as "Sir Archibald Grant of Moniemusk's Reel," thus referring to a noble patron of fiddle music and his home, but was shortened to its current pungent title within a decade (Kuntz 2012, 147 and 105). And "Killie Krankie"

Title in Scotland	New Title in Virginia Reels	Similarities, if Any
Speed the Plough	Speed the Plough	unchanged title
Johnny in the Nether Mains	Billy in the Low Grounds	close to a direct translation
Marquis of Huntley's Farewell	George Booker	local well-known persons
Duke of Gordon's Rant	Scott's Favorite	notable person; thing of theirs
Money Musk	Killie Krankie	places (in original meanings)
Flowers of Edinburgh	Old Virginia	sizable locations; modifier
Perthshire Hunt	Richmond Hill	place; short word starting "h"
My Love She's But a Lassie Yet	Richmond Blues	no parallel; function change
Madam Parisott's Hornpipe	Whiskey Barrel	no parallel; title genre change

Figure 11. Scottish tune titles and Knauff's own titles for several of the *Virginia Reels*.

also refers to a location, one of a famous battle. In a last sequence of changes with a Scottish background, a "Miss Farquharson's Reel"—not particularly common under that name—received a text from Robert Burns, becoming the common song "My Love She's But a Lassie Yet," a tune still used for dancing under that title. Then it apparently became the march called "Richmond Blues" . . . which, through its inclusion in the *Virginia Reels*, we know was still used as a dance!

What I find most remarkable about this particular array of title changes is the different, graduated levels of parallelism in meaning. Just one of these tune titles remained unchanged in its trip across the Atlantic to Virginia: the pan-British "Speed the Plough." And just one is a simple translation, the modest move from "Johnny in the Nether Mains" to "Billy in the Low Grounds": the Scottish term "nether mains" refers to a portion of the principal lands on which an affluent homeowner resides, specifically the lower portion, which quite likely would abut a watercourse. In cases where that land flooded seasonally—admittedly, less likely in hilly Scotland than in Virginia—a "nether mains" would be synonymous with "low grounds." But quite a few other title pairs are very or somewhat parallel in structure or type of content; see figure 11.

In summary, of these nine title pairs, just two—the first two listed in the table—are identical or nearly so, and just two exhibit no similarity at all. But between these extremes we find five pairs of tune names joined by an intriguing graded array of similarities. Are these similarities coincidental? Some may be, but not all! In at least a few cases, these parallels must be the residue of hazy memory, of associating tunes with *types* of titles. The details of the common ground kept during those five changes of title are also of interest: Placenames known in Scotland yield to ones in Virginia, and the same goes for titles referring to people, with an unsurprising corollary. The new titles refer not to noble landowners but rather to American soldiers, whether affluent or not, just as do a handful of other tune titles in the *Virginia Reels*. This stage in Virginia history should not now be viewed as simply "antebellum." It was postbellum too; memories of the War of 1812 and the Revolutionary War remained fresh.

The enormous published collections of Scottish fiddle tunes from the late eighteenth and early nineteenth centuries reached well beyond the straightforward function of dance accompaniment to drawing-room aesthetic pleasure and, notably, to political/cultural regional assertion. A fair number of those fiddle tunes rode the vogue for Scottish music in England both to the center of English culture, London, and to distant outposts of English culture, including the young United States. However, in the more far-flung environments, such tunes shed most of their political message along with a portion of their participation in drawing-room high culture. In the United States, fiddle tunes' numbers in terms of publication diminished as they joined all sorts of tunes in general pop music collections. In addition, the violin was often lumped in with other instruments in terms of technique; many collections were meant to be versatile, serving customers playing flute or fife or violin or clarinet, and the simple and range-restricted arrangements in these collections could indeed be performed by each instrument.

In the early nineteenth century through about 1840, a "large" American music anthology would be one along the lines of *Riley's Flute Melodies*, which included among several hundred pieces a few dozen fiddle tunes. Then the sizable—eventually enormous—collections published by Elias Howe dominated the market. These offered larger selections of melodies from all categories, including fiddle tunes, and so included more cognates of the *Virginia Reels* than had been previously published here. The chart given as figure 12 lists the *Virginia Reels* that were published in the United States during the course of the nineteenth century, and the titles with which they were associated in Howe's various collections. I also note whether these tunes had been already anthologized by Riley; Riley's and Howe's names for given tunes normally matched.

All of the tunes in the *Virginia Reels* that were printed by both Riley and Howe were hits, and had appeared previously in Scottish fiddle

Title in Virginia Reels	In Riley?	Title in Elias Howe's Various Collections
Killie Krankie	X	Money Musk
The Hero		Miss Brown's Reel
Speed the Plough	X	Speed the Plough
Old Virginia	X	Flowers of Edinburgh
Richmond Blues	X	My Love She's But a Lassie Yet
Natchez on the Hill	X	ancestor: Rose Tree;
		sibling: Old Zip Coon
Sich a Gitting Up Stairs		Such a Getting Up Stairs
Ohio River		Boatman Dance
Midnight Serenade		Buffalo Gals

Figure 12. Members of Knauff's *Virginia Reels* that were published repeatedly in other American collections.

publications under the names still employed in the American mainstream. The last three tunes (and the youngest incarnation in the "Rose Tree" family, "Old Zip Coon"), as new blackface minstrel songs, entered the repertoires of fiddlers who learned from written notation, from adjustments of the published sung melodies. But they became part of the stable body of constantly reprinted inherited pop music melodies remarkably quickly. The overall continuity of titling and intimate details of melody in the Howe-dominated stream of publications characterized the usual fate for printed fiddle tunes. Although a handful of the *Virginia Reels* took part in that path, the *Reels* versions mostly had new titles in that publication, and, as will be explored in the next chapter, were musically at least a little unusual. In short, the *Virginia Reels* was not a link in the chain of *printed* transmission of any of the tunes. Howe and his contemporaries seemed not to pay anything like the degree of personal attention to tunes (and their titles) as was typical around the turn of the nineteenth century. Melodies, especially ones that had been around for a while, were simply replicated, with reliable titling. But, even though the main reason these tunes were endlessly reprinted was to fatten (and thus enhance the perceived worth of) ever-larger collections, this practice did keep a nice selection of older fiddle tunes available to music-literate fiddlers. This nineteenth-century stream of publications, with stable tune titles and stable tunes, was known to some degree all over the United States, but had its greatest influence in New England and across the northern part of the country.

Titles in the *Virginia Reels* as Models for Contemporary Fiddle Tune Titles in the Upper South

We immediately notice that several of the tune titles in the *Virginia Reels* are the same as those tunes' titles today as played in fiddling and string band music of the Upper South. Here I am referring to music as played in two types of locations, by two groups of performers. First, there are the inheritors of the older fiddling traditions living within a few hundred miles of where North Carolina, Virginia, Tennessee, and West Virginia converge. Second, there are the folk music revivalists most of whom live in large cities throughout North America. These two groups overlap in various ways, but their different attitudes toward older fiddle music support differently shaded repertoires and ways of performing. To gather up a set of titles to compare to those of the *Virginia Reels*, I turned my attention to the largest fiddle-oriented annual festivals populated by these two groups of musicians, Clifftop (perhaps fourth-fifths revivalists) and Galax (perhaps four-fifths local inheritors of old-time music). It is a very positive development supporting the future of American old-time music that both populaces flourish.

This section of this chapter describes an experiment! For the purpose of looking at tune titles, I evaluated my lists of titles from the 2014 iterations of these large annual festivals, that is, I did a census of the titles from the following competition categories at both contests: old-time band, clawhammer banjo, and old-time fiddle. Since there are thirty-five titles in the *Virginia Reels*, I plucked out the thirty-five titles most employed from the conjoined festival tune title lists as described above. Of course, there is no guarantee that the thirty-five *Virginia Reels* are representative in the same way! Nevertheless, I bulled ahead and compared the subject matter of the titles. I first arranged the titles of the *Virginia Reels* as shown in figure 13. When titles didn't fall neatly in just one category, I tried to respond to this through the order in which I listed the titles. For instance, the last title in the group called "Salty and Outdoors" is "Mississippi Sawyer," and then the first title in the group called "Places" is "Ohio River"; the abutting titles both refer to rivers and include state names. Similarly, "Peter Francisco," which is the last title in the group dominated by military themes, is followed by "The Hero," the first in the "Persons and Places Less Specific or Unknown"; as mentioned above, "The Hero" probably referred to Mr. Francisco.

When I began to insert the names of the most common tunes played at Clifftop and Galax in 2014 to the right of the names of the *Virginia Reels*, I proceeded through several graduated layers of correspondence. The first assignments were quite simple: matching titles from the *Virginia Reels* with those some titles in modern use, here "Forked Deer" and "Mississippi Sawyer." Second, I found close parallels in meaning or syntax: "Rose in the Mountain" paralleled the current title "Fire in the Mountain" due to shape, Knauff's "Indian Whoop" and the modern "Lost Indian" included the word "Indian" and had the bonus of requiring unusual sounds (respectively the player calling "Whoo" and the use of the AEAC# scordatura, which encourages emphasis on certain double stops, left-hand pizzicato, and so on). Then I sought out less obvious parallels, such as that between Knauff's minstrel tune "Sich a Gittin Up Stairs" and the modern "Bile Them Cabbage Down": both have bits of text, and do not seem to be set outdoors, and both are simple tunes. In another, even looser level of parallel, "Gaston" and "Black-Eyed Susie" both refer to individual persons lacking a last name. As I finished the puzzle, I was surprised to find I had only one complete lack of even a trace of a parallel, the non-pair of "Lockwell" and "Ragtime Annie."

	Salty Titles; Outdoor Subjects	
Forked Deer	Forked Deer	same title (and same tune)
Speed the Plough	Grey Eagle	hooves: draft animal and racehorse
Whiskey Barrel	Polecat Blues	source and result of inebriation?
Rose on the Mountain	Fire in the Mountain	blank blank the mountain
Billy in the Low Grounds	Chinky Pin Hunting	doing something outdoors?
Mississippi Sawyer	Mississippi Sawyer	same title; tune also in VA Reels
	Places	
Ohio River	Boatman	text within song; name of that song
Old Virginia	Arkansas Traveler	state named, and flavor imparted
Natchez on the Hill	Cumberland Gap	location and topographic feature
The Island	Hell Broke Loose in Georgia	cannons vs. loud sounds (of war?)
Petersburg Ladies	Shelvin' Rock	locations, but city vs. slopes
Richmond Hill	Sourwood Mountain	locations, but city vs. slopes
	Patriotic; Military People; Other Specific People	
Richmond Blues	Soldier's Joy	soldiers, not necessarily fighting
Killie Krankie	Camp Chase	battle; Civil War prison camp

Republican Spirit	Breaking Up Christmas	patriotic feeling; festive period
22nd of February	Eighth of January	Washington's birthday, Battle of NO
Colonel Crocket	John Brown's Dream	real yet legendary pugnacious figures
Scott's Favorite	Bonaparte Crossing the Rhine	generals
George Booker	Durang's Hornpipe	less well known figures
Peter Francisco	John Henry	very strong men
Persons and Places Less Specific or Unknown		
The Hero	Hangman's Reel	type person; profession
Villalave	Walkin' in the Parlor	fancy hotel (?); nice room
Lockwell	Ragtime Annie	(no parallel)
Two Sisters	Julie Ann Johnson	women
Gaston	Black-Eyed Susie	an individual
Lady of the Lake	Yew Piney Mountain	geographic feature (+ modal music)
Nancy Anderson	Angeline the Baker	specific woman
Slighted Jenny	Lost Girl	distressed female person
Courting; Minstrel Tunes or Songs; Other Songs		
Sich A Gittin Up Stairs	Bile Them Cabbage Down	indoors and salty
Love in a Village	Fly Around, My Pretty Little Miss	courting?
Love from the Heart	Golden Slippers	cheerful courting
Flying Indian	Indian Squaw	Indian further described
Indian Whoop	Lost Indian	Indian and sounds (whoop; AEAC#)
Oh, Where Did You Come From	Cotton-Eyed Joe	text within song; name of that song
Midnight Serenade	Sail Away Ladies	women asked to move

Figure 13. Tune title roundup: titles in the *Virginia Reels*, common titles at Galax and Clifftop in 2014, and possible parallels between these.

Some of these parallels are strong, some middling, some quite strained. In the end, I remain impressed by the overall congruence of current old-time fiddle tune titles and those that Knauff quoted. Indeed, it is because of the broad similarities in both word formulas and topics between the titles of tunes in the *Virginia Reels* and those typically found in modern old-time music that I was able to use titles from the *Virginia Reels* in my general discussion of fiddle tune names at the start of this chapter.

Knauff's Tune Titles: A Partnership of Nostalgia and Fashion

Both Knauff's titles and current titles illustrate multiple historical layers. Not-so-old titles' subjects among the *Virginia Reels* include "Richmond Blues" (then a young military unit), "Peter Francisco" (the Revolutionary War hero, deceased in 1831), "Lady of the Lake" (a legendary figure, but here doubtless referring to Walter Scott's novel published in 1810), and "22nd of February" (Washington's birthday, post–Revolutionary War as a national celebration). In a very rough parallel, current fiddle tune titles include quite a few that invoke developments over the mid- to late nineteenth century and early twentieth century. Several are oral tradition adaptions of compositions with known dates, such as "Angeline the Baker" (Foster's "Angelina Baker," published in 1850) and "Golden Slippers" (James Bland's minstrel song, originally styled as a spiritual, then sped up and popularized in the late 1920s). Other current titles include the names of musical genres still far in the future when the *Virginia Reels* came out: "Ragtime Annie" and "Polecat Blues." Of course, both the *Reels* titles and contemporary titles include ones that reach back to the late eighteenth century, such as "Speed the Plough" and "Soldier's Joy." One broad difference between the two bodies of tune names is that the "new" subjects in the *Virginia Reels* are in fact closer to the date of that publication than the "new" titles in contemporary old-time fiddling are close in time to the present. As a corollary, *Virginia Reels* as a broad title names a genre not that far out of fashion; it is no surprise that several titles include names of what were already substantial cities, places in which it was easier to stay up-to-date than in small towns and the countryside.

Finally, perhaps the most striking characteristic of the titles assembled as the *Virginia Reels* is that they already evoke nostalgia. The word "old" in "Old Virginia" resonates on several levels. Fiddling had become less fashionable than flute playing decades earlier, and the genre of the reel, though far from ancient, paled in novelty when compared to more recently arrived dance types, notably the waltz and the polka. But continuity of both style and of local associations had their own powerful appeal. Most important, Virginia's past was already seen as idyllic compared to its present. By the 1830s, much of the soil was already worn out, and out-migration westwards had become a serious economic problem. "Old" Virginia was celebrated in numerous poems, some of which would be set to music. This part of the South was already the "Old South."

- CHAPTER FOUR -

"Lady of the Lake" and "George Booker"

Knauff Digs More Deeply into Local Oral Tradition

DOES THE THIRD PAMPHLET OF THE *VIRGINIA REELS* HAVE A THEME? Perhaps Knauff was merely assembling melodies he had heard at dances but hadn't put in the first two volumes. But if a plan lay behind the contents of volume 3, this might be the justification: Knauff established the economic potential of publishing local dance tunes in the first set of *Virginia Reels*. In the second set, he focused on his immediate environment: he celebrated people and places that his target audience knew. When he created No. 3, the governing principle may have been complementary to that shaping No. 2: these were local *melodies*. Most of the tunes in No. 3 had not yet been published in the United States, and the few among them that had reached print (or manuscript) here were rare enough in those notated forms that Knauff probably hadn't seen them on paper; to him, these were local oral tradition tunes.

More tunes survive from this volume than from any of the other three pamphlets comprising the *Virginia Reels*. This suggests that I focus on this group to exemplify several factors marking the flourishing of southern US fiddle tunes in oral tradition. After all, these tunes are concentrated bits of musical information, pairs of eight-measure strains containing much internal repetition. What is the essence of a tune—that is, which of the sounds that we hear make up the persisting kernel of notes and which instead belong to the temporary surface in performance? How much distinctiveness in the audible surface of a performance causes fiddlers to believe that they are playing a different tune? How do these very compact pieces strive to be larger than simple

Figure 14. "Crockett and His Fiddle," illustration by Michael Hague, and used here with his permission. This picture was first published in William J. Bennett and Michael Hague, *The Children's Book of America* (1998), a collection intended for an audience of youngsters in the third through sixth grades, children overlapping in age with Knauff's students at the Buckingham Female Collegiate Institute.

bipartite dance tunes? In sum, why do these little tunes still attract musicians' interest? The answers that I can best address with reference to this touchstone collection of southern fiddle tunes boil down to four categories: motives for fiddling, choices of tunes to play, adjustments of the surface of performances to fit prevailing styles, and renewal of repertoire through dropping some tunes and adopting or inventing others (that is, complementary attrition and creativity).

Why Fiddlers Fiddle

The melodies making up the *Virginia Reels* are dance tunes, whatever additional functions they may sometimes fulfill. Fiddling for dances can be straightforward. A satisfactory performance proceeds at a steady, appropriate pace, contributes to the dancers' energy, and has some aesthetic weight. But, apart from the inflexible need for a reliable tempo, these parameters leave plenty of room within which fiddlers can maneuver. And unless they are employees content to simply do their jobs, or for any reason are in a situation that discourages creativity, maneuver they will, in order to remain alert and perhaps challenge themselves. Elements of aesthetically based joy call out for attention: the physical motions encourage rhythmic pushes (that is, variety of note lengths and strategically placed accents consonant with a steady tempo). Also, most fiddlers through most of history have been extroverts enjoying competition; perhaps aggressiveness outside of war finds its very most natural surrogate expression in sports, but it can also mark music performance.

It was in Scotland that fiddling first landed securely within the matrix of North Atlantic music cultures that would eventually include Knauff's Virginia. Scottish fiddling would send repertoire and performance ideas along several routes to the British colonies and the young United States. Although most of the tunes in the third number of the *Virginia Reels* made their initial bow *in print* in that publication, several seem to have traveled from Scotland with little or no stopover in the world of English music publishing or its echoes in the budding United States. Others among these tunes traveled along with Scots Irish and Highland Scots immigrants. And this cannot simply have been a matter of transporting melodies: attitudes helping shape fiddling as cultural practice came too. This composite cultural transfer must have included the writing of new tunes in transplanted Scots and Scotch-Irish cultures.

When the violin arrived in Scotland in the early 1600s, it came as a young instrument newly fashionable for performing art music (Johnson 1972, 11). It was adopted in its new home simultaneously as cultivated violin and rustic fiddle. We don't know how quickly it displaced earlier bowed stringed art instruments, but violins (and thus fiddles) were being made in Scotland by the beginning of the eighteenth century. The first substantial body of *published* fiddle tunes in any North Atlantic repertoire that would presage American fiddling appeared in late eighteenth-century Scotland, even though most early American publications including fiddle tunes were on the simpler English model. Indeed, those England-echoing collections were at least partial models for the first pamphlet of the *Virginia Reels*—that is, the fiddle tunes in them had an obvious dual function of dance accompaniment and instrument pedagogy. However, I believe that late eighteenth-century Scottish fiddle tune publications illustrate the more educated layer of a broad Scottish immigrant practice that did not pass through the English filter, a practice relevant for understanding the tunes themselves—especially those making up the third number of the *Virginia Reels*—and the collective future of such tunes and the attitudes shaping their performance.

The Act of Union (1707) had a profound and lasting impact on Scottish psychology. With Edinburgh no longer a capital city, an increased inclination to cherish and foster symbols of Scottish distinctiveness and value found a ready partner in distinctively Scottish dance and its music. Strathspeys and reels were not just functional and attractive, but also "national," thus satisfying on several levels at once. Professionals helped cultivate this music. Most of the many collections from this era were issued by music merchants who also played for dances and who composed some dance tunes (Collinson 1966, 213). Concerning the larger body of fiddlers of various levels of accomplishment, Johnson stated that "folk fiddlers or bagpipers were generally established, secure members of the community; they were school masters, tradesmen in country towns, factors on estates, personal servants of the aristocracy. Most of them could read and write musical notation" (1972, 99). He was aware that referring to a musically literate group spearheaded by professionals as "folk fiddlers" was problematic.

Gelbart recently explored the evolution of intellectuals' understanding of what we now think of as folk and art ideologies and processes, with Scottish "national" dance music being important in the early stages of defining and differentiating between folk and art musics (2011). My interest complements his. Yes, we can witness the emergence of these categories, but the journey is as important as the destination. We can also observe the continued close relationship between inherited (and newly composed) tunes of Scottish dance music and the nascent aesthetics of art music. This rich cultural overlap, coupled with the sheer compactness of the populations involved, meant that many, many fancy versions of fiddle tunes were published. When this music exceeded essential function and the inherited light aesthetic weight of the two-strain dance tunes themselves, when it became also "national," performers enriched the playing style for two interrelated reasons, to bear that increased ideological load and to reward focused listening.

Published incarnations of countless strathspeys and reels in what Johnson called "drawing-room style" took on a remarkable level of refinement (1984, 34). On the other hand, the transmission of this music as followed through multiple appearances of tunes in publications and manuscripts still bore traces of the fluidity of oral tradition, partly because few copies of each book of tunes were issued. Many collections were published by subscription, and lists of subscribers included just a few hundred nobles, other landowners, professionals (teachers, architects, lawyers), and professional musicians. Music store owners ordered no more than four to seven copies (see, for example, Gow [1784], [1–2]). Having these collections on hand stimulated sales of instruments and accessories, advertised the performance and teaching skills of the compilers, and in general constituted an indispensable facet of the local music business.

If educated fiddlers were playing fancy versions of Scottish national dance music in formal settings, what were more routine performers playing for dances? The short answer is that all agile fiddlers, literate or not, knew about and had the option of playing complex forms of tunes. Indeed, since plenty of dance fiddling was done by the same men that published the drawing-room collections, much of that playing was probably of a level of complexity approaching that of concert settings. Humbler fiddlers would have tried to match this level of elaboration on occasion. Indeed, "humbler" may not be the right adjective, since countless anecdotes present Scottish fiddlers of this period as proud, aggressive extroverts—when fiddlers met, they routinely tried to top each other (McHardy throughout).

When fiddling came to the British colonies in the areas that would become the United States, it arrived in multiple streams. The English mainstream was echoed in publications by men like Blake and Riley, with fiddle tunes appearing in very plain forms, as a minor ingredient in general anthologies of popular music. What we don't get from those publications is much of a sense of fiddling practice by the Scots-Irish—whose culture set many patterns for backwoods southern culture—or of fiddling as developing on the spot in America. Since there were still far fewer people in the United States than in England or Scotland during Knauff's era, there were fewer fiddlers and less evidence of fiddling. Nevertheless, local histories provide a freckling of anecdotes that give us some sense of continuities of attitudes held by fiddlers and about fiddling.

The earliest British settlers in the colonies had little time to relax. Nevertheless, Puritan stodginess filtered down the coast from Massachusetts, and a Virginia statute of 1618 (!) outlawed Sabbath-day "dancing, fiddling, card-playing, hunting, and fishing" (Dulles 1965, 8). There must have been a significant amount of interest in each of these pursuits to make forbidding them worthwhile. Also, the ordering in this list may be significant: dancing and fiddling make a logical pair, and following fiddling with playing cards, hunting, and fishing presents a tidy roster of masculine sins.

We know about the activities of individual fiddlers from the nineteenth century largely through geographically delimited research by folklorists and historians; each of the regional collections of fiddle tunes presents many such stories. I'll give a short sample from my own research. I learned about a fiddler named Gideon Lincecum (1793–1874) because one of my English professors at Austin College (Sherman, Texas) was Jerry Lincecum, a direct descendant. Some years after I graduated, Jerry discovered that Gideon, an extrovert as an individual and as an amateur biologist, had left behind letters and serial journal publications, largely but not entirely in the sciences. A few excerpts concerned music, so Jerry asked me to take part in a broad study of Gideon.

While living near the Mississippi Choctaw, Gideon learned homeopathic remedies from the Indians, and in turn arranged a social affair for his new friends at which he fiddled. A second, longer anecdote was set further west. Like many residing in the South shortly before the Civil War, Lincecum relocated repeatedly. In 1835, he led a few neighbors on a voyage of exploration in Texas—where he would soon bring his family. One day, he encountered some Indians, then stumbled upon an impromptu picnic hosted by a family with whom he had recently stayed, on the shores of Eagle Lake (about thirty miles west of the future Houston):

> The carriages were immediately unloaded, and the negroes started back for a supply of blankets, more bread, coffee and so on. One of the younger men told the negro to bring his violin,—which was as much as to say invite the neighborhood to come. . . . Seeing the violin case thrown out amongst their pots and blankets, and not having had one in my hands for months, I was hungry for music. I opened the case and found a splendid violin, in excellent condition. I took it out, and going near to two or three ladies, said, "some of you were telling a new comer what the wild man could do. With this good violin, I will furnish you with a little story that will bear telling as long as you live." I performed "Washington's Grand March" so loud that I could distinctly hear the tune repeated as it returned from the echo on the opposite lake shore. I could feel

that my very soul mingled with the sound of the instrument, and, at the time I was about to become so entranced as to be unfit for such jovial company; the handsome lady ran up and, slapping me on the shoulder, exclaimed, "Good heavens, Doctor! Where are you going?" I was startled, and training up [tuning? positioning?] the violin, performed Gen. Harrison's march, then Hail Columbia and then the No. 1 cotillion in the beggar set. They all went to dancing ... (1874–1875, 10–12)

Knauff and Oral Tradition: Pieces Other Than the *Virginia Reels*

Although the *Virginia Reels* constitutes George Knauff's most extensive efforts in arranging rather than composing, his total output mixed these activities about equally. He was unusually careful to specify when he borrowed rather than created a tune, but did not go a step further and differentiate between the types of sources from which he arranged. His collection called *Gatherings* includes reworkings of previously published pieces, and his hit "Wait for the Wagon" came close on the heels of the original published form of that work, a song written in 1850 "by a lady" residing in New Orleans[1] (see Fuld 1971, 332). But did the anonymous "lady" compose the music? "Written by" often referred only to lyrics; songs were often described on their title pages as "written and composed by" when the composer had penned both words and music (that is, except in the many cases where a song was "by" a famous performer, who might not have had anything to do with its creation). In any case, it seems possible that the tune for "Wait for the Wagon" came out of oral tradition; it certainly thrived there. The song was popular enough to receive quite a few alternative texts, often still including the word "wagon." These could be political in nature. While exploring this thoroughly would take me too far afield, I will note that the song continued to be recast in political campaigns during the nineteenth century.

Another of Knauff's song arrangements, one that even more certainly issued from oral tradition, is his "Three Farmers Went a Hunting." Forms of the text have been found in sources as early as the mid-seventeenth century (see, e.g., Cox 2013, 623); Knauff's version is shown as figure 15.

The hook of this nonsense song (or children's song, as it is often classified today in both Great Britain and the United States) is amusing wrong identifications. In verse 1, one of the three men sees something that he believes is a frog, but another of the farmers asserts it is a "jaybird, with the feathers washed away." Parallel mistaken identifications and corrections follow. Knauff's version has seven verses, but we seem less patient today: most performances now include just three or four verses. Closely related songs—ones featuring the same text formula in each verse—include "Three Men Went a Hunting," which Helen Creighton collected in Nova Scotia (1932, 201), and "Three Huntsmen," which Norman Cazden found in the Catskills (1982, 570–73; with meticulous annotations). But it was members of this tune/text family that were most similar to Knauff's transcription that were collected closest to his home during the twentieth century, the West Virginia versions gathered up by Cox.

Knauff arranged two instrumental tunes not in the *Virginia Reels*. Neither was in simple duple time, so neither could be used as a reel. The fact that "Allegheny Waltz," the only piece he issued through a Richmond publisher (W. L. Montague, in 1849), is not known to this author is no surprise. The genre of the waltz spread through Europe and European former colonies twice, with the normal rhythmic density of the 1820s wave greater than that of the 1860s wave; current fiddled waltzes are all of the latter group, while Knauff's waltzes—composed or arranged—fall in the former group.

More interesting is Knauff's tune that is a version of the tune customarily called "Blue-Bonneted Scots." This melody has sometimes been texted, and alternative names reflect alternative texts. In figure 16, I align a version of what I believe to be the parent tune, "O Dear Mother, What Shall I Do," the pedigree of which reaches well back into the eighteenth century, with Knauff's "Blue-Bonneted Scots," and a later version of that tune (and song) from influential Boston publisher Elias Howe. This set of tunes connects with Knauff's "Billy in the Low Grounds" in a complicated way to be explored below. For now, two characteristics of Knauff's tune should be noted. First, Knauff's "Blue-Bonneted Scots" is less elaborate than the Scottish "Oh Dear Mother." The older Scottish song is in the highly ornamented drawing-room style, while Knauff's melody is meant to accompany a dance and is neither more nor less dense than the average cotillion. Second, Knauff notated a circular ending for the first strain of his tune, a practice more common in modern southern oral tradition than in published collections of Scottish tunes.

Figure 15a and 15b. Knauff's comic song from oral tradition: "Three Farmers Went a Hunting."

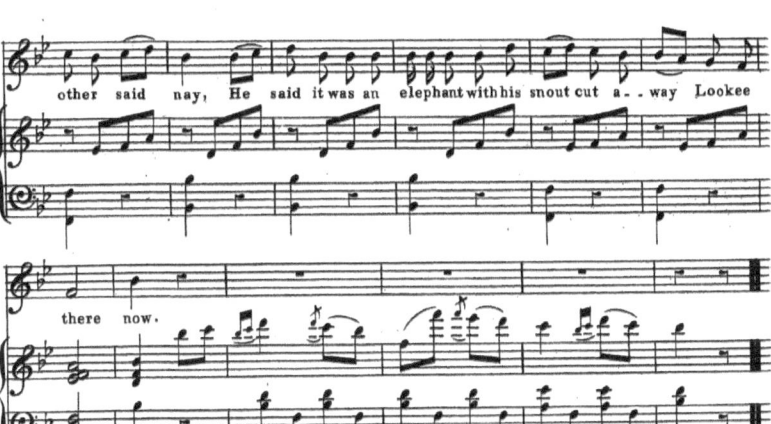

2
They hunted and they hollow'd, and the next thing they did find
Was a frog in a well, and that they left behind, Lookee there now,
One said it was a frog, but the other said nay
He said it was a jay-bird with his feathers wash'd away, Lookee there now.

3
They hunted and they hollow'd, and the next thing they did find
Was a barn in a meadow, and that they left behind, Lookee there now,
One said it was a barn, but the other said nay
He said it was a church, with the steeple cut away, Lookee there now.

4
They hunted and they hollow'd, and the next thing they did find
Was the moon in the element, and that they left behind, Lookee there now,
One said it was the moon, but the other said nay
He said it was a cheese with the half cut away, Lookee there now.

5
They hunted and they hollow'd, and the next thing they did find
Was a hare in the woods, and that they left behind, Lookee there now,
One said it was a hare, but the other said nay
He said it was a wolf with his tail cut away, Lookee there now.

6
They hunted and they hollow'd, and the next thing they did find
Was a lady in a garden, and her they left behind, Lookee there now,
One said it was a lady, but the other said nay
He said it was an angel with the wings cut away, Lookee there now.

7
And they hunted and they hollow'd, and the next thing they did find
Was an owl in a bush, and that they left behind, Lookee there now,
One said it was an owl, but the other said nay
He said it was the evil one, and they all ran away, Lookee there now.

Figure 16. Knauff's "Blue-Bonneted Scotts" and related tunes.

The *Virginia Reels*: Choosing a Repertoire for a Dance Evening in Antebellum Virginia

American fiddlers focus on duple-time bipartite tunes called breakdowns now and reels in Knauff's Virginia. The tunes' simple formal structure allows great flexibility in the length of performance. Since it takes only eight to a dozen seconds to play through a strain, the performance can be gracefully terminated very soon after a dance is over, or, conversely, a dance can be shaped to match a handy group of repetitions of strains of melody. A typical performance includes at least a handful of melodies, and probably tunes in more than one genre. At a dance, sets of physical requirements will fluctuate—that is, the specific tasks set for the dancers' muscles and lungs will match the various dance genres, and in a concert situation, there's sufficient variety both within and between tunes to entertain both fiddlers and audiences. Thus, it makes sense to look at the four collections and the *Virginia Reels* overall as organic wholes, as attempts at rounded gatherings of musical material. What contrasts between pieces are needed? How does the whole collection sound?

Figure 17 charts several aspects of the individual *Virginia Reels*. My goal is to offer data for comparison with the general flavor of late eighteenth-century Scottish fiddle publications, with the English-derived American publications roughly contemporary with Knauff's activity, and, somewhat impressionistically, with current practice in southern fiddling. What is "normal" and what is—in several obvious aspects—exceptional about these pieces, individually and in the aggregate?

In terms of key, nearly all of the *Virginia Reels* are in major, and nearly all are in the easiest, most common keys for the fiddle: D Major (fourteen of the thirty-five pieces), A (9), G (3), C (2), F (4), two in dorian mode, and one in the surprising key of Eb (actually, only unusual if evaluated as a fiddle tune key, not as one for a keyboard arrangement; pianists favor flat keys). This key distribution—apart from the incongruous insertion of "Old Virginia" in Eb—does not surprise when compared with either the earlier Scottish publications or current southern practice. The match with Scottish practice is stronger. To more closely parallel current southern practice in rough statistical terms we would add a few more pieces in A Major and take away two or three of the four in F Major. The key distribution is, however, very different from the even tighter array of keys used by Blake and Riley, among others. Knauff's contemporaries

Title	Keys	Ranges	Unusual Forms
I, 1 Killie Krankie	A	norm	
I, 2 Republican Spirit	D	norm	
I, 3 Natchez on the Hill	A	+ low	
I, 4 The Two Sisters	D	norm	
I, 5 Speed the Plough	A	norm	
I, 6 Slighted Jenny	G	+ high	
I, 7 Mississippi Sawyer [not really]	C to G	+ high	
I, 8 Forked Deer	D	+ low	
I, 9 Whiskey Barrel	D	+ high	
I, 10 Love in the Village	D circular	norm	varied, both types
II, 1 Old Virginia	Eb!	+ high!	
II, 2 Richmond Hill	A	+ low	varied, fiddle type
II, 3 Villalave	F	+ low	varied, fiddle type
II, 4 Petersburg Ladies	D	+ low	varied, fiddle type
II, 5 The Hero	C double	norm	
II, 6 Peter Francisco	F	+ low	
II, 7 Twenty-Second of February	A	norm	
II, 9 Island	F	+ low	
II, 10 The Richmond Blues	D	+ low	varied, fiddle type
III, 1 George Booker	A	+ low	
III, 2 Oh Where Did You Come From	D	+ high	
III, 3 Colonel Crocket	g dorian	+ high	
III, 4 Rose on the Mountain	D	+ high	
III, 5 Billy in the Low Grounds	A	+ high	
III, 6 Lockwell	D circular	norm	
III, 7 Lady of the Lake	a dorian	+ high	
III, 8 Scotts Favorite	D	+ high	
IV, 1 Sich a Gittin Up Stairs, Varied	D	+ high	varied, mostly piano type
IV, 2 Gaston	G	norm	
IV, 3 Indian Whoop	A	norm	three different strains
IV, 4 Love from the Heart	D	+ high	
IV, 5 Ohio River	F	+ high	three strains; var. fiddle
IV, 6 The Flying Indian	A circular	+ high	
IV, 7 Nancy Anderson	D	+ low	
IV, 8 Midnight Serenade, Varied	G	+ high	varied, both types

Figure 17. Some musical characteristics of the individual *Virginia Reels*.

and immediate predecessors in the creating of smallish instrumental anthologies for solo instruments (flute, violin, oboe, etc.) concentrated on the keys of D and G. The inclusion of numerous tunes in the slightly harder (more difficult to finger) key of A reflects the appealing resonance of the violin in that key, enhanced today by frequent recourse to the key-specific tuning of AEAE (in D Major, ADAE). Last, we will consider the pair of tunes that are not in major, but rather in dorian mode (that is, matching the series of intervals found on the piano's white keys with d as the tonic). Tunes in minor or dorian can be found in early American instrumental collections, but not many, and these are usually not common-time fiddle tunes, but rather waltzes or the occasional "dead march," such as the ubiquitous "Roslin Castle."

In sum, the key distribution for the tunes making up the *Virginia Reels* places that collection in sequence between Scottish fiddling and current southern fiddling; early nineteenth-century American printing of fiddle tunes does not fit in this series. The same goes for the ranges these tunes explore. Most fiddle tunes that reached print by the 1830s in the United States fit within the range reaching from d1 (open string d) to b2 (fourth finger on the e string in first position). While some members of the *Virginia Reels* fit this "New England" norm—such as members of the *Virginia Reels* still often played in New England today, including "Money Musk" ("Killie Krankie" in the *Virginia Reels*) and "Speed the Plough"—the vast majority of the *Virginia Reels* exceed that octave-and-a-sixth span, instead opting for an interval of a third or a fourth more. Many of these melodies require a fiddler to go into third position on the e string; the fiddler or fiddlers whose playing Knauff mined must have been quite comfortable doing that. And many other of the tunes instead extend down onto the g string. However, a span of two octaves seems to be the conventional limit: none of the *Virginia Reels* both ventures into third position and down onto the g string. This again matches fairly well with both late eighteenth-century Scottish fiddling and current fiddling in the Upper South (and urban old-time fiddling modeled on that of the Upper South), although Texas-based contest-style fiddling routinely exploits a larger range, that is, both employs third position and reaches down to the g string.

Most of the *Virginia Reels* stick to the standard two-strain form, but a few either have three distinct strains or contain written-out variations. This mild push against the bounds of convention again flouts the patterns common in American fiddle tune printing during and before Knauff's time, but is at home in the contexts of earlier Scottish and later southern fiddling. The variations are of two types. In the first case in which Knauff marked a tune as "varied" ("Sich a Gittin Up Stairs"), he presented a simplified form of piano variation technique; this was probably part of his own arranging process rather than a transcription of what his source fiddler did. Most other examples I have marked as "varied" in the right-hand column offer both a basic form of a strain (or half of one), then a form that is bit denser rhythmically, as a fiddler today might do; these changes might well come from Knauff's source fiddler(s). "Midnight Serenade" (today's "Buffalo Gals," "Alabama Gals," etc.) seems to partake of both processes.

A few tunes have circular endings for one or both strains (that is, the melodies cadence one or several notes above the tonic, so that resolving to the tonic occurs only by starting the strain again). And "The Hero" has a double-tonic structure, with the opening gesture immediately repeated a step up, although this takes the melody out of the key briefly. This tune did later enter the mainstream of American fiddle tune printing as "Mrs. Brown's Reel" and survives today under the related titles of "Wagoner," "Tennessee Wagoner," and others. Absolutely all of these exceptional features fit the same historical sequence, that is, fall in line between Scottish and modern American southern fiddling.

"Ducks in the Pond":
Exotic Elements in Fiddle Repertoires over the Centuries

Here is an obvious but important fact: fiddlers choose to learn some but not all of the tunes they encounter. As a result, personal repertoires, regional ones, and the overall body of tunes are constantly changing. And although fiddling is basically an oral tradition, the occasional alliance with print (and more recently, recordings) skews the maintenance of all levels of repertoire now and then. This section of the chapter concerns the intersection of opportunity and preference, focusing on the tune Knauff placed in volume 3 of the *Virginia Reels* under the title "Lady of the Lake," the same melody that is played in West Virginia and nearby (plus in urban old-time music circles throughout the United States) under the title "Ducks on the Pond."

When Knauff anthologized "Lady of the Lake," this was the first printing of the tune. That it is in dorian mode (with the tonic of *a*) separates it from the mainstream. It survives today because it—now with the slightly changed title "Ducks on the Pond"—was in the repertoire of fiddler Henry Reed (1884–1968) when young folklorist Alan Jabbour (b. 1942) apprenticed with him in the 1960s. Jabbour, an accomplished fiddler, brought much of Reed's repertoire into the folk music revival and made it available for the long term in his elegant website, "Fiddle Tunes of the Old Frontier: The Henry Reed Collection" (http://www.loc.gov/collection/henry-reed-fiddle-tunes/about-this-collection/). Quite a few of Knauff's *Virginia Reels* were in Reed's repertoire, though often under other names. Jabbour discovered that conjunction, and became both the link between Reed and the folk revival (through his own performances, and, for many years, his playing with the Hollow Rock String Band) and his being first scholar to study the *Virginia Reels*.

Many contemporary fiddlers who play tunes from the *Virginia Reels* that were in Reed's repertoire learned from Jabbour, or from the Hollow Rock String Band's recordings, or directly from Reed (after they learned of Reed's existence from Jabbour). Betty Vornbrock (b. 1954) remembers learning "Ducks on a Pond" from Alan one way or another—probably via a combination of the routes mentioned! She grew up in the Midwest in an art music environment; what she enjoyed about being in school orchestras was the playing with others. She roved quite a bit in her young adulthood, including stints in West Virginia and Texas. She now lives in Hillsboro, Virginia, on her and her husband's Christmas tree farm, makes beautiful cloth instrument cases, and fiddles for the Reed Island Rounders. Why does she choose to play this particular tune? She, like many fiddlers with a foot in the folk revival, favors "crooked" (irregularly phrased) and modal tunes. These players did not learn a body of tunes from relatives or neighbors while growing up, and so select among the galaxy of tunes they hear guided by their own aesthetic preferences, which often point them toward especially striking tunes like this one. However, after decades living near the source of the tune, Vornbrock remains part revivalist but has also become part insider in the tradition, and a respected fiddle teacher. The lines between local inheritor and urban revivalist blur, but don't disappear entirely.

Vornbrock's "Ducks on a Pond" is much like other versions played in the area; they all stem from Henry Reed's playing, in many but not all cases via the agency of Alan Jabbour. Reed's home in tiny Glen Lyn, Virginia, near the border with West Virginia, is due west of Knauff's Farmville, about 175 miles away and, situated on a pass through the Blue Ridge Mountains (the East River and the New River meet there), is on a migration route from Piedmont Virginia. I imagine that a fiddler connected in some way with either the fiddler(s) who was/were Knauff's source, or someone in that fiddler's musical lineage, or someone who owned that sheet music moved out that way.

All fiddlers I have asked who know both this melody and "Lady of the Lake" from the *Virginia Reels* agree that the two are the same tune.[2] The implied harmonies match. The contours do, too, but look out of phase, that is, similar gestures often occupy different parts of a given measure. The changes are the sort that typically manifest themselves when a tune not widely played moves through oral tradition: inexact memory plays a role in recreating a tune, and the essentials persist, but may be freely treated.

Betty Vornbrock plays in a West Virginia idiom. While there are several styles competing for allegiance in that state, these styles seem to me to be poised between assuming a banjo will be present in performance (as is true eastward, where Virginia, North Carolina, and Tennessee meet) and expecting that the fiddle part will be melodically self-sufficient. In Vornbrock's performance of "Ducks on a Pond," she plays both strains in their home ranges—the two, though contrasting, are fairly high—and also in forms an octave lower. This adding of depth through transposition, more common among West Virginia fiddlers than in the tristate intersection, thus replaces some of the energy granted by the melodic fiddle and banjo duet (fading in and out of unison) of the latter area.

Adjusting Style: From "The Marquis of Huntley's Farewell" to Knauff's "George Booker" and Beyond

Part of the thoughtful ordering of tunes within the second through fourth pamphlets of the *Virginia Reels* is that Knauff paid special attention to choosing the first melody of each (and also the last melody in pamphlets 2 and 4). The first tune in the second volume, "Old Virginia," could be argued to be a version of "The Flowers of Edinburgh," a tune well known in its original home of Scotland, and also endlessly reprinted in the young

Figure 18. "Lady of the Lake" and its descendant "Ducks on a Pond."

United States (and copied into numerous music commonplace books). But Knauff's version is unusual in more than its name: he has cast it in the key of E-Flat Major, which is definitely not a fiddle key, and the melody challenges the fiddler's left-hand technique by exceeding third position (a handful of the *Virginia Reels* do require third position, but only this one goes higher). Neither the range nor the key present a problem to pianists. The first melody in the fourth pamphlet, "Sich a Gittin Up Stairs," started life as a common and uncomplicated blackface minstrel song, but it is just one of two melodies that Knauff himself asserted was "varied," and indeed, illustrated a procedure akin to that shaping piano variations of the day. The special characteristic of "George Booker," the first member of the third pamphlet, is something quite different. The key of A Major is the normal one for both the tune's immediate ancestor and today, and no formal variations are appended. Instead, in this tune—the first one in the pamphlet and one fully allied with oral tradition—it is the amount of rhythmic detail that stands out.

"George Booker" is the only member of this volume of the *Virginia Reels* that has an ancestor with a continuous history in print in Scotland. Although "The Marquis of Huntley's Farewell" fell out of the world of publishing in the United States during the early nineteenth century, the tune under its new name survives in oral tradition in several styles of southern fiddling. It illustrates many aspects of the strong link between how tunes were shaped and performed in late eighteenth-century Scotland and today in the American South. This tune fills the fiddle's available range in first position. The two strains contrast in range, as is conventional, and that contrast is especially vivid, with the first strain spending lots of time on the *g* string, and the responding strain spending an especially high percentage of its time up on the *e* string. The savoring of the low range in the first strain must be one reason that "The Marquis of Huntley's Farewell" did not become one of the handful of tunes that entered early nineteenth-century mainstream English and American practice: to join that club, tunes dared not dip below the note *d* that then marked the lower edge of most flute and fife performance.

Much of the reason that rhythmic detail—including plenty of Scotch snaps—permeates these pieces is that "The Marquis of Huntley's Farewell" is a strathspey, which is the most stately of the Scottish country dances, and thus with the most time for variety in rhythm. In figure 19a, the top two examples of this well-known Scottish tune are from late eighteenth-century publications representing the playing of prominent Scottish fiddler/composers. The two fiddlers agreed on the contour of the tune, indeed on many details, but had different opinions concerning which ornaments to employ as melodic accents (trills or alternatives or nothing). Also, and of more interest, comparison of the two versions reveals frequent small differences in rhythms: when there are two pitches played within the total time span of a quarter note, the point of arrival on the second pitch is often different. In the first strain, that lack of a unison appears in the fourth beat of many measures, while in the second strain, this takes place in the inner beats of the measure; this is one of the subtler ways the strains contrast. This may seem an insignificant difference, but it matters for two reasons. First, these small differences between versions emphasize that these fiddler/composer/publishers did think through their versions of tunes and presented personalized forms (possibly even more distinctive in performance than in print). Second, the nature and position of the tiny rhythmic differences demonstrate how important these fiddlers considered rhythmic detail in the push from weak beats forward, in the overall propulsion of this music.

The third version of "The Marquis of Huntley's Farewell" given in figure 19a comes from a single sheet published by George Willig Jr. in Baltimore circa 1843 (this date marked in pencil on the one copy I have seen, which was deposited at the Library of Congress to record the copyright).[3] Willig was Knauff's first and main publisher, so perhaps Knauff had seen the piece, but I have no evidence of this. The single sheet has "Marquis of Huntley's Farewell" at the top, identified as a strathspey, and "Braes of Balquhither" below, called a reel, which in Scottish practice was a more rapid common-time dance (a reel was often danced immediately following a strathspey). In this American printing, "Marquis of Huntley's Farewell" has retained rhythmic punch, but lost some variety. No pitch ornaments are marked, and there is more Scotch snap than in the Scottish versions. This sheet seems to have been designed as an attractive exotic item, as distinctively Scottish, so that the most audible Scottish feature is emphasized to a fault.

Figure 19a demonstrates that, while Knauff's "George Booker" presents more intimate rhythmic complexity than do the other *Virginia Reels,* it is nevertheless less detailed than was typical of the parent tune. At least part of the reason for this must have been that the tune is now a Virginia *reel,* which Knauff probably heard played at a tempo leaving less room

Figure 19a. From "Marquis of Huntley's Farewell" to Knauff's "George Booker."

for rhythmic nuance than the automatically slower parent strathspey enjoyed. (For this figure, I changed the time signature to common time for ease of comparing the various forms of the melody, even though the cut time in Knauff's arrangement gives a better feel for the pace of performance.)

As dotted rhythms faded from southern American fiddling over time, how did performances *not* fade in terms of rhythmic power? Different contemporary fiddle styles offer different solutions. In the central styles of the Upper South, rhythmic complexity is maintained in part through the nature of the blackface minstrel fiddle/banjo duet (with guitar and bass nowadays). I'll examine how that works in the next chapter. Elsewhere in the South, fiddle styles based more completely on the solo fiddle find specific ways to keep that momentum. Figures 19b and 19c return to the tune "George Booker," once as played in one of the modern West Virginia styles, and once as played in Texas contest style.

West Virginia fiddler Jake Krack (b. 1985) came from Indiana to West Virginia as a teenager because of his love of the old-time fiddling of that state (his father became an owner of a music store to support Jake's enthusiasm). He has studied carefully with Lester McCumbers, Melvin Wine, and Bobby Taylor, very different iconic fiddlers of West Virginia. Although Jake now has a day job as an Americorps Vista special projects coordinator, he spends at least as much time fiddling as a soloist, ensemble member, teacher, and more. He has won each of the appropriate championships in his and neighboring states several times. He was kind enough to spare me some time for interviews when he was sixteen (at Clifftop) and twenty-six (at Galax). He played "George Booker" during that second interview at my request.

Jake plays the high strain first, which has the effect of abruptly inserting the listener into a shining moment of bright energy. This strain includes no pitches lower than that of the open a string. Thus, the very low start of the next (usually first) strain, emphasized by held notes, is quite bold. Further, the frequent use of c natural rather than $c\#$ adds a downward tilt to this already low strain (there is no g to be sharped—or not—in this strain). This double source of increased contrast between strains serves to replace the intimate complexity of rhythms permeating its ancestor, "The Marquis of Huntley's Farewell."

The other version of "George Booker" in this figure is in contemporary contest style. Alita Stoneking Weisgerber, daughter and musical heir to

100 • "LADY OF THE LAKE" AND "GEORGE BOOKER"

Figure 19b. "George Booker" as played by Jake Krack during an interview at Galax in 2012.

Figure 19c. "George Booker" as played by Alita Stoneking Weisgerber, Hallettsville, 2015.

Figure 19c concluded.

Figure 19c. "George Booker" as played by Alita Stoneking Weisgerber, Hallettsville, 2015.

Missouri fiddler Fred Stoneking, adopted Texas contest style, applying it to both traditional Texas repertoire and some Missouri pieces. She married Tom Weisgerber, also a champion Texas-style fiddler, and they live in Petersburg, Minnesota, where he grew up. The curious reader can find plenty of performances by both Weisgerbers (as well as of Jake Krack, and most of the other living fiddlers mentioned in this book) on YouTube as of this writing. Indeed, carefully listening through Alita Weisgerber's output as revealed on YouTube will expose at least one other performance of "George Booker," one that is handy to compare with the one I recorded at the Texas State Fiddle Contest in Hallettsville in April 2015, and transcribed in figure 19c. This performance is a little shorter than the norm, but is otherwise typical of her playing and of Texas-style contest fiddling in general.

Contest fiddling stemming from Texas style is essentially linear and full of variations large and small, routine and dramatic. There's a bit of swing permeating the overall rhythm, and the accompanying guitar chords are jazz derived. In this and most performances, the principal strain (usually the lower one, but almost always the more striking one, whether low or high) is played twice, the other strain twice, the first twice, and so on for roughly two minutes. Thus, the form of this performance could be diagrammed A1 A2 B1 B2 A3 A4 B3 B4 A5 A6 (many performances are a few strains longer). The "story" offered by the performance combines the principles of alternating the strains, general building of effect, and internal symmetries. Very near the start, the toying with mode that Jake Krack employed *between* strains happens *within* the strain through Alita Weisgerber's near-juxtaposition of the *g#* proper to the key and *g* natural. The beginning of A2 offers long notes—a common rhythmic thinning for dramatic effect—while the beginning of B2 turns a line into an arpeggio, and reemphasizes the harmonic element by then outlining a B Major chord, V/V in the home key of A Major (already done in B1). A3 further departs from A1 in the greater dwelling in the low range in its third measure, and greater use of *g* natural in its fourth measure, but A4, after its first measure, returns quite literally to A1. B3 replaces a line with a sawtooth pattern, then B4, following the model of A4, returns to the original form of the B strain (again after the first measure). A5 exaggerates A2, then A6 largely mirrors A1. Thus, on top of the pulsation between strains, the stories offered by both the A and B strains involve establishment, departure, and return, with exaggeration some two-thirds of the way through the series of each strain. There are many musical subplots too, as one can discover, for example, by comparing the effects of strains B3 and A5.

Nikos Pappas recently read a paper linking the elaborate variation technique employed in Alexander Camel "Eck" Robertson's iconic and seminal 1922 recording of a tune now standard in Texas contest fiddling, "Sally Goodin," with late eighteenth-century Scottish variation techniques. He cited small, tantalizing bits of evidence suggesting that there may have been some continuity of practice over the centuries (2012). My own cautious endorsement of this stems from my belief in some degree of continuity in fiddlers' attitudes that could have preserved variation technique or repeatedly inspired reinventing some form of that practice. Fiddlers on the moving frontier of the South were generally bold and often artistic, and, like their Texas descendants, less apt to have dances to accompany than were fiddlers in settled areas. Playing quite a bit for their own entertainment, early Texas fiddlers occasionally met in the context of weekend gatherings punctuated by rodeos and other competitions. It is no wonder that they cultivated a style heavily reliant on variation, and equally unsurprising that that style is now the favorite of fiddlers in much of the United States.[4] Since we are so much less apt to dance to fiddling than to listen intently to it, complicated forms of tunes are welcome.

Scottish fiddling of the late eighteenth century and continuing through Knauff's era featured variation of several kinds. Although contours of multiple printings of given pieces remained nearly identical, ornaments (especially trills) and rhythmic niceties (dotted rhythms, Scotch snap, etc.) varied between published forms of those tunes, and probably even more so in performance. Much less often, fiddle tunes were presented in variation sets, generally Italianate in character, with stable harmonies but progressively denser rhythms, just as Knauff tentatively explored in "Sich a Gittin Up Stairs." And many fiddlers improvised variations of some kind. For instance, one Pate Baillie is said to have been traveling on a ferry when "a gentleman" promised him cash if he could immediately improvise ten variations on a tune, which Baillie easily exceeded (McHardy 55). But that tale from oral tradition gives us no clue concerning the nature of the variations. Perhaps they were Italianate. But at least one Scottish fiddler made fun of the "hahas of Italian music" (McHardy 76). Perhaps instead Baillie's variations were more like those that Knauff notated in the *Virginia Reels* but did not mark as variations.

I should note that articulating music analyses is quite foreign to most fiddlers! They express themselves through the art/craft/compulsion of fiddling, not in prose reflections and certainly not in technical vocabulary. And the fact that modern contest fiddling is susceptible of analysis like that applicable to art music does not make contest styles better than other manners of performing: the best fiddlers in every style make tremendous music. The point I wish to make through discussing these two transcriptions of modern performances of "George Booker" is that a tune with a memorable melodic hook can don different stylistic garbs and continue to make a powerful impact. Knauff's "George Booker," though looking simpler on paper than the late eighteenth-century versions of "Marquis of Huntley's Farewell," would have been similarly strong because of its transformation from stately strathspey into brisk reel. And Krack and Weisgerber's performances of "George Booker" are neither more nor less impressive than those earlier forms of the tune. The fiddlers are just using different strategies to move the music powerfully forward.

"Billy in the Low Grounds," "Old Virginia," and "Mississippi Sawyer": The *Virginia Reels* and Creating New Tunes from Old

The lives of several of the individual tunes in the *Virginia Reels* illustrate the wild variety of tune's fates within what fits under the broad umbrella term *oral tradition*. On one end of a continuum of relative stability there are melodies that survive with little or no change over the centuries. In the *Virginia Reels*, these include tunes with documented earlier histories such "Money Musk" (Knauff's "Killie Krankie") and "Speed the Plough," plus stable tunes appearing first in this collection, such as "Forked Deer." On the other end of that continuum, there are newly composed tunes that don't catch on, like "Lockwell." Such tunes—ones that simply didn't catch the attention of enough performers to survive—are oral tradition's casualties. In between these extremes are all kinds of relationships, not easy to classify. The primary authority on melody relationships in British-American folk song was Samuel P. Bayard. As part of his studies of Child ballads, he defined the "tune family" as "a group of melodies showing basic interrelation by means of constant melodic correspondence, and presumably owing their mutual likeness to descent from a single air that has assumed multiple forms through processes of variation, imitation, and assimilation" (1950, 33).

Bayard was also the father of the study of American fiddling, but did not propose that the concept of tune family would work well for the Pennsylvania instrumental repertoires he had so meticulously collected and organized. He linked just under a third of the tunes published in *Dance to the Fiddle, March to the Fife: Instrumental Folk Tunes in Pennsylvania* (1982) to what he believed, due to very close resemblances, were direct ancestors. He described many more relationships with a carefully graded array of impressionistic terms, each of which appeared many times in the tune annotations in that massive collection. Resemblances were called just that, or were qualified as being—in order of intimacy— slight, elusive, "bearing some," possible, general, considerable, "quite a bit," "double-edged," especial, striking, substantial, close, or unmistakable (in all cases his words). I reviewed that book long ago, hoping to find in it some overarching theory of tune relationships that worked for fiddle tunes. I mentioned in the review that Bayard hadn't articulated a parallel to the tune family theory he knew better than anyone else; he wrote me hoping that I had one in mind! I didn't—and don't—but will sample the situation with three case studies here.

Knauff's "Billy in the Low Grounds" survives under that and closely related titles; Henry Reed called his version "Billy in the Low Lands." There is a clear antecedent, the Scottish "Johnny in the Nether Mains," and clear examples of the same tune under other names in early America, such as "New Haven Green." Uncommon tunes like this one do not merely attract numerous titles, the melodies themselves are more apt to change, since fiddlers' memories are less frequently reinforced. Is this tune related to "Blue-Bonneted Scots," which Knauff also arranged? The harmonic progress and the general contour seem similar, but the change of time signature seems to have been enough to qualify this as a different tune in Knauff's view. Now I'd like to travel a tenuous path in hearing tune relationships. "Blue-Bonneted Scots" seems clearly descended from "O Dear Mother, What Shall I Do" (see fig. 16). A Scottish fiddle tune in C Major called "The Braes of Auchtertyre" was noted by Nathaniel Gow to be related to "O Dear Mother" ([1802], 20). "The Braes of Auchtertyre"

106 ✦ "LADY OF THE LAKE" AND "GEORGE BOOKER"

"Johnny in the Nether Mains." Gow & Sons 1802, 2.

"New Haven Green." Seward 1807, 31.

"Billy in the Low Grounds." Knauff 1839, III, 4.

"The Beaus of Albany." Howe 1843, II, 37; 1844, II, 69, and in dozens of his (and others') later publications.

Figure 20. Knauff's "Billy in the Low Grounds" and relatives.

crossed to the United States under that title, and also often was printed as "The Beaus of Albany" (see fig. 20). Today, that C-Major tune survives under the title "Billy in the Low Grounds." In fact, that tune is much more common than Knauff's and Reed's tune, and has largely usurped the title. All of these tunes share an implied harmonic underpinning, and, if one is generous, a very broad contour. But shifting from the G Major of the rare modern performances of Knauff's "Billy in the Low Lands" to the C Major of the Braes/Beaus/Billy complex encourages the tune to traverse more of the available range of the violin. Perhaps the broad similarity of tunes allowed the C-Major tune to borrow the title, and perhaps the greater drama allowed in the C-Major tune made it more popular.

The second tune I'd like to speculate about in this section is Knauff's "Old Virginia." The only section that differentiates this tune from a normal "Flowers of Edinburgh" is the beginning, as shown in figure 21. Is that enough to make it a new tune? This "Old Virginia" is unique; we can't know if there was a cumulative opinion about this among tradition insiders. It does seem that Knauff's source fiddler liked arpeggios. His "Natchez on the Hill" differs from typical versions of the minstrel standard "Old Zip Coon" in precisely the same way: "Natchez on the Hill" starts with arpeggios, then joins the contour of the more common tune. Of course, arpeggios are easy on the piano, so that may have been a reinforcing factor.

In "Old Virginia," as in "Flowers of Edinburgh," the second strain comprises quite a long melodic loop, one stretching through the entire strain. A prominent and creative Ozark fiddler of the mid-twentieth century, Art Galbraith, found that the grand contour wouldn't fit in eight measures, so he let the power of the melody rather than formal fiddle tune conventions rule, with a result that his B strain stretches well past the conventional length of eight bars (see a transcription in Marshall 2012, 104). Galbraith's rhapsodic, convention-defying form has been frequently copied; I especially like the version played by clawhammer banjoist Adam Hurt (2009, cut 6). This enduring, well-disseminated take on "The Flowers of Edinburgh" seems to me to be at least as much of a departure from the conventional identity of the melody as is Knauff's "Old Virginia." Is that tune, or is the Galbraith/Hurt/et cetera stretched version a new tune? I often hear the latter referred to as "Galbraith's 'Flowers of Edinburgh.'" In the world of biology, this would be called a distinct subspecies.

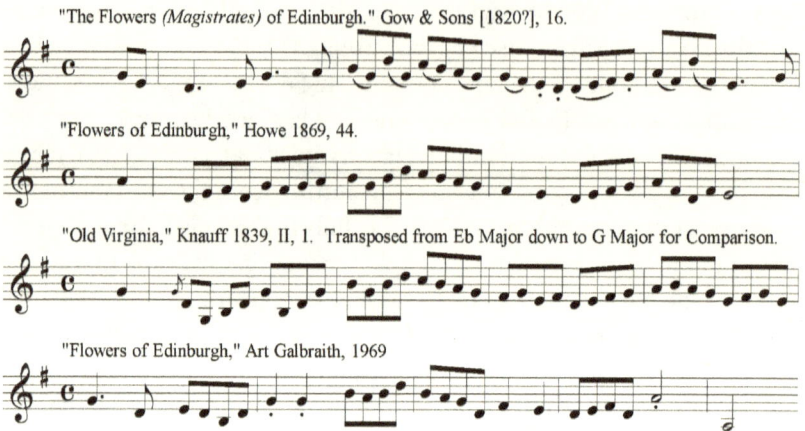

Figure 21. "The Flowers of Edinburgh": the first four measures of various versions.

I'll close this section with a look at possible tune relationships stemming from stretching a tune sideways, as in Art Galbraith's performance of the high strain of "The Flowers of Edinburgh" (1980). However, in this case, what I suspect started as a stretch resulted in a break and reformulation! Knauff's is the first publication of the tune "Mississippi Sawyer." Yes, there is some associated confusion: Knauff assigned that title in the first number of the *Virginia Reels* to a tune that doesn't survive today, then placed the tune that we now call "Mississippi Sawyer" in the fourth pamphlet with the title "Love from the Heart." Perhaps this was an error on the part of his source fiddler(s) or on Knauff's part; William Sidney Mount wrote down a version of the usual tune "Mississippi Sawyer" under that title at about the same time. I do think that it is reasonable that tune and title were associated back then as they are now.

Fiddlers have images of contours that may be concrete or fluid, and also have each internalized formal conventions into which a remembered (or deliberately modified, or misremembered and accidentally transformed) contour would likely be pressured to fit. Another common old-time tune, one often performed with scraps of text, is "Old Molly Hare." It is also in D Major, and the signature strain, the high one, has the same general contour as that of "Mississippi Sawyer," but proceeding twice as fast (see fig. 22). "Old Molly Hare," unlike "Mississippi Sawyer," does have a clear Scottish antecedent, "Largo's Fairy Dance," which was published and likely composed by Nathaniel Gow (1809, 19). Might "Largo's Fairy

"Largo's Fairy Dance," Gow 1809, 19.

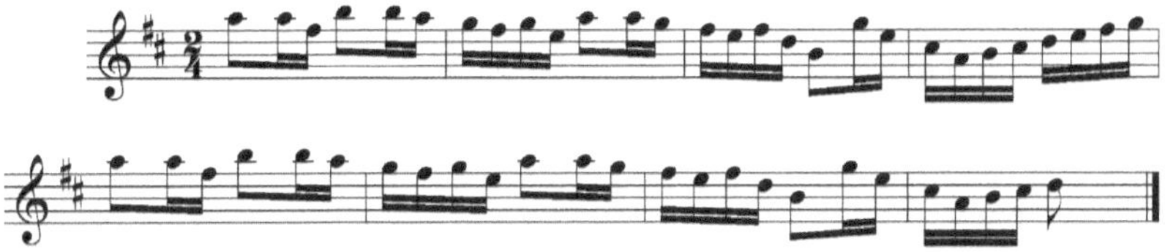

"Old Molly Hare," William Sidney Mount manuscript collection, 1850s?

"Love from the Heart," Knauff 1839, he mistakenly (?) labels another tune "Mississippi Sawyer."

"Mississippi Sawyer," Tim Donley, interview during Galax, 2001

Figure 22. From "Largo's Fairy Dance" to "Mississippi Sawyer," high strain only.

Dance" have survived with its current proportions in American oral tradition, and eventually gained a text during the blackface minstrel era, and subsequently have been known here as "Old Molly Hare?" Sometime before Knauff learned "Mississippi Sawyer," might his source fiddler for this tune have separately remembered "Largo's Fairy Dance," but imprecisely, in a stretched form, so that the contour that was played through twice in the high strain of the older dance was doubled in length? That would then be the high strain of "Mississippi Sawyer." This seems possible to me, but we don't have intermediate stages to situate along a slow evolution of change.

- CHAPTER FIVE -

Knauff's "Ohio River" and "Indian Whoop"

The Rhythmic and Timbral Puzzles of Blackface Minstrelsy and of Modern Old-Time Fiddling

THE FOURTH, FINAL PAMPHLET OF THE *VIRGINIA REELS* MAY HAVE been published over a decade after the first three pamphlets appeared; the rare extant copies bear a plate number suggesting it came out in 1852. But the graphics for the Willig edition of pamphlet 4 match those of pamphlet 3. Was number 4 printed originally in a set without plate numbers, perhaps as early as 1839 or so, when a plate-number-less first pamphlet (and perhaps 2 and 3) came out? Or was the artwork for pamphlet 3 filed for over a decade, then resurrected for the title page of 4? While the most frustrating mystery in the history of *Virginia Reels* is not knowing the identity of the fiddler(s) from whom Knauff appropriated the tunes, this dating problem is a close second.

During the possible extended pause in the publication of the series, blackface minstrelsy transformed the American music environment, shifting from being primarily street fare—mostly but not entirely performed by and for members of the working classes—to dominating popular entertainment. "Boatman Dance" ("Ohio River" in the *Virginia Reels*) may have been around for some time before Knauff printed it; the move into a broader range of acceptability of minstrelsy may have changed his opinion of these particular tunes. Music that he might not have initially considered marketable to his affluent neighbors and to the parents of his female students may have become not only acceptable but fashionable.

Figure 23. After the first publications of "Boatman Dance," boatmen were often depicted dancing. This picture (by an unknown illustrator) is of the title page of "Song of the Negro Boatman," written by J. W. Dadman (1862). The lyrics are a poem by John Greenleaf Whittier, his dialect celebration of approaching freedom entitled "Song of the Negro Boatmen." Note that in this illustration, the female figure gestures toward the Union army in the distance. Image from and used by permission of the Frances G. Spencer Collection of American Popular Sheet Music, Crouch Fine Arts Library and Baylor University Digital Collections, Baylor University, Waco, Texas.

Black Fiddlers and the Early Shaping of Blackface Minstrelsy

Blackface minstrelsy was the most distinctively American entertainment of the nineteenth century and our first significant cultural export. Performers in blackface worked as solo acts in circuses and similar shows for decades before the four men in the Virginia Minstrels created the first evening-long program in 1843. That quartet's instrumentation remained the minimum for decades: fiddle, banjo, tambourine, and bones, with all performers singing during choruses of songs. When minstrel troupes became much larger later in the century, such quartets survived as one among the acts making up those shows, an act old-fashioned but still enjoyed.

When white minstrels in blackface copied and parodied black practice, they drew on several streams of black performance. There were many slave fiddlers; hearing them play was the easiest route for these white entertainers to sample black music making, at the same time that it presented slaves' least specifically African American sounds. There were plenty of slave fiddlers as early as the late seventeenth century (Wells 2003, 135). Also, free black fiddlers were common in the North (Wells 1978, 3). And we should keep in mind that when Gideon Lincecum visited the 1835 picnic at Eagle Lake in barely settled Texas, the hosts "called up the Negro fiddler and tried to dance awhile" (1874–75, 12). After painstaking research, Dena Epstein concluded that there were more black than white fiddlers in the antebellum United States (1983, 99). I find that easy to believe in the case of Knauff's Virginia. Socializing centered on dancing in "Old Virginia," and none of the planters present at a dance wanted to be stuck in a corner fiddling: they wanted to dance and visit with their family and friends.

Blackface minstrelsy, although more a northern than southern product at first (Lott 1993, 38), had audiences nationwide. Quite a few minstrel pieces circulated as sheet music well before the Virginia Minstrels' big splash of 1843; many lyrics described the narrators playing musical instruments. One such piece was issued in New York in 1833: "Sambo's 'Dress to the Bred'rin. As Sung with the most Enormous Applause, Mr. Davis' Musical Parties, on Friday Evenings, Broadway House, by Mr. Brower, the Celebrated Comic Singer" (Taylor 1833). The lyrics describe how much better life could be if the protagonist and family and friends could go to "Hettee" (Haiti). There they would "be receve, Gran as Lafayettee"; there they would "feel no rod," and "lib so fine." Verse 6 begins:

> Dar smoke de bess segar, Fech from de havanah,
> Wile our dorters fair, Play on de Pianah.

Verse 9 continues:

> Dar we hab partys big, Dar dance an play de fiddle,
> Dar wales and hab de jig, Kast off an down de middle.
> Den in de gran saloon, We take de blushing damsull,
> Were eyes shine like de moon, An ebry mouf dey cram full.

Two years later, a song came out with lyrics naming even more instruments: "Jim Brown. A Favorite Comic Song." In the first two verses, the narrator refers to leading a brass band and mentions playing cymbals and a drum. Verses 3 through 5 mention stringed instruments:

> De way I larnt to play de carry ob de sword,
> I practis on de Banjo sugar in de goard;
> De niggers all dance when Jim begin to play,
> Dey dance from de morning, to de closing ob de day.
> I plays upon de fiddle and I plays de clarinet.
> I plays upon de cymbals till I make de nigger swet.
> I was born on Long Island close to Oyster Bay,
> I worked upon de farms for three cents a day;
> De genius ob dis nigger, was sure to be disciver,
> I jump't upon de pine raft and floats down de river.
> I land at Coarlers hook, de music in my hand,
> Quick I get de leader ob de famed Brass Band.
> I caution all de New York niggers not to stop my way,
> For if he play de fool wid me dey in de gutter lay;
> For when I was at New Orleans and only three feet high,
> I run before old General Jack, and make de red coats fly.
> Den I play upon de corn stalk de true Yankee fiddle,
> Lick'd lasses from de punkin blow, and sugar from maple.

Narrator Jim Brown brags about both his fighting ability and his musical skills. He refers to the cornstalk fiddle, then also to what is presumably a regular fiddle with its greater volume for dance accompaniment. His band instruments include the clarinet, cymbals, and drum. The banjo figures importantly, of course (1835).

Dale Cockrell, while immersed in the holdings of the American Antiquarian Society, came upon a newspaper article from the early 1840s that illustrated informal, lower-class use of venerable fiddle tunes along with minstrel items in a mixed-race entertainment. This article, entitled "Grand Trial between Nance Holmes and Suse Bryant, on Long Wharf, Boston," narrated a dance competition between two prostitutes, accompanied by a "half-Negro fiddler" (1997, 8–10). The tune to accompany a hornpipe was "Fisher's Hornpipe," which goes back at least to the 1780s in England (see Kuntz 2012). Tunes played for a dance named a "Virginia Breakdown" included minstrel standards: "The Camptown Hornpipe" (from Foster's "Camptown Races"), "Grapevine," "Lucy Long," and "Jenny Get Your Hoecake Done" (Cockrell 1997, 10). Even earlier than this "contest"—well before the Virginia Minstrels became famous—John Hill Hewitt arranged eight minstrel tunes as *The Crow Quadrilles*, including "Sich a Gittin Up Stairs" and "Long Time Ago," "Sittin' on a Rail," "Clare de Kitchen," "Zip Coon," "Jim Brown," "Gumbo Chaff," and "My Long Tail Blue, Arranged with Figures for the Piano Forte" (1837).

In short, *well before* the Virginia Minstrels asserted that their show would be newly refined and morally unassailable, the minstrel repertoire had established a beachhead in polite society.[1] This tug-of-war between piquant roughness and gentility would be central to shaping minstrelsy and especially how it was advertised: The genre was based on raunchiness, but to be profitable needed to appeal to all classes in terms of both concert attendance and sheet music sales. How could performers—who were often composers and arrangers, too—consistently find that mercantile sweet spot?

Black Musicians and Blackface Minstrelsy in Knauff's Virginia

Knauff, arriving in the United States in the mid- to late 1820s, heard black fiddlers, black banjoists, *and* early minstrel music before his first venture into arranging and publishing sheet music, before 1839. When

Figure 24. John Hill Hewitt, *The Crow Quadrilles* (1837), title page.

he sold music at his Farmville store in the 1830s, he must have encountered the early minstrel pieces I quoted above, or similar ones. And Prince Edward County's black population certainly included musicians, although evidence remains spotty. I haven't found documentation of a black fiddler—or any fiddler—living there when Knauff did, but Melvin Ely, in his study of an antebellum community of freed blacks in that county, touched on this topic while discussing a Farmville court case from 1858. The disputants "appeared to share a culture: much of the testimony resolved around black men playing the fiddle for gatherings of their peers" (2004, 348). Regarding the "shared culture," Ely noted that "as in earlier times, whites and free Afro-Virginians in the 1850s could readily find themselves rubbing shoulders at estate sales, public events, or places of business" (364).

The banjo, a conflation of West African plucked stringed instruments, embodied slaves' collective memory, although as seen through outsiders' lenses and as transformed with the aid of Euro-American technology. Just as Knauff would have encountered black fiddlers at dances, he also must have heard banjos played. One narration of black banjo playing in Prince Edward County during his day must stand for many similar events. A doctor, one William B. Smith, while waxing eloquent about the virtues of the persimmon tree and its fruit, described music accompanying the consumption of persimmon beer:

> Some years ago, I rode in the night to visit a patient, and as I passed the house of Mr. Samuel Poe, in the lower end of Prince Edward [County], I heard the tones of a banjor, and was told by the old gentleman (Mr. Poe), that his servants had brewed a barrel of persimmon beer, and he gave them the privilege of having what they called a "beer dance." . . . Here the banjor-man was seated on the [persimmon beer] barrel, in an old chair. A long white cow-tail queued with red ribbon, ornamented his head, and hung gracefully down his back; over this he wore a three-cocked hat, decorated with peacock feathers, a rose cockade, a bunch of ripe persimmons, and to cap the climax, three pods of red pepper as a top-knot. *Tumming* his banjor, grinning with ludicrous gesticulations and laying off the wild notes to the company. Before him stood two athletic blacks, with open mouth and pearl white teeth, clapping Juber to the notes of the banjor . . . the clappers rested the right foot on the heel, and its clap on the floor was in perfect unison with the notes of the banjor, and palms of the hands on the corresponding extremities; while the dancers were all jigging it away in the merriest possible gaiety of heart. (1838, 58–61)

Knauff also must have heard the banjo as transformed into a blackface minstrel instrument. Joel Sweeney (1810–1860), the first white banjo player that we know of, grew up on a farm about thirty miles from Knauff's home in Farmville and just as close to Knauff's later base, the Buckingham Female Collegiate Institute. Sweeney said he learned the banjo from local blacks; he certainly could have visited the persimmon beer dance described above. He started performing publicly in the 1830s, just when Knauff was getting established in Farmville (Fischer and Kelly 2000, 66). He played at local court sessions—an intriguing thought!—and toured Virginia and North Carolina with a circus. By the time Knauff brought out the *Virginia Reels,* Sweeney was in New York performing in various blackface venues. Indeed, a piece of sheet music from about that time has Sweeney performing a tune also anthologized in the *Virginia Reels.* The title page reads: "Whar Did You Cum From? Knock a Nigger Down. The Celebrated Banjo Song, as Sung by J.W. Sweeney with Great Applause at the Broadway Circus" (n.d.).[2] In any case, Knauff probably knew plenty of blackface tunes by 1839; gaining access to the music would not have been a barrier to publishing number 4 of the *Virginia Reels* that early, even if pamphlet 4 didn't come out physically until later. In one scenario, he might have been hesitant to publish the "minstrel" volume of the *Virginia Reels* before minstrelsy made the jump to fashionable national entertainment. The counter argument: he might have hurried to get in on the profits earned by the early arrangers of blackface tunes.

The next bit of speculation shouldn't be dignified by being labeled a conclusion! Knauff linked his name with those of his friends and neighbors—his potential patrons and customers—whenever he could through dedications on the title pages of his music. He also mentioned specific local youngsters in the lyrics of "The Toothache or the Quilting." Why didn't he name his source fiddler(s) for the *Virginia Reels?* It must not have been proper or useful to identify that/those individual(s). My best guess is that the *Virginia Reels* represents Knauff transcribing the playing of musician(s) low in the socioeconomic picture, probably black fiddler(s), whether slave or free.

How did black fiddlers sound? Many of them learned to fiddle from their owners or from traveling violin tutors. Lower-class white Virginians may have been in the mix, too, among them Scots-Irish immigrants, many of whom filtered through Piedmont Virginia on their way to the mountains and better chances of landownership. I suspect that slave fiddlers and other black fiddlers might well have been favored the Scottish component of British fiddling, since Scottish tunes and Scottish ways of performing seem to have been more rhythmically dense and varied. Supporting this scenario is the fact that quite a few Scottish fiddle tunes turn up in minstrelsy (see Goertzen 1995).

In addition, would-be minstrels visiting slave quarters saw and heard banjos at events like the Persimmon Dance. Although such occasions would have been rarer than those visitors witnessing slave fiddling, the banjo was visually distinctive, and entered the minstrel quartet for symbolic and visual reasons as much as for its music. Last, the African and African American predilection for clapping and otherwise adding percussive effects to music was perpetuated in the incorporation of the tambourine and bones into the basic blackface minstrel quartet.

"My Love She's But a Lassie Yet": When Fiddle and Banjo Interact

Can we piece together how those minstrel quartets sounded? Robert Winans has tried, invoking evidence remaining from the early minstrel period (1976; 1984). And current old-time fiddling in the Southeast typically takes place within quartets (or somewhat larger groups) built around a fiddle and banjo duo, with the banjo playing in what are called clawhammer and/or frailing techniques, which descend from minstrel banjo playing. There are critical differences between nineteenth-century minstrelsy performance and modern old-time playing, of course. The tambourine and bones have been replaced by harmonizing instruments—the guitar and bass—and the banjo has evolved significantly through employment of European-derived construction techniques, so its sound has gradually changed. But the connection between minstrel quartet and contemporary old-time string band is undeniable.

In those antebellum blackface minstrel quartets, just as today in old-time southeastern ensembles, the fiddle and the banjo played in heterophony. Both instruments were conceived by the minstrels as being producers of melody; neither performed a harmonizing function. I specify *heterophony* rather than unison because the banjo is less flexible than the violin in terms of easy availability of all pitches, and it also has a second responsibility. The banjoist must add an unchanging pitch with a rhythmic element. That is generally called a "drone," but that term needs to be refined here. The banjo is a plucked stringed instrument, and inefficient in the sense that its notes die out swiftly: it cannot "drone" in the sense of emitting a pitch constantly, but rather must reiterate that note many times. Precisely when the short string rings matters greatly. The banjoist's plucking that high-pitched "drone" string as the fourth (and sometimes second) of many sets of four eighth notes adds an off-the-beat accent, in propulsive syncopation. Those notes automatically displace melody notes. Also, even when the fiddle and banjo approached a melodic unison, the general effect would still lean toward heterophony, since the fiddle can sustain pitches at a steady volume and timbre, but banjo notes quickly change in character during their passage from clanging attack through swift decay. And the tambourine and bones of the minstrel ensemble added their own punctuation and rhythmic enlivenment, though this remained in the world of oral tradition.

Published notation is less helpful in imagining the sound of antebellum blackface minstrel fiddling than for fiddling in late eighteenth-century Scotland or in the younger United States. Figure 25a illustrates this. This figure follows a tune from late eighteenth-century Scotland through early America and through antebellum minstrelsy to current southeastern fiddling. "My Love She's But a Lassie Yet," although known in Scotland from the late eighteenth century primarily as song with lyrics by Robert Burns, started its published life decades earlier as "Miss Farquharson's Reel" (Bremner 1757, 19). Since the reel was a relatively fast dance, little ornamentation attached itself to those published versions, and the tune remained similarly streamlined as "My Love She's But a Lassie Yet" in English and American collections, as illustrated in the example from Winner. Perhaps some fiddlers "swung" the rhythms, but we can't be sure of that. Any additional excitement when this tune was played by black fiddlers and by their imitators/exaggerators on the minstrel stage must have reposed in elements of fiddle performance that were not susceptible of transcription (rubato, glissandos, accents), in the heterophony with the banjo, and through the contributions of the percussion.

Today this is not one of the very commonest tunes in the string band repertoires of the Upper South, but many musicians know it. Its various current titles reflect the message of the text—that the desirable young woman in question, the narrator's "love," isn't old enough to become a wife: "Too Young to Marry," "Sweet Sixteen," "Darling Child." At Clifftop 2014, I requested a performance of "Too Young to Marry" from fiddler Scott Prouty (a fiddler and fiddle teacher now living in West Virginia), banjoist Frank Evans, of Toronto, Canada, and friends in the "Canada" neighborhood of the Clifftop campground. I asked that the performance proceed in an artificial order: first a fiddle solo, which would then yield to a banjo solo (so that I could reliably transcribe the banjo line, parts of which are apt to become indistinct in the ensemble sound), then to the ensemble sound. The fiddle and banjo parts are given in figure 25b.

The power of a modern string band performance (and older string band performances, and, in terms of the fiddle/banjo partnership, all the way back to blackface minstrelsy) reaches beyond the fiddler's limning of the melody; it exists in a series of equilibria that pervade every measure. First, concerning drone versus harmony: The fiddle's moving line implies harmonies, but chords don't appear in the violin part. Instead, many fiddlers drone on convenient open strings, which are generally tuned to the tonic or the dominant in both strains (in A Major, the E and A string drones work well; the fiddle is tuned AEAE). In this way, Scott Prouty's sparing use of open-string doubles is exceptional; for more typical drones, see the performance by Eddie Bond in figure 25c. The drone versus harmony factor is also acted out in the other instruments: the drone-heavy banjo versus the harmonizing guitar and bass. In the realm of rhythmic texture, the violin, guitar, and bass accent the first and third beats of the measure, while the banjo drones push toward those accents by accenting the immediately previous eighth notes.

There is also a visual rhythmic element in live performance, the contrasting yet synchronized ways that the instrumentalists' hands move. But the trickiest element is texture, the layered heterophony. As in minstrelsy, the fiddler and banjoist in a modern string band both play the melody in a way proper to their instrument. The tuning and technique of the banjo played in the older southeastern style, the clawhammer style directly inherited from blackface minstrelsy, produces a less linear version of any melody, so that the fiddle and banjo mesh and part from a unison in a lovely way. So, that is a historically inherited heterophony between versions of the melody.

But there is more of what one might term intimate heterophony within individual notes as combined vertically. That is, the violin has a firm attack and as much sustain as desired, while the notes that are hit at the same time on the plucked instruments have more biting attacks but quicker decays (different for each of the three instruments). In particular, the banjo attack made by the performer's index or second finger

Figure 25a. Versions of the tune best known as "My Love She's But a Lassie Yet."

Figure 25b. "Too Young to Marry" in fiddle and banjo heterophony.

has that finger pushing out, the hand opening. As a result, the nail hits the string while it has a bit of vibration left over from the last time it was hit. That adds some clank you don't get from the deployment of the player's thumb, which activates the string as if the hand were closing, as in most European finger-plucked string performance: the flesh of the digit in question dampens the string the instant before the continued motion has the nail activating the string. The guitarist uses a flat pick—held more firmly for individual notes hit on the beat than for the chords played between—so we witness two kinds of attacks there. In sum, there is complexity in the attacks, just as in the composite timbres when some instruments' notes die out faster than others. We hear all four instruments, with their four subtle patterns of decay, regularly reenacting very tricky matrices of timbre and volume. When all of this occurs at once, the results are no less complex and no less satisfying than in the best fiddling in Texas contest style, even in performances when there is little or no variation of melody.

Knauff's version of "My Love She's But a Lassie Yet" bore the title "Richmond Blues"; this spritely and rhythmically spare tune worked

Figure 25c. "Darling Child," played in the Galax substyle of old-time style by Eddie Bond.

Figure 25c, concluded.

well enough for the marching of the Richmond Blues militia (and social) unit that the young men claimed it as their own. One of the noteworthy features of this "Richmond Blues" is that it illustrates two types of variation. The first is the general rhythmic filling in that we expect when a song becomes a fiddle tune: the extra notes replace some of the interest subtracted when the singer and lyrics go away, and yield a good fiddled overall texture. But also, and of special significance here, are the bits of rhythmic "densification" inserted in measures nine, eleven, and thirteen. In those locations, just a brief fillip of extra push was superimposed. These little moments of variation that Knauff chose to reproduce in this, the last piece in the pamphlet, must stand for plenty more that he didn't put into notation. These moments are clear precedents for the kind of variation enlivening the modern version of "Darling Child" placed last in this figure.

I omitted some minor bits of variation in the transcription of Prouty's and Evans's performing of this tune, but focused on variation in a 2011 performance of "Darling Child" by one of the best fiddlers in Galax style, Eddie Bond, a graceful performance done under trying circumstances.

On this day at the Old Fiddlers Convention, a storm had come in. A tornado warning siren blared repeatedly, and an authoritative voice echoed over the loudspeaker system, entreating us to move from the campground to the covered bleachers. Nevertheless, Bond and a nervous guitarist played a few tunes for me before we took cover.

In this transcription of Bond's "Darling Child," I put each "new" series of notes (that is, figures substituting for gestures as played during the first pass through each of the two strains) under dotted lines. The general trend in these little bits of variation is toward greater density, as in the Knauff "Richmond Blues" and as in most types of variation in western art or western folk music. More specifically, many of the changes accented the second or fourth beats. This looks back in history: it imitates and adds to the mid-half-note syncopation found in many of the old Scottish tunes and echoed in some American versions of those tunes; compare measures two, four, ten, and twelve of "Miss Farquharson's Reel" with measures two and ten of Winner's "My Love She's But a Lassie Yet." At the same time, Bonds's approach to rhythm can be understood as both growing out of and interacting with the fourth-of-four eighth-notes drone of a banjo.

"Boatman Dance" and the Dissemination of Black (and Blackface) Fiddle Style

Quite a few boatmen lived in Farmville and environs during Knauff's lifetime, an era during which Prince Edward County remained primarily agricultural, like the rest of Virginia. To set the scene: The 1850 census of this county identified 529 men as farmers, in addition to 43 overseers, 44 carpenters, 24 blacksmiths, and 22 wheelwrights. In less primary occupations, there were 52 merchants, 25 shoemakers, 24 doctors, 20 tailors, 19 factory hands, and 16 each schoolteachers and clergymen listed. Finally, there were handfuls of millers, bricklayers, lawyers, cabinet makers, clerks, and "tobonists" (tobacconists, I presume), plus one or two representatives of each of various occupations marking Farmville as an established city. These included the professions of jeweler, confectioner, mattress maker, gunsmith, butcher, druggist, tavern keeper, and boot maker.

Workers in transportation-related occupations included—in addition to the wheelrights listed above—eleven coach makers and three carriage makers. There were just five wagoners listed, compared with a grand total of fifty-four boatmen. According to Ely, Prince Edward County boatmen might be slaves, free blacks, or whites (2004, 68 and 155), as were the fewer wagoners (2004, 144–45). Knauff could not have avoided knowing some of the boatmen; their crowded quarters in Farmville were just a few blocks from his home. And in a town with a population of only about eight hundred in the mid-1830s (Ely 2004, 345), he must have had at least a general sense of what these men were like, and likely knew some of them personally.

This lively interracial assemblage of boatmen bore reputations for being rowdy, not any more respectful of private property than they needed to be, and liable to dance! Christopher Smith, in his study of William Sidney Mount and early minstrelsy, credited waterways with great importance in spreading minstrelsy. He noted that "mobile boundaries and arteries—rivers and canals, harbors and bays, wharves, highways and early railroads—were both the earliest incubators and the ongoing conduits by which minstrelsy's urban synthesis could reach out again across the North American continent, more extensively, comprehensively, and far earlier than has been presumed" (2013, 33). And the importance of waterways for the spread of traditional music certainly did not start or end with minstrelsy; fiddling was at the center of this picture for centuries. Mark Twain peppered his description of *Life on the Mississippi* with evidence for vernacular music traveling there. One anecdote from his days as a steamboat pilot reads:

> Once at night, in one of those forest-bordered crevices (behind an island) which steamboatmen intensely describe with the phrase "as dark as the inside of a cow," we should have eaten up a Posey County family, fruit, furniture, and all, but that they happened to be fiddling down below and just caught the sound of the music in time to sheer off, doing no serious damage, unfortunately, but coming so near it that we had high hopes for a moment. These people brought up the lantern, then, of course; and as we backed and filled to get away, the precious family stood in the light of it—both sexes and various ages—and cursed us till everything turned blue. (1917, 88)

Twain felt that music was so essential to river life that he had Huckleberry Finn witness fiddling boatmen: "They stumped back and had a drink around and went to talking and singing again. Next they got out an old fiddle, and one played, and another patted juba, and the rest turned themselves loose on a regular old-fashioned keelboat breakdown" (1917, 23).

Within the *Virginia Reels*, waterway-related titles abound, particularly in the first and third numbers. To name the cities Natchez, Richmond, and Petersburg is to evoke images of ports, although that doesn't really set those towns apart, since most substantial cities in the United States were located on rivers or bays. More specifically, the titles "Mississippi Sawyer" and "Two Sisters" probably referred to navigational hazards on the Mississippi. "The Island" was in the bay on the way to Knauff's part of Virginia, "Lady of the Lake," although referring to a book about chivalry, does have a "lake" in it, and "Billy in the Low Grounds" refers to land that is fertile due to regular flooding; "low grounds" are parts of watercourses seasonally.[3]

In the final, minstrelsy-related number of the *Virginia Reels*, the only title that mentions a waterway is "Ohio River," a retitling of the then ubiquitous "Boatman Dance." That's the river mentioned in the lyrics of the song, and the word "Ohio" scans and rhymes, but we should also keep in mind that this major river was a major boundary between slave and free states, and thus likely of special importance to Knauff's source fiddler(s), if they were black.

Many factors come together in "The Boatman's Dance." It came out in 1843; Virginia minstrel Daniel Decatur Emmett claimed authorship. But he also said he wrote "Dixie," which Howard and Judith Rose Sacks have demonstrated probably came out of Emmett's visits with the Snowdens, a black family living in Emmett's home town of Mt. Vernon, Ohio (1993).[4] Robert Winans believes that "Boatman's Dance" is also among Emmett's compositions that "were at least partially 'borrowed' for the [Virginia Minstrels'] shows from preexisting oral tradition" (1984; 88). Did Knauff's fiddler(s) get the tune from pop music, that is, from minstrelsy, or instead from some part of the oral tradition that may have separately supplied serial-adapter Emmett? Whatever the case, Knauff's employing the unusual title "Ohio River" suggests some oral/aural connection.

Soon after the Virginia Minstrels gave blackface minstrelsy a strengthened profile, the group's hits were sold as sheet music, and then, in the way of hits, were arranged countless times. I chose a widely distributed arrangement to illustrate "De Boatman Dance," the second in a collection entitled *Ethiopian Quadrilles,* arranged by the oddly named—perhaps apochryphal—A. Nagerj Onyqjva (1843).[5] A quadrille was a society dance: just as the Virginia Minstrels advertised their act as morally and aesthetically elevated (my!), this dance placed blackface minstrel songs in the same situation that I described for "McPherson's Blues" in the second chapter and for *The Crow Quadrilles* in this chapter—that is, music for affluent, fashion-conscious couples to dance to. Most of the tunes gathered up in the *Ethiopian Quadrilles* were already hits; the total sequence included "Lucy Long," "De Boatman Dance," "Massa is a Stingy Man," "Old Dan Tucker," and "Ginger Blue." Rather than alternating between pieces in simple duple and compound duple time, as was the custom for quadrilles, these are all in 2/4—the constituent tunes being in fashion outweighed the lack of contrast in meter.

The cover is marvelous and disturbing (fig. 26a). Of the seven main pictures on it, four include a banjo. In two sketches, the owner just holds the banjo, but in one he is playing for a dancer, and in one preparing to brain an alligator from his perch in a bateau (in a smaller picture, he's riding the alligator, and using his banjo as a quirt).[6] Of the minstrel instruments, the banjo clearly has the most visual appeal: it is easy to draw simply and is specifically attached to minstrelsy.

Why do I claim this version of "Boatman's Dance" was widely distributed? This collection of *Ethiopian Quadrilles* is the second of four sharing a title page in early editions. The contents of all four collections were listed on a later title page; I've seen this done on the first and the fourth number of the twelfth (!) edition (1848). The first number contained "Gwin' Ober de Mountin," "Jonny Boker," "De Old Jaw Bone," "Jumbo Jum," and "Jim Along Josey," the second as listed above, the third "Whar Did You Cum From," "Jenny Get Your Hoe Cake Done," "Charleston Gals," "Dandy Jim from Caroline," and "Old Tare River," and the fourth "Lucy Neal," "Mary Blane," "O Carry Me Back to Old Virginny" (the older 6/8 tune), "Rosa Lee," and "Stop That Knockin." This is quite an array of minstrel tunes to be gathered up and employed as elegant quadrilles!

Another collection of quadrilles shows just how fancy quadrilles that assembled minstrel melodies could be considered to have become. This is *The Ethiopian Quadrilles,* by Henry Oakey of London. It's undated, but the repertoire places it in the early 1840s. In it, one of Knauff's melodies,

Figure 26a. Cover of *Ethiopian Quadrilles*, arranged by A. Nagerj Onyqjva, 1843.

Figure 26b. "Boatman Dance," from the *Ethiopian Quadrilles*.

132 ♦ KNAUFF'S "OHIO RIVER" AND "INDIAN WHOOP"

Figure 26c. Knauff's "Ohio River" and a modern performance of "Boatman."

Figure 26c, concluded.

Ends with C7-8 (same as C1). Total form: A B C C A B C C A (low) B (low) C C A B C C.

the tune "Buffalo Gals," is associated with the dance "Le Pantalon," "Lucy Long" with "L'été," and so on, with a "Finale" danced to "The Boatman's Dance" and "Railroad Overture" (which turns out to be a version of "Money Musk"). The French titles referred to customary quadrille dance figures; pairing them with minstrel airs leaves a bizarre impression.

In figure 26c, I aligned a fine modern (2014) fiddled performance of "Boatman" from the contest stage at the Tennessee Valley Old Time Fiddlers Convention with Knauff's "Ohio River." I modified his "Ohio River" to ease the process of comparison: I reordered the strains and transposed the tune from F Major (a common key for the song "Boatman's Dance" in Knauff's day) to A Major, the key of most modern performances of "Boatman's Dance." Knauff's "Ohio River" does have the pianistic repeat within one strain that we saw in the 1843 publication photographed for the previous figure. However, in the original key of F Major, that would not have been an obstacle for Knauff's source fiddler(s). In F, the Knauff's version tops out at the d on the e string, that, the note stopped by the fourth finger in third position; quite a few of the *Virginia Reels* go precisely that high. Fiddler Tyler Andal enriched his modern old-time version with a generous complement of open-string double stops, anticipations, and versions of strains placed at lower octaves. It's quick and full of life, matching well with a picture of boatmen having a grand time during slack periods in their strenuous lives.

When we compare the Knauff "Ohio River" and Tyler Andal's "Boatman" with the "Boatman" representing the mass of versions of "Boatman's Dance" from the 1840s and 1850s—the photographed arrangement was chosen partly because it could represent such an average—neither seems more "arranged" than the other, given the different styles in which the arrangers worked. Both versions are rhythmically more dense than were the earlier versions, as befits moving from a well-known song to a fiddle tune; both arrangers vary contours enough to demonstrate independent thinking at some point in the oral tradition process. The main difference between the arrangements would have been in the nature of the source. In Knauff's day, "Boatman" was a big hit. Robert Winans, in a tally of songs advertised as going to be performed in blackface minstrel concerts during 1843–1852—he examined some 151 printed programs that specified tunes to be played—found that "Boatman's Dance" was in the top ten (1984, 81–82). But today, "Boatman" is quite rare in the local stream of fiddle performances in the Upper South; it is played much more often by revivalists at Clifftop than by inheritors at Galax. Although known in school songbooks of my generation, it's now an illustration of exotic nostalgia rather than of widespread taste in the world of old-time fiddling.

How did we get from early blackface minstrel performances of fiddle tunes to string bands of the modern Southeast? The essential blackface quartet constituted a workable small ensemble in the late 1830s and into the next decades, but larger groups were soon common; sheet music covers show that some of those groups included guitars. At the same time, the world of fashion exerted complicated influences. On the one hand, minstrelsy was putatively wild entertainment. For instance, the modern onomatopoetic extravagance of fiddlers' "Listen to the Mockingbird" and "Orange Blossom Special" was anticipated in minstrel violinist James Buckley's "celebrated imitations of the farm-yard," which included some twenty different bird cries (1855). On the other hand, when minstrel tunes became hits, they immediately were issued as individual items of sheet music, sometimes still advertised as being raw-edged authentic minstrel tunes (thus, with pictures of ensembles in blackface on the covers, and/or with boldly swirling title page decorations), but often with refined title page decorations and rhetoric encouraging genteel parlor piano performances by ever-so-proper debutantes, a critical sheet music demographic. The tug-of-war between rustic exuberance and pretty performances of minstrel tunes befitting cultivated drawing rooms continued through and after the nineteenth century.

"Indian Whoop" and "Sich a Gittin Upstairs, Varied": Knauff and the Rough and Smooth Edges of Minstrelsy

Should we be surprised to see the titles "Indian Whoop" and "Flying Indian" in a volume of the *Virginia Reels* that focuses on blackface minstrel tunes? The basic factors are these: Indians were rare in Knauff's part of Virginia by this time, but had left important cultural traces and had at least a double presence in local consciousness. The well-established noble (and conveniently doomed) Indian of fiction and the visual arts was already celebrated in many songs. That figure coexisted in American psychology with the threatening (and less spiritually elevated) living Indians with whom there was sporadic friction on the not-so-distant frontier. And a third thread emerged during Knauff's lifetime, one that reoriented the infinitely dignified and mysteriously wise pagan of legend toward rollicking entertainment—the patent medicine and thus the medicine show connection with minstrelsy. In short, there was not just one informed and coherent image of the Indian in the air, but rather bizarrely coexisting and interlaced models: the eternal Indian, the inconvenient Indian (both frontier warlike savages and peaceful Indians who owned land whites wanted), and the knowledgeable jester embodied in the medicine show Indian, that is, the shaman demoted to clown.

Let us consider a widely distributed set of seven pieces of sheet music from 1843 collectively entitled "The Indians, Consisting of King Phillips Quick Step, Song of the Red Man, On-ka-hye Waltz, Osceola Quick Step, Keocuck Quick Step, Black Hawk Quick Step, Nahmeokee Waltz." These publications, which shared a title page, consisted of a mixture of compositions and arrangements by German immigrant Simon Knaebel.[7] The Indian names invoked include three war chiefs who had not been dead for more than a few years. However, the first listed, King Philip (Metacomet) had died in 1676. But his image had been freshened: Washington Irving wrote a biographical sketch that was popular in Knauff's day. The "noble savage" image in this vignette is explicit: King Philip was "free from the restraints and refinements of polished life, and, in a great degree, a solitary and independent being, obey[ing] the impulses of his inclination or the dictates of his judgment; and thus the attributes of his nature, being freely indulged, grow singly great and striking" (1842, 148; originally published serially in 1820). Significantly, such noble savages are as doomed as they are virtuous; King Philip joined those "brave and noble hearts of Nature's sterling coinage, [which] were broken down and trampled in the dust" (149). At about the same time, a popular play came out relating a version of King Philip's story, *Metamora, or the Last of the Wampanoags: An Indian Story in Five Acts*, by John Augustus Stone, written and widely performed in 1829. In that play, King Philip was renamed Metamora, and a fictional wife appeared. Her name, Nahmeokee, also was one of the pieces within Knaebel's *The Indian*, emphasizing the importance of this literary connection in shaping this musical compilation.

Several scholars believe that Stone's play implicitly supported the Indian Removal Act: "The mere deployment of the noble-but-doomed savage motif may have operated in Jacksonian society as a cultural code for anti-Indian sentiment and thus support for removal" (see M. Scott 1999, 89); in any case, if "Indian decline and demise [were] inevitable, [there was] no cause for guilt or for further debate" (80). Further, in a trope on this interpretation, Martin Scott notes that "a white actor's portrayal in redface of a noble savage would tap into racist assumptions and support removal in much the same way that white entertainers in blackface pandered to and promoted antiblack feeling" (87). This factor dovetailed with the growth of homeopathic medicine: Indians were thought to know the secrets of natural remedies, which held more than a germ of truth. The first American patent medicine, from 1811, was labeled Tuscarora Rice, associating it—rightly or willfully—with that Iroquoian-speaking people who lived in Virginia and the Carolinas at the time of contact, then in New York by Knauff's day. A stream of Indian-associated nostrums followed, such as Wright's Indian Vegetable Pills (1837+), and Dr. Morse's Indian Root Pills (1850+).[8] However, in advertising terms, the "natural" ingredient in the noble savage ideological complex was more important than that truth. And entertaining prospective customers for what came to be known as patent medicines brought all of these factors together: minstrel performers made up as Indians became part of medicine shows, and these "Indians" therefore accrued a comic aspect.[9] This rather than the noble-but-dignified mainstream seems the best fit for the titles "Flying Indian" and especially "Indian Whoop."[10] Of course, that these two titles appeared in the fourth, minstrel-oriented pamphlet of the *Virginia Reels* supports this train of thought.

The raunchy side of minstrelsy exemplified by "Indian Whoop" coexists curiously with attempts to tap the genteel market for minstrel airs in pamphlet number 4 of the *Virginia Reels*—that is, having "Sich a Gittin Up Stairs" and "Midnight Serenade" ("Buffalo Gals") presented in "varied" versions. These do not exemplify how *fiddlers* typically ornamented tunes during repetitions, but rather were Knauff's attempts to plug into piano variation technique. The point of average theme and variation sets in the pop sphere was not nuanced musical eloquence, but rather progressive difficulty, the conquering of which ideally made the listener's amazement and pleasure grow. Typical examples might or might not start with a brief, flowery introduction akin to those often introducing songs. Then, the real beginning was a well-known tune played in a simple form. Ever more difficult elaborations of that theme followed, generally contrasting in techniques and therefore effects, but departing progressively further from the theme. Such variation sets presented problems of technical facility rather than of interpretation to the performer and carried the listener on a straightforward journey from the familiar to stunning skill.

Knauff's essays in this form were easy in comparison with any of the independent theme and variations published at about this time, but nevertheless have a bit in common with those flashy monstrosities. "Sich a Gittin Up Stairs" is the closer of these two arrangements to the common practice. The sections are these: introduction, thinly textured theme, and just a few easily negotiated variations. What is most striking is that the last two variations have the pianist's right hand hitting chords off the beat. Such variations were a common option in the big variation sets of the day. They were harmonically based, and distant enough from the main theme to require some distance from the initial presentation of that theme. But they were not so hard that they ought to go near the end of the form; they normally were placed near the middle of the sequence of variations. Knauff used this option twice, both times ending with it. His concentrating on this figure is clever: this variation type belongs to conventional variation practice, but is also syncopated, suiting the fact that the "varied" tune belongs to minstrelsy.

"Indian Whoop" Further Considered: Tune Titles, Musical Sound, and Widened Appeal

The most notable feature of "Indian Whoop" is the "whoop!" If we see minstrelsy as ranging from rough-hewn to somewhat more refined approaches that wouldn't alienate crinoline-clad debutantes and other upper-crust customers, it is the whoop that places this tune near the rustic end of the continuum, despite Knauff's choosing to insert it in the female-student-oriented *Virginia Reels*. In addition, "Indian Whoop" belongs to a select group of tunes that have served as a bridge between fiddlers and a broad popular audience over centuries: tunes based on a gimmick, on featuring a sound plucked from the world outside of music. Because of the enormous importance of such effects within minstrel fiddling and, on a more general level, in widening the appeal of fiddling, I'll now digress to consider how tune titles can be reflected in musical sound, using the members of the *Virginia Reels* as illustrations.

Most correspondence between tunes' titles and melodies takes place on some very general level: short titles announce these brief tunes, and an epigrammatic pungency marks both titles and music. Of course, a genre designation like "hornpipe" or "waltz" identifies a dance, and thus a meter and a tempo. But what about the rest of a given title, and what about titles omitting genre names? Proper names as parts of titles—as was so common among late eighteenth-century Scottish tunes—often indicate little or nothing about the nature of a tune, instead marking patronage or history. And the general "salty" character of so many titles corresponds only in the broadest way with the crisp brevity of most 4/4 tunes that could have been considered "Virginia reels" by Knauff and are classified as breakdowns today.

Fiddle tunes that had been songs retain some of the rhythms required by their former lyrics. And in an overlapping handful of tunes, the characters of the melodies are plausibly congruent with the meanings of their titles. For instance, the thinned, assertive rhythms of "Richmond Blues" are inherited from the lyrics of the parent song, "My Love She's But a Lassie Yet," but those same rhythms now infuse what is now a dance tune with military meaning proper for its association with the militia unit called "Richmond Blues." A similar reinterpretation works for "George Booker." Its dotted rhythms in the *Virginia Reels* derive from those permeating the parent tune, the strathspey "Marquis of Huntley's Farewell," and assertive dotted rhythms also remind us of a march, and so suit the tune's probable new namesake, Prince Edward County's Lieutenant George Booker. Perhaps the motoric intimate contour of "Speed the Plough" matches the steady, energetic effort of ploughing. Also, even though the entire fiddle repertoire is shot through with looping contours and even though the two strains of most tunes contrast in tessitura, these characteristics match up especially well with certain tune titles. In the *Virginia Reels*, these include "Natchez on the Hill," in which the contrasting ranges of strains could be taken to portray the parts of city by the river and high above on a bluff, and "Forked Deer," in which lively gestures in contrasting ranges could be imagined to paint the young buck pawing on the ground and jumping. Last, in "Old Virginia" (almost the same as "Flowers of Edinburgh"), the second strain lacks the usual internal repeat, instead consisting of a very broad contour that could be interpreted as congruent with the physical and historical expanse of "Old Virginia."

These thoughts are summarized in figure 27. Am I pushing too hard to identify correspondences between title and tune? Perhaps, but I invite the reader to reassign titles within the figure, and see if they work nearly as well as with the tunes with which they are normally linked. I should note that such tune/title associations are strongest in the Upper South. In Texas-style fiddling and in associated contest styles, so much has been invested in shaping tunes into certain new kinds of variation sets that title/tune links have been largely obscured.

During Knauff's era, this was a fun way to create a piece that would grab a customer's attention. Of course, pictorial music goes back centuries. During the nineteenth century, the practice certainly continued in both art and popular music. As an example of this, I'll discuss a tune from Knauff's era that belonged to the pop sphere, but had no connection with minstrelsy. An immigrant whose parents were Italians living in Russia continued the family's peregrinations by moving to the United States. In 1839, "The Grasshopper's Waltz, Composed by Nolcini" came out. As a subtitle, Nolcini asserted that "The Subject of this Composition Was Derived from the Motion of the Insects Whose Name It Bears." Double-dotted rhythms and extravagant melodic gestures permeate the piece.

Within blackface minstrelsy, how unusual was "Indian Whoop?" Actually, imitating sounds from nature—and eventually sounds made by people—became a regular feature of minstrel fiddling. James Buckley, leader of Buckley's Serenaders, transcribed his "Celebrated Imitations of the Farm-Yard" at the end of his collection of violin music. He included several dozen bird imitations (hen, blackbird, hawk, pea-hen, etc.) but he also offered imitations of animals ranging from crickets and "cat, in the night" to cows (1855, 71–75). Elias Howe, in his *Quadruple Musician's Omnibus*, drew on a larger minstrel corpus of sound effects by adding considerably to the range of animals imitated ("Bark of a Mastiff Dog," "Laughing Hyena") and approximating human noises ranging from "Mother Calling Daughter" (two versions) to "Out of Breath" to eight different versions of "Child Crying" (1869, 169). Such collections of sounds remained regular ingredients of instrumental collections throughout the rest of the century.

Knauff's "Indian Whoop" is the first use of that title that I've found. William Sidney Mount wrote down the same tune by the same title in his large music commonplace book a few years later, entering it just below the minstrel tune "Old Molly Hare." He annotated his version of "Indian Whoop," noting that he had gotten it "from the brothers Pfeiffers"

Title of Tune in Virginia Reels	Characteristic of Tune Congruent with Meaning of Title
Indian Whoop	Actual vocal "whoop" written into score
Love in the Village	Chromaticism for sentiment; this probably not a fiddle tune
Villalave	Variation technique, suggesting drawing-room elegance
Sich a Gittin Up Stairs	As above, even though this was a blackface minstrel tune; Also, some rhythmic correspondence to that of song's text
Midnight Serenade (Buffalo Gals)	Same incongruous (?) use of variations in blackface tune; Also, some rhythmic correspondence to that of song's text
Ohio River (Boatman Dance)	Has some rhythmic correspondence to rhythm of song
George Booker (Marquis of Huntley's Farewell)	Rhythms: dotted through inheriting rhythms of Scottish tune, but perhaps now with military import instead
Richmond Blues (My Love (is but a Lassie Yet)	Rhythms: thinness inherited from setting of text probably now goes well with dual use as march and dance
Speed the Plough	Rhythms: intimate motoric effect to suggest effort?
Natchez on [under] the Hill	High/low tessituras of the two strains: shore vs. hill?
Forked Deer	High/low tessituras. A strain: speedy? B strain: paws ground?
Old Virginia (~ to Flowers of Edinburgh)	Second strains lacks internal repeat; broad contour may paint large expanse of land

Figure 27. Titles in the *Virginia Reels* that may be depicted to some extent in the music.

(fiddlers from his home in the Stony Brook area of Long Island, and he wrote sideways to the left of the tune: "As sung & played by some of the musical Southern Negroes." I expect that Knauff either notated "Indian Whoop" firsthand from a local black fiddler or secondhand from Joel Sweeney or some other local blackface minstrel.

I give the first few measures of the "Indian Whoop" and relatives in figure 28. James Bryan does a grand job of turning Knauff's sheet music into idiomatic southeastern fiddling; his changes are additions of drones and strategic bowings. Lewis Thomasson's "Indian Whoop" and Eck Robertson's "Lost Indian"—both illustrating fiddling in Texas during the early twentieth century—both have "whoop" sections that closely resemble what Knauff wrote down, and their other two strains are similar in general character to the Knauff tune. What gathers these tunes and others with titles including the word "Indian" together isn't close melodic correspondence, but rather aiming at one or more special effects, at its easiest in the tuning of AEAC# (Robertson does that down a step; I've transposed his version up to concert pitch for ease of comparison). This tuning is a special effects scordatura in several North Atlantic fiddle repertoires, since it facilitates drones and pizzicato (both right- and left-hand varieties).

Knauff's "Indian Whoop" is not an intriguing melody, and neither are its various embodiments later in history. Its hook is its gimmick: anyone can enjoy the catchy "whoop." In that way, it's the ancestor of "Listen to the Mockingbird" (Winner 1855) and even "Orange Blossom Special" (Rouse 1938). Fiddlers grow impatient with constant requests for those tunes, and contests seldom allow them except in specific "trick fiddling" categories, but countless outsiders know and enjoy these flashy numbers (see Noles 2002 throughout).

Mississippi fiddler Hoyt Ming's version of "Indian War Whoop" (1928) was his most-requested piece. There's some similarity to Knauff's "Indian Whoop": the whoop itself, and the general shape of the piece. Ming's tune is loosely phrased. He repeats a measure-long idea for some time, then the idea with the whoop, then the other idea for a while, then he more or less repeats. Perhaps he learned a tune very like Knauff's "Indian Whoop," then didn't care enough about the parts other than the whoop to keep them stable. In any case, the Ming tune (and as reconstituted and re-regularized by John Hartford, and as inserted in the movie *O Brother Where Art Thou* (Coen and Coen 2000) clearly belongs to this group of gimmick-centered tunes that still appeal to audiences outside of the core fiddle constituency.

In the end, that is the lesson of pamphlet 4 of Knauff's *Virginia Reels*. These tunes show fiddling reaching out into various musical and cultural spheres and being rewarded by support from outside of the central constituency of fiddling. "Ohio River" ("Boatman") celebrates physical travel on real waterways, the spread of fiddling through minstrelsy, and the complex overlapping of working-class and upper-class sensibilities and those classes' entertainments. "Indian Whoop," at the rough edge of minstrelsy, makes a journey in subject matter from labored ideology—the noble, doomed Indian figure with its positive and negative aspects—to slapstick and to audiences of minstrelsy. "Sich a Getting Up Stairs," in this arrangement targeting the complementary, genteel edge of the nineteenth-century popular music audience, helped define multiple simultaneous uses for pop music items in general and for fiddling in particular. And the first example in this chapter, "Richmond Blues," from an earlier pamphlet of the *Virginia Reels*, shows that the minstrel tunes

Figure 28. "Indian Whoop": beginnings of three strains by three fiddlers.

of pamphlet number 4 do not stand alone in such historical and cultural adventures. Following this tune through the centuries has shown how fiddle tunes flex to please multiple audiences, and serve multiple uses: this fiddle tune started as just that, then became a song, then a march and a dance, and today still meets a combination of uses.

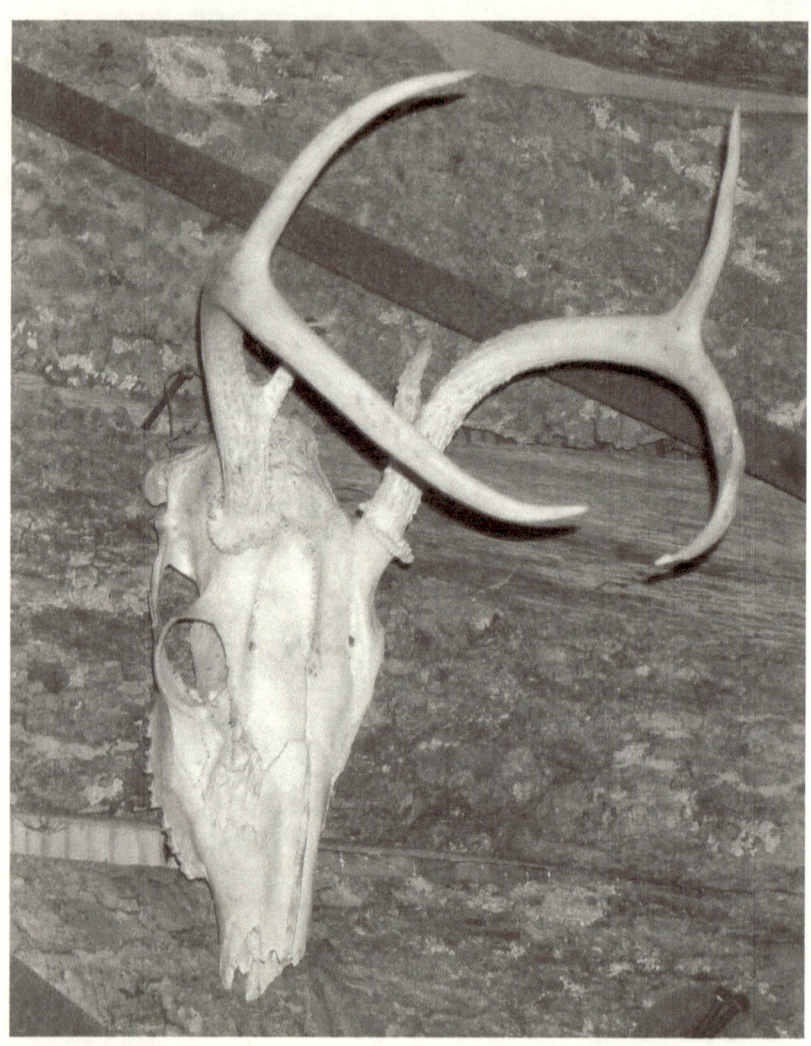

Figure 29. A "Forked Deer," successfully hunted.

Epilogue

"Forked Deer," Multivalent Nostalgia, Sustainability, and the Edge Effect

"FORKED DEER" STARS IN THIS FINAL CHAPTER. IT IS ONE OF VERY few fiddle tunes that now flourish in southern fiddle styles ranging from straightforward to quite fancy, and throughout the United States—in old-time fiddling in the Upper South, in exuberant West Virginia styles, and in the melodic improvisations of the modern contest fiddling originating in Texas. Both the title and the melody of "Forked Deer" enter the historical record in Knauff's *Virginia Reels*. Yes, it is a pleasure to research those of today's southern fiddle tunes that reach back to the late eighteenth century in Scotland, tunes anthologized in the drawing-room publications of that era; documented age lends a patina of authenticity to oral tradition materials, even when the evidence is of activity outside of oral tradition. But most American fiddle tunes postdate that early heyday of Scottish fiddling. Yes, "Forked Deer" could conceivably belong to some coterie of tunes that did not get into the early Scottish tune books despite being in regular use; however, it is probably instead an American tune from its birth.

The Tune "Forked Deer"

Knauff's "Forked Deer" consists of the normal complement of two strains contrasting in range. In fact, that juxtaposition in "Forked Deer" is especially bold. The first strain largely stays in a restricted range and sits on an A chord (the dominant in D Major, the tune's usual key). This strain has the effect of an extended announcement of the higher, more expansive strain, which stays as stubbornly high (until its cadential measures) as the low strain had obstinately remained low. This is not a melody fraught with ambiguity or indecision! Knauff emphasized "Forked Deer's" brash character in his arrangement of it in the *Virginia Reels*. During the pounding on the A chord in the low strain, he inserted many g# neighbor tones in the piano's left-hand part, thus further emphasizing the A chord. In many of his arrangements, he buttressed the contrast *between* strains by opting for opposed effects—particularly densities—in the accompaniment. Here he does that *within* the first strain. Then, in the second strain, he lets the left hand match the energy of the frolicsome melody by being busy throughout.

Like most southern fiddle tunes, "Forked Deer" did not make it into the nineteenth-century mainstream of instrumental anthologies, those issued by Elias Howe. In fact, this tune found its way into just one publication later in that century. The second entry in figure 30a is a photograph of a page from a publication from 1876, *Coes Album of Jigs and Reels. Something New for Professional and Amateur Violinists, Leaders of Orchestras, Quadrille Bands, and Clog, Reel, and Jig Dancers; Consisting of a Grand Collection of Entirely New and Original Clog-Hornpipes, Reels, Jigs, Scotch Reels, Irish Reels and Jigs, Waltzes, Walk-Arounds, Etc., for the Violin*. The key word in this volume's extended title comes late: "Walk-Around," which advertises a blackface minstrel connection. I reproduced the entire page on which this "Forkedair Jig" appears to illustrate that link. First, it is not just *called* a jig (meaning "Negro jig" in this context), but includes notated syncopation, just as do many "jigs" from the minstrel repertoire. The type of rhythmic exploration differs from tune to tune, as among the three on this page, the other two of which are even more explicitly blackface minstrel tunes—one is connected with minstrel banjoist Joel Sweeney, and the other attributed to Zeke Backus, who belonged to minstrel troupes in the 1840s and 1850s, notably Christy's Minstrels. This "Forkedair Jig" is just different enough from Knauff's "Forked Deer" to suggest that Coes transcribed it from oral tradition rather than copied it from some other publication.

Alexander Camel "Eck" Robertson recorded "Forked Deer" during the 1922 sessions that produced the famous and influential, extravagantly varied "Sally Goodin." Unfortunately, his "Forked Deer" was not issued. Several other early twentieth-century fiddlers also recorded the tune

"Forked Deer," Knauff (1839)

Page on which "Forkedair Jig" appears in Coes (1876)

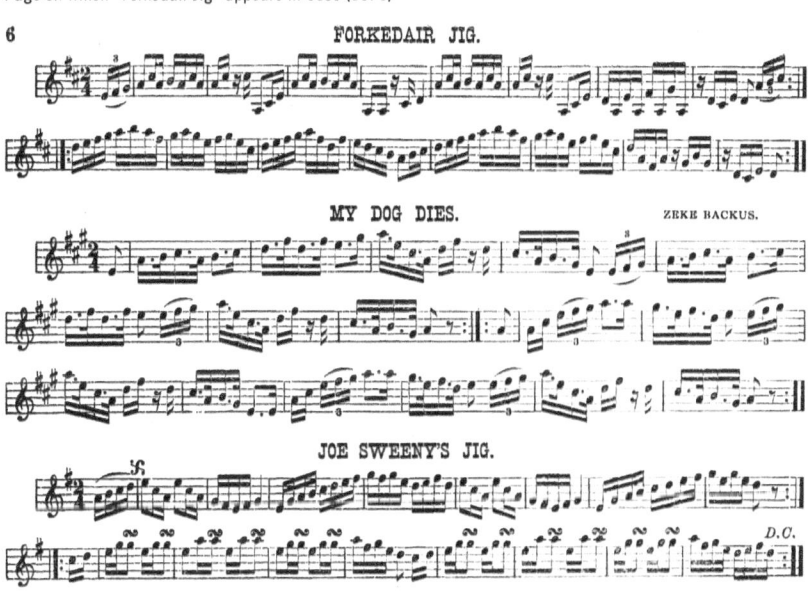

"Forked Deer" by Richard Bowman (interview at Galax 2001)

Figure 30a. "Forked Deer," simple versions.

Figure 30b. "Forked Deer," played in a West Virginia style by Bobby Taylor.

EPILOGUE ✦ 149

Figure 30b, concluded.

during the 1920s–1930s (see Kuntz 2012), and it has remained a staple of southern fiddling since. We will skip ahead to the present in order to take advantage of the fact that this tune is one of very few that is still frequently played in each of the major styles of southern fiddling.

One could not ask for a more straightforward or more powerful contemporary Upper South "Forked Deer" than that of Richard Bowman, the fiddler for the Slate Mountain Ramblers, a family string band working out of Mt. Airy, North Carolina (transcribed from a 2001 interview, but also see Slate Mountain Ramblers 2006, cut 9). The rhythmic anticipations we have seen in other old-timey performances are here again as upward slides that reinforce the banjo accents (and drone) on the second half of the fourth beat, performed by his daughter Marsha Bowman Todd. This strong push forward makes the performance work. Richard Bowman's vigorously accented rhythms reflect the essential link between the mid-nineteenth-century minstrel quartet and today's old-time fiddling as cultivated in its core geographical area, within a few hundred miles of where Virginia, North Carolina, and Tennessee meet.

Bobby Taylor's West Virginia version of "Forked Deer" is also in the broad world of what insiders consider "old-time" fiddling, but illustrates the opposite end of the spectrum of variation found in performances that fit under that umbrella. He incorporates a profusion of small but cumulatively energizing accents through adding density here and there. In sheer quantity, the amount of minor variation matches that which Eddie Bond put in his performance of "Darling Child." (Bond's own "Forked Deer"—not transcribed here—mirrors his "Darling Child" in amount and flavor of variation.) The details of Taylor's version (and of many other modern West Virginia versions of "Forked Deer") begin to push this piece toward having more than two strains. In that way, it resembles the Texas version by multiple state champion Wes Westmoreland, the most celebrated Texas fiddler in his prime as of this writing. However, the general feel of Taylor's style leaves it close enough to those current in the Virginia/North Carolina/Tennessee old-time locus that Taylor served as fiddler for the New Ballard's Branch Bogtrotters—the top string band associated with Galax, Virginia—before Eddie Bond joined the group.

Wes Westmoreland's "Forked Deer," recorded at the Texas State Championship in Hallettsville in 2014, exemplifies the best current Texas contest fiddling through its general feel (pace, degree of swing, specific timbres, accompaniment), his illustrating of style-specific variation technique, and in his shaping of form on both broad and intimate levels. Belonging to contemporary contest style are the freedom of figuration and the general progress of the form: A A B B A A B high B high A A B stretch B stretch A A B high B high A is an unsurprising sequence of strains. In the area of intimate form, the beginnings of the A strains offer an easy illustration. The start of A2 is slightly more linear than the start of A1. Then A3 begins as did A2, setting the scene for the widened form of the opening gesture that leads off A4. A5 and 6 are free mild variations on earlier forms of A, but with A5 more dense than A6 (mirroring the relationship of A1 and A2). A6 incorporates a short opening stretch (preparing the listener for the major stretch in B5 and B6). A7 is a dramatic return to A1, with A8 closer to A2. Then, A9, the final strain is a coda of sorts, summarizing the previous shots through A by combining some new material (thus affirming the continuous variations) with A5, A6, and A1. Thus, the progress of A strains is rounded, while the more dramatically contrasting forms of the B strain offer a sequence that is instead more progressive. The combination is quite elegant.

I've talked with Wes briefly about these tightly woven forms, and he has politely professed mild surprise at the symmetries I find fascinating. He prefers to focus on the factor of improvisation, although he and another fine Texas fiddler (and multiple state champion) Carl Hopkins have studied recordings of other fiddlers intently together and have played all of the core Texas tunes—including "Forked Deer"—many hundreds of times. The results are much more systematic in terms of variation than the West Virginia version of Bobby Taylor; both are much more oriented toward overall form than is Richard Bowman's version. But when the extraordinary vigor and clarity of Taylor's form and the ensemble complexity of the form played by Bowman and the Slate Mountain Ramblers are taken into account, all three performances end up offering similar amounts of total musical energy. These are equally convincing performances.

I don't think it's too far-fetched to see these three versions as parallel to Knauff's three approaches to shaping tunes in terms of amount of variation. The straightforward majority of Knauff's arrangements assembled as the *Virginia Reels* anticipate Bowman's style, the tunes varied in terms of density ("Richmond Blues" and others) parallel Taylor's version, and the more systematic variation in "Midnight Serenade" ("Buffalo Gals") and especially "Sich a Gittin Up Stairs" offers a precedent for the elaborate variations of Westmoreland and other Texas stylists.

Following Strains A1 and B1, new material is under dotted lines.

Figure 30c. "Forked Deer," played in Texas style by Wes Westmoreland III.

EPILOGUE ✦ 153

Figure 30c, concluded.

(closing tag incorporated in strain)

The Title "Forked Deer"

This tune's name has been as stable as any other fiddle tune title over the centuries, perhaps because it is packed with meaning. "Forked" is pronounced "four-cud" to avoid any scatological misunderstanding of the first word ("Forked-Horned Deer" has occasionally served as an ultraclear if awkward alternative title). A "forked deer" is a young buck, or any buck early in the annual process of growing antlers, one whose antlers have each branched into a pair of main tines. Images of youth, late spring, hunting, and tasty meals all merge in this title, which thus fits nicely into the dominant general type of fiddle tune titles, the "salty and rustic" group.

"Forked Deer" may also have a geographical link, whether original or added over time: There is a Fauquier County in northern Virginia (thus "Fauquier Deer"), a sizable Forked Deer River in western central Tennessee, and a Forked Deer Creek about fifty miles northeast of Knoxville, Tennessee. These two watercourses may have been named "Forked Deer" for how they appear on a map (visibly "forking" like antlers' first tines), might have been assigned their names to commemorate an explorer seeing a buck with appropriate antlers in the vicinity, or both. Also, one of the rare renamings of the tune specifies a famous southerner and is also an ironic military reference: "Bragg's Retreat." Andrew Kuntz explains that this title

> undoubtedly refers to the unfortunate Confederate general Braxton Bragg of the western theatre of the American Civil War. Bragg commanded the Army of the Tennessee from mid-1862 to the end of 1863, and was neither well-liked nor well-respected. He could often be irascible, sullen and rigid, and was consistently out-generaled by his Union opposites. Private Sam Watkins, who served in the Army of the Tennessee during Bragg's tenure wrote in his memoirs that one of the common sayings among the men of his company while on march was "Bully for Bragg! He's hell on retreat!" The source for the tune under this title is Meridian, Mississippi, fiddler Stephen B. Tucker, who recorded it for the Library of Congress in 1939. (http://www.ibiblio.org/fiddlers/BRAB_BRAM.htm)

Thus, the multivalence of the title "Forked Deer" plus this particular retitling of the tune touch most of the normal categories for fiddle tune titles in the American South: the salty title with outdoor subject, geographical (in the important subgroup naming watercourses), referring to a person, and invoking a military connection. What types of fiddle tune title have been left out? I have not encountered modern performances of this tune that are texted, or which bear titles having anything to do with courting. However, there is a version of "Forked Deer" called "Come and Kiss Me" in the same late nineteenth-century publication for solo violin by George H. Coes that includes "Forkedair Jig," suggesting that the tune was given lyrics at least once, and that that text concerned courting (just the melody is given by Coes: 1876, 34–35). So, if we add "Come and Kiss Me" to the roster of tune names, the melody of "Forked Deer" has been associated with absolutely every major type of fiddle tune title. Kuntz lists yet more titles (2012), but one result of eased communications during the last century is increased standardization of tunes titles: all younger fiddlers and the vast majority of senior fiddlers know this tune as "Forked Deer."

One factor distinguishes Knauff's titles from those characteristic of contemporary fiddling—a fascinating hybridity of military and chivalric/nostalgic references in many of his titles, a mixing of affect reflecting a real-life overlay of ideology and behavior in the antebellum South. Among the *Virginia Reels*, the most obvious example is the title "Richmond Blues." That title refers to a militia unit, but one devoting more energy to pageantry—to dressing elaborately for ceremonial occasions, at which these young men of good family did some marching, but more preening and dancing—than to military training or exercises. Their activities had much more in common with the "knightly" tournaments held at Amelia Springs than with practical military matters. Mark Twain believed that the ideology of chivalry as adopted in the South turned out to be harmful, in fact leading to foolish, vainglorious entry into the Civil War and inevitable defeat. He railed against what he saw as the fatal infection of southern thought by the stunningly popular writings of Sir Walter Scott, the author of romances set in reimagined medieval Britain such as the novel *Ivanhoe* (1820) and the poem *The Lady of the Lake* (1810). In Twain's words, Scott did:

> measureless harm; more real and lasting harm, perhaps, than any other individual that ever wrote. Most of the world has now outlived good part of these harms, though by no means all of them; but in our South they flourish pretty forcefully still.... There, the genu-

ine and wholesome civilization of the nineteenth century is curiously confused and commingled with the Walter Scott Middle-Age sham civilization, and so you have practical common sense, progressive ideas, and progressive works, mixed up with the duel, the inflated speech, and the jejune romanticism of an absurd past that is dead, and out of charity ought to be buried. . . . It was Sir Walter that made every gentleman in the South a major or a colonel, or a general or a judge, before the war; and it was he, also, that made these gentlemen value these bogus decorations. For it was he that created rank and caste down there, and also reverence for rank and caste, and pride and pleasure in them. . . . Sir Walter had so large a hand in making Southern character, as it existed before the war, that he is in great measure responsible for the war. (1917, 275–76)

How hyperbolic were Twain's claims? Actually, the trappings of romantically reshaped medieval chivalry were enjoyed in Virginia long before Scott entered the picture; Scott's writings at most crystalized and amplified ways of thinking that were already in place. In 1845, William Caruthers penned a romantic celebration of a famous expedition of 1716. Alexander Spottswood, the acting governor of the British colony of Virginia, had led an expedition of about fifty men (plus horses, dogs, and ample supplies) due west, up the Rappahannock River Basin, and across the Blue Ridge Mountains into the Shenandoah Valley. This group enjoyed sumptuous hospitality along the way and paused to hunt and to drink toasts frequently—the portable liquor cabinet never disappointed. Later, Spottswood sent each of the participants a small gold pin; they became known as the Knights of the Golden Horseshoe. When Caruthers wrote about this early eighteenth-century "knightly" quest for land during Knauff's day, he was looking fondly back over a century at a trip already infused with this brand of self-indulgent and well-lubricated nostalgia (see Davis 1949).

Knauff may or may not have been sensitive to the chivalric resonance of the titles of several of the *Virginia Reels*. That he placed "Scotts Favorite" right after "The Lady of the Lake" suggests some level of familiarity with the body of literature that Twain later indicted; Scott's works were already well known in German-speaking areas while Knauff was growing up. Several of the military and/or chivalric titles in the *Virginia Reels* did not last, but what about the general topics and attitudes celebrated in this early nineteenth-century slanting of chivalry? Paul Christopher Anderson summarized this antebellum reformulation as part of his analysis of the cultural forces surrounding a celebrated guerrilla cavalryman of the Confederacy: *Blood Image: Turner Ashby in the Civil War and the Southern Mind*. Anderson described "the cult of chivalry" as "a systematic preternatural devotion to good manners, hospitality, respect for family lineage, personal integrity and independence, and military prowess" (2002, 24), in which individuals' most noble traits were shaped by the natural world, and one in which "spirit mattered more than science" (2002, 148).

A thorough exploration of how central characteristics of the modern South echo or develop antebellum factors would outweigh this book! However, since Knauff gathered up several tunes the titles of which belong to the military/chivalric/nostalgic complex, and even included a tune named for Scott's *The Lady of the Lake*, I decided to enter this arena in a small and tentative way.[1] I chose to compare how the ingredients of southern chivalry—as summarized by Anderson—appeared in Scott's poem with how those qualities are expressed today in southern fiddle contests, that is, juxtaposing values as expressed in literature with how modern behavior illustrates the persistence of these values. This is summarized in figure 31.

A few of today's fiddle tune titles do retain some redolence of the nineteenth-century interpretation of medieval chivalry, though this can be subtle. For instance, the fiddle tune title "Lady of the Lake" became "Ducks in a Pond." What originally was a mystical and legendary literary reference lost its punch as widespread acquaintance with Scott's poem faded. However—and here I am again launching into an intellectual adventure—perhaps the "ducks" in the new title should not be pictured exclusively as Disney ducks, happily gliding on the surface of the pond, sieving food and quacking contentedly. The ducks are certainly outdoors and resting on water . . . moving through the use of invisible power on an only partially visible and constantly moving other world. Some species have evolved in the direction of low buoyancy, enabling them to feed through diving. Their disappearances underwater to feed create suspense: how long will they be gone, what have they seen, where will they reappear? A section of a webpage describing this group of ducks, a page belonging to a site conjoining hunting and conservation interests, leads off with description that could have been lifted from romantic literature:

Value	In Scott's Lady of the Lake	In Modern Fiddle Contests
Martial prowess	Skilled and willing fighters	Skilled contestants exhibiting similar competitiveness
Individual bravery	Battles often reduced to fighting alone, to duels	Most competition is solo
Hospitality; manners	Incognito king sheltered; Combatants sup together, etc.	Fiddlers often accompanied on guitar by their opponents; gracious, generous demeanor
Respect for family lineage	Loyalty to family and clan members unto death; trumps all other values	Family bands; great respect for older family members and for fiddlers' music antecedents
Personal integrity and independence	Individual bravery and sacrifices	Fiddlers create their own versions of tunes
Spirit more than science	Rely on bravery and character; numbers/resources don't matter	If music literate, competitors downplay; it's oral tradition, and matters of character
The natural world as the source for individuals' best character traits	Celebrates woods and wildlife of Scotland throughout; King met while hunting, well before various battles commenced	Nature reflected in tune names; lack of artifice stressed in informality of dress and in other aspects of event ethos

Figure 31. Chivalric values in Scott's *The Lady of the Lake* and in modern fiddle contests.

Cold wind, slate-gray sky, and angry water—most of us, if we know divers at all, know the birds on days like this. Squadrons of 'bills boring in on the deck like WWII torpedo planes: rising, falling, dropping their landing gear, hesitating, then exploding over the decoys in every direction as they sense that something isn't quite right.

Scaup, canvasbacks, redheads and ring-necked ducks—the freshwater diving ducks, or pochards—have stirred every hunter who has known them. There's nothing subtle about a flock of divers, whether they are cans rocketing in from big water to a sheltered sago pondweed bed on a dirty, windy day; redheads streaking from freshwater ponds to beds of shoal grass in a coastal lagoon; or ring-necks pitching down to a bed of pad plants in a Florida swamp. (M. Anderson 2015)

Hunting is certainly the route through which the title "Forked Deer" can be argued to connect with early nineteenth-century chivalry as expressed in literature. Matching wits and endurance with deer was the logical and ubiquitous recreation for the men of Scott's *The Lady of the Lake*. Yes, that poem is a conventional nineteenth-century entertainment: While loosely grounded in fact, the story—just like the plot of *Ivanhoe*—moves forward not just through historic rivalries and armed struggles, but also through the explication and eventual simplifying of love tangles, includes a tournament, and depends on improbably successful disguises; it's no surprise that Rossini found this poem easy to turn into an opera. But Scott's narrative starts with a hunting scene and references that manly sport several times. Each of the poem's six "cantos" describes the action of a single day. The story commences with the incognito King of Scotland pursuing a "stag" variously described as an "antlered monarch," as "noble," "gallant," and "stalwart" (Canto First, sections 1, 5, 6, and 19). In a festival placed much later in the narrative, greyhounds pull down another "gallant stag," who then endures into the next phase of the celebration as venison (Canto Fifth, section 25). Last, two soldiers with bit parts in the narrative look back on happier times, one described as "in peace, a chaser of the deer" (Canto Sixth, section 4), another lamenting "I wish I were as I have been, hunting the hart in forest green" (Canto Sixth, section 24).

In sum, in Knauff's day, the tune name "Forked Deer" bore a straightforward and sturdy consonance with the southern attachment to Sir Walter Scott's celebration of chivalry. But how strong is that connection today? As the cultural functions of hunting have changed, the semantic resonance of tune titles connected with hunting has also been rearranged—perhaps "reproportioned" would be the best way to put this. In *The Lady of the Lake*, hunting was a refuge from the constantly roiling mortal dangers of war, an activity representing both the safe harbour of home and the sweet pains of nostalgia. In dramatic contrast, hunting in modern America offers some peacefulness but more adventure; it's a manly outpost in the prosaic landscape of daily life. Knauff's "Forked Deer" offers a waystation between reimagined medieval life as enjoyed in antebellum psychology and the equivocal patterns of modern life, with nostalgia running like an always bright yet constantly reshaped thread through all of this history. The immediacy of hunting has ebbed, and thus the proportions of the syntactic ingredients of early nineteenth-century tune titles including "Forked Deer" have shifted, with nostalgia for rural life still emphasizing nature, but with diminished emphasis on man's struggle within and mastery of the outdoors. In the end, this and many other fiddle tune titles remain evocative and common within the "salty, rustic" mainstream of fiddle tune titles largely because nostalgia is nearly as malleable as it has been important in European and American psychology for centuries.

"Forked Deer" Today: Multiple Styles (and Substyles) Reflecting Multivalent Nostalgia

Tides of change continue to push all of southern fiddling in certain shared directions, at the same time that regional influences and regional loyalties continue to flex their muscles. What do today's performance styles have in common? First, today's fiddling consists of loosely linked subcultures. Fiddling attracts a much smaller audience than do mass-media-driven genres of popular music, and the events available for that audience to attend garner publicity only in the small towns in which most fiddle-based events take place. Of course, once you attend one fiddle contest or festival, you can enter the complex of subcultures easily, simply by gathering brochures advertising cognate events at a well-stocked table generally present for precisely that purpose.

Knauff's activity couldn't anticipate our modern contest-driven fiddle subcultures, but the fate of the *Virginia Reels* pointed in that general direction by suggesting that the main current of southern fiddling after his time would lie outside of commercial popular culture. The *Virginia Reels*, the first collection to illustrate the forming of a distinctive repertoire of southern fiddle tunes, didn't spark imitation. Indeed, while a generous handful of copies of Knauff's *Virginia Reels* sold, many more copies of the 1839 Willig edition survive than of the early 1850s revision published by Benteen. The collection reveals that southern fiddling was on the cusp of becoming distinctive during the same era during which American fiddling as a whole was being shunted away from participation in the mainstream of popular music. Fiddle tunes were losing the small but formerly secure niche they had in English-derived publications, the same connection that we also saw in the commonplace books like those of Philander Seward and Samuel Watkins, young American enthusiasts fiddling during the first decades of the nineteenth century during the generation just before Knauff came to the United States. Fiddle tunes would continue to be published in the nineteenth century in the pop music collections issued by Elias Howe and his followers, but were clearly anthology fatteners rather than hits. And the importance of fiddle tunes as an ingredient of blackface minstrelsy—this overlaps with Howe's publishing activity, since he worked both under his own name and as minstrel figure "Gumbo Chaff"—faded as minstrelsy gradually turned to new repertoires and eventually dissipated into variety and vaudeville. Coes's collection of 1876, noted above as containing two versions of "Forked Deer," turned out to be another exception, reflecting the survival of fiddle tunes within the oral tradition of minstrel performers, but, like the *Virginia Reels,* not finding enough commercial success to inspire imitation.

In short, that the *Virginia Reels* was only temporarily and marginally successful shows that southern fiddling was entering a nineteenth-century antecedent of subcultural status at the same time that it was becoming distinctive. That is, fiddle tunes were no longer of great interest to the rather small percentage of the population who could afford to buy sheet music. A much larger slice of the population got to participate in commercial popular culture beginning in the early twentieth century. Because of that widening of participation, even though fiddling attracted the attention of fewer people, the commercial net stretched enough to assure a role for fiddle tunes in the early, "hillbilly" phase of country-western music. And some affection for fiddle tunes and performance habits and materials of fiddling survived the modernization of that commercial outlet—which progressively minimized the ingredient of fiddling—and then the later inundation of life by rock music. Enough interest survived to provide the raw material for the reshaping of fiddling as a contest-based subculture by the middle of the twentieth century.

The same broad historical forces have changed and continue to transform the sound of each of the styles making up southern fiddling in parallel ways. Increased leisure, increased access to good models for performance, and the shift away from dance accompaniment to playing for attentive listeners are all factors that affect every style. Fiddlers today have more opportunity than ever before to receive formal or at least regular lessons and to practice. Compared with past generations of fiddlers, they use longer bows held in more relaxed grips (and with more fluid wrist movement), have better instruments on the average, and play more "in tune" (closer to the art violinist's species of near-equal temperament). They produce timbres which, while distinctive, are in a general way increasingly closer to those associated with art performance (that is, they have a somewhat less nasal sound, one favoring extreme upper partials less), and attacks are more calculated in terms of bite and general effect.

At the same time, the principle of separation of styles corresponding to geographical area that started with the differentiation of southern from northern repertoires, as first illustrated in the *Virginia Reels*, has continued. Several regional and local styles have survived the communications revolution of the last hundred years, although those styles continue to change, and new styles are emerging. True, complaints are reliably, regularly, even loudly aired among fiddlers about pernicious standardization enforced by the spread of contest style. And within the old-time sphere, there are complaints about dominant trends, for instance, bemoaning the spread of the influence of North Carolina fiddle stylist Tommy Jarrell. The commonest verbal formulation, regardless of which fiddle style is being criticized, is: "That stuff all sounds alike." But close examination of good performances in any style—that is, music making by the fiddlers whom insiders in the style consider strong and representative—shows that that complaint never holds water. Contrasts of personal musical preferences and influences, the variety of reasons people with all sorts of musical choices opt to fiddle, and surprising historical factors all contribute to skillful playing in a luxuriant array of styles.

For instance, contest-style fiddling as cultivated in Texas remains the touchstone substyle of contest style, but it is not the only substyle flourishing today. The self-named "National Fiddle Contest," held annually in Weiser, Idaho, also focuses on Texas style, but with primary reference to an earlier generation. Benny Thomasson (1909–1984), a pivotal figure in the shaping of Texas style, retired from his auto repair business in Dallas in the early 1970s, and moved to Washington State to be near a son. He participated in the National Old-Time Fiddler's Contest in Weiser, Idaho, for several years starting in 1972. Some of his students had already started reorienting that influential contest toward Texas style; Thomasson's arrival accelerated that trend. A form of Texas-style contest fiddling that stems directly from his playing dominates there today and radiates out in the western United States, especially in Idaho and Washington; this species of contest style has at least as many adherents as Texas-style proper.

Thomasson's variation technique included the basic ingredients of Texas style already discussed in this book in connection with Tom Weisgerber's "Money Musk," Alita Stoneking Weisgerber's "George Booker," and especially Wes Westmoreland's "Forked Deer." This includes incidental melodic variation that doesn't violate a tune's standard harmonization, a strain or two returning at an octave different from the original one (usually higher, though rarely requiring more than third position), a few strains starting with a stretch (held notes substituting for part of a melodic gesture), and various internal symmetries created within the variation process. Thomasson didn't invent these ingredients—they were present to some degree in the fiddling of his father and his uncle and of friends such as "Eck" Robertson—but he systematized them, and through musical example and force of his gently charismatic personality brought the general Texas style into a considerable degree of alignment. However, the subsequent history of Texas style in Texas is one of steady building on his style, of continually denser variation technique. In my transcription of Westmoreland's recent performance of "Forked Deer," I put dotted lines over material that was appearing for the first time. Roughly three times as many measures are "new" here as in a performance of the tune by Thomasson recorded four decades earlier (in the late 1960s; reissued on Thomasson 2005, cut 13). A version of "Forked Deer" played in 1987 by a much-respected fiddler of an intermediate generation, Terry Morris, features an intermediate number of "new" measures (2000, cut 7).

I compared these statistics with ones gathered from multiple performances of a half dozen other contest standards, and the results are clear: The sheer amount of variation (and consequent possibilities for nuanced refinements of form) has been continually rising in Texas, although the basic techniques remain those standardized by Thomasson. The process of change has been quite different in the Weiser/Northwestern turf. The "National Fiddle Contest" there has grown to be quite large and efficiently run. Since the schedule is crowded, each contestant gets a mere four minutes to perform three tunes, a breakdown such as "Forked Deer," a waltz, and a tune of choice (perhaps a rag). Although these fiddlers pause briefly between tunes, the effect is of a medley, not a fully developed variation set. The breakdown usually occupies less than three-eighths of the four-minute span, usually less than one and a quarter minutes. There's much less time for variation than in Texas (where there are no statutory time limits; typical performances last two to four minutes). In Thomasson's versions, the second in each pair of strains often replicated the first in that pair almost exactly, and quite a few subsequent passes through a given strain are precise repetitions of earlier versions. As a result, a modern fiddler needing a compact version of a tune could simply design a performance like one of Thomasson's but omitting most of the repetitions; that's approximately what the winning fiddlers in Weiser do.

The champions in Weiser—generally also influential teachers—thus have stylistic pedigrees stemming directly from Benny Thomasson in terms of variation technique and are in that specific way as legitimate Texas contest fiddlers as are the champions in the top events in Texas. But the contrast in sound only starts with the contrasting approaches to crafting variations. Weiser-oriented fiddlers are more apt to have listened to and even played classical music; Texas fiddlers instead all spend some time with Texas swing. The first difference affects details of timbre, the second nuances of rhythm.

Repertoire choices can be partly shaped by who the fiddlers are, and thus what manner of nostalgia motivates them. In terms of socioeconomic level, the vast majority of Texas players range from blue collar—Carl Hopkins is a welder—to lower rungs of the medical field: Wes Westmoreland, after a decade fiddling in a country-western band in Branson, Missouri, became a pharmacist, and rising star Bubba Hopkins has a day job as an optometrist's assistant with a growing business as a fiddler, fiddle teacher, and fiddle tune transcriber. Many of the Weiser fiddlers are blue collar, but quite a few others are white collar, and they are somewhat less likely than the Texas fiddlers to have learned fiddling from members of their family. In these ways, the Weiser champions parallel the urban revivalists who have gravitated to fiddling in old-time southeastern styles, while most Texas fiddlers from Texas are more like the direct inheritors of tradition among old-timey musicians.

Perhaps the most interesting factor here is that of differential nostalgia. Fiddlers who do not grow up among traditional musicians, who do not take on fiddling as part of assuming the artistic attitudes and behaviors of their family and neighbors, do have differently proportioned motivations, a fact that has consequences for both style and repertoire. Nostalgia looms large among all fiddlers' motivations, but nostalgia is far from uniform in strength or detail. The non-inheritors tend to be more self-conscious—indeed more scholarly—about how they play and which tunes they seek out. They possess more generalized feelings of nostalgia and are inclined to favor what is distinctive among the choices available. Thus, the non-Texas Texas-style fiddlers and the old-time urban revivalists will stick more closely to older performance styles when they can and will fill out their repertoires with tunes that are modally or formally or historically from outside of the mainstream. I say "fill out" their repertoires because all fiddlers will know the common tunes such as, among those that made an appearance among the *Virginia Reels*, "Forked Deer" and "Wagoner" (Knauff's "The Hero") for fiddlers in all styles, and "Mississippi Sawyer" for the old-time fiddlers. But among contest-style fiddlers, it's the non-Texas crowd who are more likely to play less central tunes like "George Booker" frequently, and among old-time fiddlers, it's the urban revivalists who will play both "George Booker" and "Ducks in a Pond" (though seldom the more straightforward "Mississippi Sawyer," a favorite among the old-time inheritors). Thus, the proliferation of American fiddle styles first witnessed by the publication of the *Virginia Reels* has spawned and nurtured further diversification and vitality of repertoire.

The fiddler or fiddlers from whom Knauff gathered up the *Virginia Reels* were probably not music literate, or at least not accustomed to using printed music regularly. They certainly didn't see themselves as in a position to make money from printing the music they performed for dances. Black fiddlers, though plentiful through the early part of the twentieth century, have become extraordinarily rare today. This again is a matter of nostalgia, the main ideological fuel for the modern cultivation of fiddling. African Americans have relatively little reason to look back fondly at many of the threads of American history that relate to fiddling, and so that impetus to fiddle is lacking.

Might we find some degree of parallelism with today's fiddlers—that is, with the inheritors versus the revivalists—among Knauff's students? These young women lived in a social environment where fiddling for dances was routine; some but not all of them likely had fathers who fiddled, even though probably not during those dances. So Knauff's *Virginia Reels* would have meant different things to different girls. Some form of the future difference between outsider and insider enthusiasts may have already been in place among them. Also, they probably came from families whose feel for nostalgia was different for quite a variety of reasons. In the extended family of Knauff's wife, the originally Huguenot

Bondurants, was some fraction of their nostalgia for France? Did farmers with worn-out land look more longingly at the past than those whose crops were still plentiful?

The Edge Effect and the Vitality of Southern American Fiddling

The tug-of-war between rough-edged putative authenticity and pretty performances of minstrel tunes befitting cultivated drawing rooms continued through and after the nineteenth century. Complexities in the sustenance of fiddling in the past—ones foreshadowing the different populations of fiddlers and the controversial characteristics of modern fiddle contests—have appeared regularly through history.

These rich situations, parallel to the productive complexity of the "edge effects" of ecology, have, by inspiring manuscript and printed replication and modification of fiddle tunes, allowed a much more detailed understanding of the history of fiddling than would have otherwise been possible. But "edge effects" in fiddling are not just a matter of historiographic convenience: they offer what I believe to be the strongest theoretical model for understanding how the history of American fiddling has been and remains bound up with the interaction of the borders of different cultural spheres and the linked repertoires and performance practices. I will draw on a recent online resource, Levin and colleagues' *Princeton Guide to Ecology*. The concepts and specific quotations I cite below are all from the section of that massive work entitled "Principles of Reserve Design," subsection "Reducing Edge Effects" (Levin 2013, V.4.6).

Levin notes, "The single best approach to preserve biodiversity is to conserve or restore large habitat areas." The parallel recommendation for fiddling would be for the practices and repertoires of American fiddling to somehow return to some broader cultural sweep, to a larger percentage of the music heard in North America ... which seems no more likely than the return of Montana to a completely wild state. American fiddling, while far and away the most vigorous branch of venerable American traditional music in terms of both number of participants and size and liveliness of public venues, cannot be more than a family of subcultures today, with little prospect of meaningful or lasting expansion. But the complex of fiddle subcultures remains strong because of the positive action of what ecologists call "edge effects," which for the current purpose translate as phenomena associated with interfaces between popular, high, and traditional cultures rather than geographical and biological habitats.

In ecology, we worry about habitat loss and consequent constriction of biodiversity. In the case of fiddling, the parallel would be the shrinkage of social settings friendly to fiddling, and the related loss of repertoire and of participants. Ecologists see "a key goal of reserve design [being] to reconnect habitats that have been fragmented to allow the habitats to function as a whole rather than as a set of independent pieces." Doing this entails the creation of physical "corridors, or long and relatively thin strips of habitat." For the composite fiddle subculture, the parallel to those physical corridors are linkages between fiddle areas and populations including publicity, common choices among leisure activities, and travel that delivers fiddlers to multiple contests and other festivals. Ecological "conservation targets are likely to be a handful of species of conservation interest—charismatic or rare species—or unique geographic or hydrologic features with which those species are associated." Interestingly, there are parallels in fiddling for both the species and the geographic features, but response to these factors is separated by regional style. Texas-style contest fiddling focuses on relatively few tunes that are especially rich in content to start with, and especially welcoming to variation techniques; thus, we would call "Forked Deer" and "George Booker" something like "charismatic." In contrast, many of the old-time local tunes played at, for instance, the Tennessee Valley Old Time Fiddlers Convention tend to be chosen in part for their rarity, and their titles may accrue value through specific or generic geographic references (thus, respectively: "Buffalo Gals" and "Billy in the Low Grounds").

The extraordinary adaptability of the music of fiddling has helped it travel through time, travel better by the series of repertorial and stylistic alliances explored in this chapter. That is, at the same time that fiddle tunes retained a strong connection with rural dance for centuries, many melodies hitchhiked through eras and through space by linking up with art music and nationalism, as in eighteenth-century Scotland; with the broad category of popular music, as in late eighteenth- and early nineteenth-century England and the young United States; or with a specific body of popular music, as in the rich flourishing of fiddle tunes in blackface minstrelsy in mid-nineteenth-century America (and throughout the English-speaking world). This is quite a series of cultural edges, and each has been productive for fiddling.

Today, with the link between fiddling and dancing much weakened, we have returned to how fiddle tunes were sustained in late eighteenth-century Scotland—that is, to a combination of the sentimental attachments of nostalgic nationalism with aural intricacy and attractiveness reminiscent of that of complex art music. At the same time, precisely which bodies of pop or art or ethnic music are used by given groups of fiddlers to supplement their breakdowns and waltzes tend to color style, just as minstrelsy affected the rhythms of fiddling during the nineteenth century. Different nourishing "edges" mark different styles and can also be distinguished by location. Texas fiddlers play swing tunes, while quite a few non-Texas-contest-style fiddlers have a background in classical violin, and others play a bit of bluegrass. Old-time fiddlers in the inheritor category hear bluegrass regularly and may also play bluegrass tunes, while the old-time fiddlers who are urban revivalists often have the most varied fiddling experiences of all. Many revivalists are classical violinists, too. Harry Bolick, a fine revivalist fiddler who regularly attends Clifftop, took part in jam sessions in the 2014 festival that concentrated respectively on mainstream Upper South fiddle tunes (but more often than not in unusual versions), new tunes, Texas tunes from repertoires in place before contest fiddling took over that state, klezmer, Cape Breton style, Hawaiian, Cajun, minstrel, and calypso! I played guitar in some of these sessions and was struck by how brand-new tunes whose fiddler/composers hoped could join the old-time repertoire seemed designed to fit best with the most unusual old-time tunes.

Today's fiddlers have access to fiddling in all styles; their allegiance to one (or two, sometimes) is a matter combining ease of access, yearnings for community, and personal character. Given fiddlers may be generous in their talk about styles other than their own, or may instead be dismissive; these can be rough, complaint-filled edges. But, celebration, tolerance, or grumpiness aside, the results are good: lots of people with different takes on nostalgia in general and the desirable qualities of fiddling in particular all remain enthusiastic participants. Also, allegiances are muddied in the specific histories of a growing number of individual fiddlers. That is, sometimes the divisions between fiddle styles (and their performers) are clear and sometimes not. In the contest-style sphere, some Texas fiddlers compete now and again in Weiser, and rather more northwestern fiddlers come to Hallettsville, Texas, to compete in the separate "Gone to Texas" bracket in the state fiddle contest. Indeed, a steady stream of them move to Texas, and eventually, with the acquisition of a state driver's license, are allowed to enter the main brackets at that contest. On rare occasions, such an immigrant has become the Texas state champion.

Similarly, in the Upper South, a smallish overlap between the populations of inheritors who attend Galax and the urban revivalists who dominate Clifftop gets trickier when those categories mix in individuals' backgrounds and attitudes. Some revivalists start as such, then contact elderly relatives whom they learn belatedly are traditional musicians. Yet other revivalists are the children of revivalists and have grown up listening to their parents and friends jam; they are inheritors within that revivalist community. And many of the Galax area inheritors sample revivalist performances in person or through the Internet. Differences do remain; the simple fact that many musicians can only take a week off from work at a time has played a role in the fact that Clifftop and Galax have actually grown more different during the last decade. Some fiddlers I talk to regularly at Galax refer to Clifftop as being for "northern" old-time musicians, and some Clifftop attendees complain about tepid welcomes and low competition scores they've received in Galax. Nevertheless, Betty Vornbrock comes to both festivals to support her many students and competes in the senior bracket at both, and Jake Krack is widely respected at both, often winning top prizes in both festivals.

Fiddling and Music Pedagogy Today: Perpetuating Knauff's Wishes for the *Virginia Reels*

Knauff was arranging oral tradition fiddle tunes, probably from the playing of one or several black fiddlers, for affluent girls to play on the piano. The *Virginia Reels* were simply his most successful essay in publishing, a business experiment closely allied to his professional endeavors in the area of piano pedagogy. He had put together a set of tunes he hoped would find a place in the young industry of popular music, an anthology intended to be purchased for and played by well-bred future planters' wives. Perhaps this limits what we can understand about the tunes, though it would have been unrealistic to expect Knauff to have been inclined toward and skilled in ethnography. In fact, putting a good face on what initially could be considered an impediment to the study of the

Virginia Reels is not hard. It is one among countless symptoms of why fiddling has lasted so well, that is, that the materials and practices have regularly received outside sustenance—in that remarkable series of edge effects—while not losing track of fiddling's essential musical content and cradling ideology.

Knauff's use of fiddle tunes as raw material for learning art instruments was not new, as shown in early American instrumental publications like those of Blake and Riley. And such employment of fiddle tunes continues today, especially for violin students learning through the Suzuki or O'Connor methods. Many beginning students are exposed to a few fiddle tunes in the books and then pay an initial visit to the world of fiddling in some of their first public performances.

I will close with a visit to those violin students' first nervous occasions on stage, as contestants in the beginners' brackets in current fiddle contests. A few very young competitors come from situations that preserve the simplest inherited way of cultivating tradition: learning face-to-face in family or neighborhood environments full of fiddles, fiddle tunes, and attitudes encouraging learning fiddling as a straightforward, un- or little-questioned part of growing up. Many more of the kids on stage come from outside of any family or local tradition. They are violin students being taught through what is now the dominant school for teaching bowed stringed instruments to American kids, the Suzuki method, or through a recent entry into the violin instruction world, the O'Connor violin method. Mark O'Connor is a prominent figure in the northwestern substyle of Texas-based contest fiddling. He studied with Benny Thomasson and won numerous high prizes, most in the northwestern fiddle circuit. He presented fiddle camps at which he honed detailed instructional techniques and a specifically American repertoire centered on fiddle tunes, and he began publishing his violin method in 2009 (four of a projected ten books are available as of this writing). His carefully graded repertoire in these books includes many fiddle tunes—in the first book, just "Buffalo Gals" from the *Virginia Reels*, but also such standards as "Soldier's Joy," "Old Joe Clark," and "Bonaparte's Retreat," with "Boil 'em Cabbage Down" in seven versions.

We will visit these young violinists at my favorite fiddle contest, the Tennessee Valley Old Time Fiddlers Convention. This event takes place early in October in Athens, Alabama, on the campus of Athens State University. First thing Saturday morning can be a taxing time for the judges at this contest. It's chilly when the contest launches early that day, and the judges, themselves fine fiddlers, were up late Friday night playing. After all, although the fiddle contest has become the dominant public forum for traditional American instrumental music, competitors and officials at such events agree that jamming informally is more important than the formal competition. However, the main reason that judging early on Saturday can be an excruciating marathon is because that is when the youngest fiddlers compete.

In most American fiddle contests, competition is divided into brackets. As in many contests held in locations between the central fiddle areas of the southeastern United States and of Texas, the Tennessee Valley Old Time Fiddlers Convention offers both brackets defined by performance medium, as is customary in the Southeast (thus, categories for mandolin, harmonica, fiddle, "classic" old-time fiddler, old-time band, bluegrass band, etc.) and brackets for contest-style fiddlers sorted by age (here, two sets of youngsters aged below sixteen, the central category of junior fiddlers—aged sixteen to sixty—and seniors (see www.Athens.edu/fiddlers). Each competitor plays a bipartite dance tune or two, generally with guitar accompaniment.

Both broad aspects and some of what seem like esoteric aspects of the *Virginia Reels* are still with us in gatherings of fiddlers like this one. The atmosphere is wholesome, and family oriented, and explicitly nostalgic. It's an artificial village—one celebrating a somewhat mythical southern past—that lasts a weekend ... then is reconstituted elsewhere on many other weekends during the year. It's a southern world like that explored in the first, third, and last pamphlet of the *Virginia Reels*, rather than the tight local one of the second pamphlet. And the rosily represented southern past mixes the somewhat old (a few generations) with the much older (nearly two centuries), whereas the *Virginia Reels* drew on the present and recent generations in the people and culture of "Old Virginia." The difference between the fiddle world of the *Virginia Reels* and of the Tennessee Valley Old Time Fiddlers Convention can thus be characterized as one of geographic and temporal immediacy. But the haze of nostalgia goes a long way toward obscuring such distinctions!

One ingredient of fiddling that may seem inessential but is not is the minority report of tunes that imitate sounds from outside of music, or at least outside of conventional fiddling. I didn't hear Knauff's (and Ming's, and Hartford's) "Indian Whoop" at the 2015 Tennessee Valley Old

Time Fiddlers Convention. However, it seems that every railroad line in America passes through Athens, and train whistles regularly interrupt the competition. On one of the many, many times that this happened this particular year, senior fiddler Roy Crawford had just gotten seated on stage, but couldn't proceed due to the whistles and clattering. He played just a few bars of "Orange Blossom Special," and almost everyone in the audience laughed knowingly. Interestingly, the chuckles came from both people knowledgeable about fiddling and quite a few individuals who knew less about this music, who were present to support the university or simply to enjoy a wholesome activity in town. They might not know fiddling well, but they certainly knew that particular "trick" tune. In addition, three tunes played in the competition imitated non-fiddle sounds: "Cluck Old Hen" (glissandos and pizzicato), "Bumblebee in a Jug" (a rapidly twisting melody), and "Whistler's Waltz" (a section employing harmonics). But the most impressive unconventional effect was during the playing of the "Star-Spangled Banner" that opened Saturday evening's competition. Bluegrass fiddler Aubrey Haney (who had headlined two shows here shortly before the Friday night competition commenced) had dismantled his bow, and reattached it with the fiddle strings between the stick and the horsehair. The hair touched all four strings, so that Haney offered a sustained melody plus a legato combination of harmonizing and drones. Much of the fiddling was virtuosic during the competition, but sometimes even fancier outside of it! This border between what fiddlers could play in the competition and what was inappropriate but entertaining constituted one important "edge" of fiddling enlivening the weekend; the mixed motives and backgrounds of the beginning fiddlers illustrate another.

Many of the youngest children who play early on Saturday morning are violin students whose teachers bring them to compete because "it is good for them" rather than because they have yet become fiddlers—or for that matter, violinists—whose audiences should rightly encompass more than loving relatives. In recent years, versions of "Bile 'em Cabbage Down" from the O'Connor violin method have come to outnumber those of "Twinkle, Twinkle, Little Star" from Suzuki students. In any case, the judges must treat this as they do all of the official competition, and meticulously rank dozens of achingly tentative attempts at these tunes as well as other simple versions of, for example, Irish tunes.

O'Connor, through emphasizing American tunes and encouraging some improvisation, has moved to a middle point between violin and fiddle cultures, although Suzuki remains the method of choice nationwide. The joke can be on the Suzuki violin teachers in the long run. They expect that a few fiddle tunes can come in handy as waystations along their students' inexorable group march toward emulating Paganini. However, many of these violin students find the fiddle world convivial and musically satisfying, and they convert to fiddling. And the flexibility of motion introduced in the early stages of the Suzuki violin method (see Suzuki 2007 and Kendall 1999) can be as useful in fiddle technique. It is later in the learning process that fiddle and violin part in terms of not just repertoire and of oral versus written transmission, but also regarding preferred timbres, nuances of both attacks and of sustained bow strokes, and subtle proclivities in intonation. By my informal tally over the decades, this well-populated "edge" between art music and fiddling produces the majority of recent generations' legions of fine fiddlers.

✦ ✦ ✦

When George P. Knauff moved to rural Virginia, he stepped into a time and place of rapid change. Depleted soil and shrinking incomes were pushing many of Virginia's more enterprising citizens west. Knauff's daughter married in Virginia; his son pursued promising prospects in Arkansas. Knauff himself had come from a Germany with little to offer an ambitious young man to a place not as much better as he must have hoped. He worked hard and tried to fit in, with mixed results but with unflagging energy and creativity. We who are curious about the history of traditional music in the South can be grateful that his orderly mind and integrity caused him to be clear about when he was composing and when he was arranging music. And we are doubly lucky that his balance of following convention and inventive search for new products to sell led him to issuing the *Virginia Reels*. This collection previewed the future of southern fiddling in many ways, ranging from the nature of the tunes and of today's variety of regional styles to tune titles and, especially, the extraordinary durability of this music.

Why are many of the tunes published as part of the *Virginia Reels* still with us? More generally, why has fiddling lasted so well? Cultural materials and practices endure when they serve ongoing (or shifting but not waning) cultural and emotional needs, and offer aesthetic satisfaction as well. Fiddling provides opportunities for self-expression that is wholesome and available to both the academically talented and to individuals that don't do as well in formal schooling. It is now nationalistic in a noncontroversial way, and serves multivalent nostalgia well. The aesthetic materials are solid: the essences of tunes are sturdy and alluring, survive numerous changes of surface style and performance venue, and persist through constantly reforming alliances with popular culture. Every one of these salutary qualities was already present in antebellum southern fiddling as reflected in George P. Knauff's *Virginia Reels*.

Appendix

The Willig Edition of Knauff's *Virginia Reels*

P r. 75 C.   Nº I .

Published and Sold by George Willig Jr.

Property of the Publisher

KILLIE KRANKIE.

REPUBLICAN SPIRIT.

APPENDIX ✦ 177

NATCHEZ ON THE HILL

THE TWO SISTERS.

SPEED THE PLOUGH.

Allegro

SLIGHTED JENNY.

MISSISSIPPI SAWYER.

FORKED DEER.

WHISKEY BARREL.

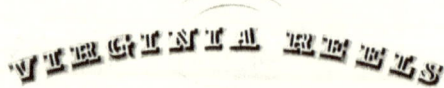

Selected and arranged for the

PIANO FORTE

BY

57 C^{ts} Nt.

Published by GEO. WILLIG, Ballimore.

N.º 1 Contains	N.º 2 Contains
Killie Krankie.	Old Virginia.
Republican Spirit.	Richmond Hill.
Natchez on the Hill.	Villalave.
The two Sisters.	Petersburg Ladies.
Speed the Plough.	The Hero.
Slighted Jenny.	Peter Francisco.
Mississippi Sawyer.	22.ᵈ of February.
Forked Deer.	Island.
Whiskey Barrel.	Richmond Blues.
Love in the Village.	

VILLALAVE.

PETERSBURG LADIES.

TWENTY SECOND OF FEBRUARY.

ISLAND.

THE RICHMOND BLUES.

VIRGINIA REELS
Selected & Arranged for the PIANO FORTE
by G. P. KNAUFF.

BALTIMORE,
Published by George Willig Jun.

Pr 50¢.

N.º 3 Contains

George Booker.
Oh where did you come from.
Colonel Crocket.
Rose on the Mountain.
Billy in the low grounds.
Lockwell.
Lady of the lake.
Scotts favorite.

GEORGE BOOKER.
A VIRGINIA REEL
ARRANGED BY GEORGE P. KNAUFF.
BALTIMORE Published and Sold by GEO. WILLIG Jr.

OH WHERE DID YOU COME FROM.

COLONEL CROCKET

A VIRGINIA REEL

BY GEO P KNAUFF

BALTIMORE Published and Sold by GEO WILLIG Jr

ROSE ON THE MOUNTAIN

Entered according to act of Congress in the year 1839 by G Willig Jr in the Clerks office of the District court of Maryland.

LADY OF THE LAKE
A VIRGINIA REEL

ARRANGED BY G. P. KNAUFF.

BALTIMORE, Published and Sold by GEO WILLIG Jr.

SCOTTS FAVORITE, A VIRGINIA REEL

Entered according to act of Congress in the year 1839 by G. Willig Jr. in Clerks office of the District court of Maryland.
1537

VIRGINIA REELS
Selected & Arranged
for the
PIANO FORTE
by
G. P. KNAUFF.

BALTIMORE,
Published by George Willig Jun.r

N.º 3 Contains

George Booker.
Oh where did you come from.
Colonel Crocket.
Rose on the Mountain.
Billy in the low grounds.
Lockwell.
Lady of the lake.
Scotts favorite.

N.º 4 Contains

Sich a gittin up stars, varied.
Gaston.
Indian Whoop.
Love from the heart.
Ohio River.
The Flying Indian.
Nancy Anderson.
Midnight Serenade, varied.

APPENDIX ✦ 197

INDIAN WHOOP

GEORGE P. KNAUFF

Published by G. WILLIG, Baltimore.

LOVE FROM THE HEART.

OHIO RIVER.

APPENDIX ✦ 199

THE FLYING INDIAN.

Published by G. WILLIG Baltimore.

NANCY ANDERSON.

Notes

PREFACE

1. I didn't understand the place of Farmville in the riverine transportation system well enough when writing the article and also was wrong to assign a definite date for the fourth, final pamphlet of the *Virginia Reels*.

CHAPTER ONE

1. Baltimore is the significant seaport nearest to Richmond, although more northern ports accepted the bulk of antebellum immigration. Knauff maintained business connections in Baltimore, and was rumored to have come from there (Shepard 1940, x).

2. The classical languages were also offered at the Buckingham Female Collegiate Institute, though the romance languages seem to have remained more popular. Only Spanish and French were mentioned in the few students' letters home that survive (see West 1990 and Shepard 1940).

3. This piece was printed many times in the 1840s through the 1860s, both in England and in the United States. The full citation of the edition that survives in the most copies in US libraries reads: "I'm Afloat! I'm Afloat! A Song. The Music Composed and Respectfully Dedicated to Hon. Mrs. Leander Starr by Henry Russell." Boston: Geo. P. Reed, 1861. But there were copies of earlier editions of the song circulating in America in the early 1940s; Ms. Malloy could not have graduated later than 1843, the year that the institute closed the first time. Did she perform the song as such? The letter describing her graduation only mentions her playing the piano. Among the many editions of the song were variation sets, including an undated one by British composer H[enry] W[illiam] Goodman, who was active beginning in the early 1840s ([184-?]). But whether Ms. Malloy sang and accompanied herself or played any sort of transcription or variation set, this must have been a heart-on-the-sleeve moment.

4. This was Kocswara's Op. 23, printed in London by J. Lee as early as ca. 1788 ("The Battle of Prague, Sonata in F Major for Pianoforte with [optional] accompaniments for Violin, Cello, and Drum"). There were many dozens of printings in the United States,

often of the whole piece, but often of excerpts (and often with Kocswara cited as composer, but often not, in which cases the piece was characterized as "A Favorite Sonata"). One such version was adorned with a fine picture of George Washington: "The Battle of Prague. Favorite Sonata for the Piano Forte." Boston: Graupner, n.d. This juxtaposition should not surprise, since one war could symbolize another, and both the Revolutionary War and the War of 1812 still resonated strongly.

5. Was this "Mr. Loving" married? An H. G. Loving was co-owner of the institute at one point, along with the Reverend Aristides H. Heustis (doubtless father of or otherwise related to the Sarah A. Heustis who was on the 1839 faculty as governess and English teacher). Reverend Heustis was on the "Committee of Examination" as listed in the 1839 catalogue, and at some point on the faculty (West 1990, 19).

6. These letters were written on September 4, 1843 (concluding with the appeal cited here), and June 9, 1844. They are part of the Spraggins family papers, 1809–1967, Virginia Historical Society Mss 1Sp7166–133–134.

CHAPTER TWO

1. My thanks to Robert Flippen of Farmville for showing me his copy of this piece of sheet music, and kindly allowing me to photograph it.

2. I urge the reader to keep in mind that the attachment of themes to these pamphlets is not something Knauff ever mentioned or implied in any way; the themes are mine, emerging from my own analysis of the four pamphlets.

3. Paul F. Wells (2010) describes how a one-time employee of Howe's, William Bradbury Ryan, seems to have drawn directly on Boston's fiddlers (including members of the city's large community of Irish immigrants) for *Ryan's Mammoth Collection* (1883). This important publication then reappeared nearly intact as Cole's *1000 Fiddle Tunes* (1940), known in one or another edition to many influential twentieth-century American fiddlers.

CHAPTER THREE

1. The title "Love from the Heart," oddly assigned to the usual tune for "Mississippi Sawyer" in the *Virginia Reels*, was certainly in the air. Knauff might have seen a piece of sheet music, a song in 6/8 time—no musical relation to anything he wrote or arranged—with the title "Love from the Heart, Arranged for the Spanish Guitar," written by one L. Meignen (1832).

2. There is a small chance that "Villalave" referred to a person, an acrobat and leader of a circus troupe in New York and environs in the early nineteenth century. The text of an ad in the *New York Evening Post* of June 27, 1814, reads: "New York Circus. Corner of Broadway and White Street. M. Villalave has the honor to inform the public that he intends opening the NEW YORK CIRCUS on Thursday evening, the 30th instant, to perform with his company the art of ROPE DANCING, TUMBLING in all its branches. M. Villalave further informs the public that the Circus has been thoroughly repaired;

elegant scenery provided, and every convenience made for the reception of those who will honor him with their presence." An ad from the *Hagerstown* (Maryland) *Torch Light* of August 6, 1822, shows that the troupe traveled, and mentioned that Mme. Villalave would play guitar, and that M. Villalave would dance a Spanish Fandango (blindfolded, not crushing any of a profusion of eggs set out as hazards) while she did so. My thanks to Steve Green for sending me copies of those ads!

My best guess is that if Knauff's "Villalave" represented this stage performer's last name, that title would have been enriched with some sort of modifier, as in the *Virginia Reels* titles "George Booker," "Colonel Crocket," or "Slighted Jenny." But a tune in the fourth pamphlet is just called "Gaston."

3. As a resident of the New Orleans metropolitan area, I am reminded of the social and administrative structures, the prestige, and the high costs to members characteristic of Mardi Gras krewes.

4. Another fine example of a tune title naming a blue-uniformed military unit also being used for dancing comes from Philadelphia. The same George E. Blake who issued *Blake's New and Complete Preceptor for the Violin. With a Favorite Selection of Airs, Marches &c. Fourth Edition* [1810s?], cited at length in the previous chapter, came out earlier with a *Collection of the most favorite Cottillions* [sp] *for the Piano Forte, Violin, or German Flute* [1804?]. A cotillion was a sequence of about a half dozen tunes to which were attached dance figures; tunes unsystematically alternating between ones in simple duple and compound duple meter. In this book, the "Fourth Sett" includes eight melodies with figures: "The Black Forest" (in 6/8), "Le Killerman" (6/8), "The Deceiver" (2/4), "McPherson's Blues" (2/4), "The Smile" (6/8), "The Blush" (2/4), "The Valentine" (6/8), and "Mrs. Edmonton's Reel" (2/4). A Lieutenant William McPherson of Philadelphia was on active duty sometime during 1777–1780 (Pennsylvania State Archives [n.d.], item 1). On another tack—not applicable here, but fun—Cockrell quotes an African American reporting that "In the 1840s, whites frequently employed the term 'blue' or 'blues' to describe a depressed mental state" (1997, 201).

In an earlier example, one predating the *Virginia Reels*, one David L. Downing, a member of Dodworth's Cornet Band, wrote a piece for that group's performance entitled "City Blues Quick Step" (New York: William Hall and Son, 1851). The title page of yet another similar piece reads: "The Blues Quick Step, as performed by the Boston Brass Band, Composed and Respectfully Dedicated to Cap't James Hunt, Officers and Members of the Light Infantry Company Winslow Blues, by John Holloway" (Boston: John Ashton & Co., 1836). There were also many infantry units with "Greys" in their titles, and plenty of marches celebrating those units. Indeed, the vast majority of quicksteps published in the antebellum United States were named for or dedicated to specific military units.

5. While "The Two Sisters" may have been actual women, Mark Twain mentions a pair of islands in the Mississippi named that, ones that presented navigational hazards (1917, 213).

6. In addition, Rossini wrote a popular opera based on Scott's poem in 1819: *La donna del lago*. Tunes presumably drawn from that opera made their way to the United

States, and at least one of these had a dance named for it. A commonplace book of dance figures on deposit in the Essex Institute, Early Music Collection (manuscript B-2) includes among its sixty-two sets of figures one entitled "Lady of the Lake," as well as several other titles of tunes that appear in the *Virginia Reels*, including "Money Musk," "Speed the Plough" (several different sets of figures bearing that title), and "Beau's [Beaux] of Oak Hill" (the usual title of Knauff's melody "The Two Sisters"), plus one set of figures simply called "Virginia Reel" (http://www.colonialdancing.org/Easmes/Index.htm). For an extended discussion of the title "Lady of the Lake" in the United States, see Finson 1994, 15.

7. Twain's 1874 description of this bifurcated city reaches back to Knauff's day: "Famous Natchez-under-the-hill has not changed notably in twenty years; in outward aspect—judging by the descriptions of the ancient procession of foreign tourists—it has not changed in sixty; for it is still small, straggling, and shabby. It had a desperate reputation, morally, in the old keelboating and early steamboating times—plenty of drinking, carousing, fisticuffing, and killing there, among the riffraff of the river, in those days. But Natchez-on-top-of-the-hill is attractive; has always been attractive" (1917, 324–25). I have been to Natchez recently. The under-the-hill portion features harmless tourist shops, and the casino is regulated, but "small, straggling, and shabby" still seems apt.

8. A medicinal spring just a little closer to Farmville would be in regular use later, from 1877 to 1945. Local historian Robert G. Flippen wrote a history of "Lithia Water" (1994), water bottled at a spring in Cumberland County (a short distance north of Farmville) and sold widely. "Lithia Water" was advertised as "Nature's Own Remedy, for the cure of Dyspepsia, Bright's Disease of the Kidneys, Gout, Billiousness, Nervous Prostration, Calculus or Stone in the Bladder, Indigestion, Rheumatism, Dropsy, Inflammation of the Kidneys, Albuminuria Gravel, Piles, Torpid Liver, Female Weakness, Malaria, etc." What could the "etc." have included? These claims, like those of many mineral waters employed in "hydrotherapeutics," that is, mineral waters treated as patent medicines, were certainly overblown, but, as turns out to have often been the case, were based on fact. This water contains bicarbonate of Lithium ($LiHCo_3$). Lithium unites readily with uric acid, so that "Lithia waters are notably useful in cases of gout and kidney stones, as they aid in the expulsion of urinary concretions" (1994, 4). Flippen further notes that "today, medical science uses lithium carbonate in the treatment of manic depression" (1994, 10).

9. I'm not sure how to interpret this part of the title: "composed by . . . Mrs. J.E.C. of L. Co., Va. Arranged by Geo. P. Knauff." Perhaps "Mrs. J.E.C." whistled a melody, and Knauff took it from there, but gave credit where credit was due to that lady (or curried favor with her). In any case, Mrs. J.E.C. would have enjoyed having her talent recognized, but it would not have been seemly for her to descend socially to the profession of composer.

CHAPTER FOUR

1. Knauff's main publisher in the 1850s was F. D. Benteen of Baltimore, who often put out pieces of sheet music (including Knauff's version of "Wait for the Wagon") in

partnership with New Orleans music publisher W. T. Mayo. That relationship between publishers probably placed this song, originating in New Orleans, into Knauff's hands.

2. The more common "Ducks on the Millpond" is not related.

3. I have also seen two manuscript versions of "The Marquis of Huntley's Farewell" that I am confident were owned by Americans during the early to mid-nineteenth century. One version was recorded in an undated music commonplace book on deposit in the New York Public Library. It was given by a Scot to an American, and was meant to introduce the recipient to Scottish fiddling. The title page reads: "Selected by John Martin for Alex[ande]r Anderson, first wood-engraver in America, a worthy man—a gentleman of the old school and a most ingenious mechanic, withal possessing great musical talents." The version seems quite similar to the second one in figure 20, though the ink has run too much to allow diagnosing all details; a very few melodic turns are clearly different from those in that publication. The other manuscript version I have seen—I believe a later one—was in the extensive music notebook of William Sidney Mount, who was primarily a painter but also a fiddler. Except for details of bowing, his version matches the other manuscript version, as well as I can tell.

4. See Goertzen 2010 and 2012 for a more thorough treatment of Texas contest fiddling's variation technique.

CHAPTER FIVE

1. The figures for "Sich a Gittin Up Stairs" were the same attached repeatedly to this tune: All eight forward and back. First lady, opposite gentleman cross over. Chassez to the right and left and cross to places. Balancez and turn your partners.

2. This is the same piece; other songs with similar titles but dissimilar music also appeared at this time. The words constituting the title also are included in the lyrics of the twentieth-century string band tune "Cotton-Eyed Joe," there is no melodic relationship. This particular "Whar Did You Cum From," published by Firth and Hall, has one of the many illustrations from the 1833 edition of the *Ethiopian Quadrilles* as its one large illustration, the one on the lower left of the *Ethiopian Quadrilles* title page of a banjoist facing a corpulent, well-dressed black citizen.

3. If we leave out the names of river-associated cities, there are still 6 out of 35 titles in the *Virginia Reels* that have something to do with bodies of water. In a casual comparison, I looked again at my census of tune titles that were played in the fiddle, banjo, and old-time band categories in the festivals at Galax and/or at Clifftop in the summer of 2014. By my count, there were 19 such titles, out of a total of 261. Though this is a modest sample, it comes as no surprise that the watercourses were more important in the titles of members of the *Virginia Reels*, 17 percent versus 7 percent. The waterway-referencing titles from the pair of 2014 contests were "Big Scioto" (a river), "Billy in the Low Ground," "Boatin' Up Sandy," "Boatman," "Bonaparte Crossing the Rhine," "Breakin' Up Ice in the Alleghenies," "Cripple Creek," "Duck River," "Falls of Richmond," "Head of the Creek," "Horseshoe Bend," "Keep the Ark a Movin'," "Mississippi Echoes," "Mississippi Sawyer," "Polka River Blues," "Sail Away Ladies," "Salt River," "Snake River Reel," and "Three Forks

of the Cumberland." There was significant overlap between the 1839 and 2014 arrays of water-referencing titles, including "Billy in the Low Ground," "Boatman" ("Ohio River" to Knauff), and "Mississippi Sawyer."

4. According to Howard Sacks, the Snowden Papers contain no mention of "Boatman's Dance" (e-mail, August 2, 2015).

5. If this name is respaced "A nager jony jva," perhaps we are seeing a deliberately obscured "A nigger Johnny Juba."

6. The animals in the pictures deserve at least passing mention, since the accuracy of their depiction may suggest a parallel assessment of how carefully the banjo was drawn: why don't we see a fifth string? The two cows in one frame are nicely sketched, and the large catfish (catfish can exceed a hundred pounds easily) seem carefully portrayed. The alligators seem caricatures, however, and the snake surrounding pictures at the top could be one among many. To my eye, the pattern most closely resembles that of the red cornsnake (*Pantherophis guttatus*), but the visible cheek of the snake suggests it is meant to be a pit viper, possibly an eastern cottonmouth (*Agkistrodon piscivorus piscivorus*), or, most likely, a copperhead (*Agkistrodon contortrix*). My conclusion: since some animals' pictures are more carefully rendered than are others, we can't be sure how seriously to take the fact that the banjo seems not to have a fifth string.

7. The lovely title page, depicting an elaborately clad "noble" Indian, can be found a number of places on the web, including as of this writing https://jscholarship.library.jhu.edu/bitstream/handle/1774.2/6385/165.017.000.webimage.JPEG?sequence=5.

8. See Odell's *Indian Bottles and Brands* for literally hundreds of such listings (1997).

9. Cockrell reproduced a picture from the cover of a minstrel songster entitled *De Kickapoo Whoop, or Pee Wee Warbler, by Santa Claus,* from 1840: the Indian as comic figure was already entering the picture (1994, 48).

10. F. J. Hübner published a pair of tunes together in 1842: "The Flying Indian, or Daniel Boone, and the New Basket Cotillion." "The Flying Indian, or Daniel Boone," a 6/8 tune, bears no resemblance to Knauff's "Flying Indian." Perhaps the flying Indian was a recurring minstrel show or medicine show character who danced to several tunes.

EPILOGUE

1. Scott's own use of the title "Lady of the Lake" references several eras. Ellen, Scott's heroine, lives by a lake, which does play a part in the story repeatedly. One of her suitors in the story was James V of Scotland (1512–1542; reigned 1513–1542). This real-life monarch looked back in time for his pleasures—he loved jousting and the associated pageantry—and legend places the original Lady of the Lake a millennium earlier: she was said to have given the sword Excalibur to King Arthur.

References

Anderson, Mike. "The Big Four—Diving Ducks." http://www.ducks.org/conservation/waterfowl-biology/the-big-four-diving-ducks. Accessed September 22, 2015. Part of a website complex named *Ducks Unlimited: Banding Together for Waterfowl*.

Anderson, Paul Christopher. 2002. *Blood Image: Turner Ashby in the Civil War and the Southern Mind*. Baton Rouge: Louisiana State University Press.

Anderson, William F., Jr., Abstractor and Indexer. 1999. *1850 Census of Prince Edward County, Virginia, Including Slave Schedules*. Farmville, VA: Southside Historical Press.

Barlow, Milton. 1802. Untitled manuscript music commonplace book, on deposit at the New York Public Library.

Bayard, Samuel P. 1950. "Prolegomena to a Study of the Principal Melodic Families of British-American Folk Song." *Journal of American Folklore* 63: 1–44.

———. 1982. *Dance to the Fiddle, March to the Fife: Instrumental Folk Tunes in Pennsylvania*. Urbana: University of Illinois Press.

Bennett, William J., and Michael Hague. 1998. *The Children's Book of America*. New York: Simon & Schuster.

Biographical and Historical Memoirs of Eastern Arkansas, Comprising a Condensed History of the State, a Number of Biographies of Distinguished Citizens of the Same, a Brief Descriptive history of Each of the Counties Named Herein, and Numerous Biographical Sketches of the Prominent Citizens of Such Counties. 1890. Chicago: Goodspeed Publishing Company.

Blake, George E. [1810s?]. *Blake's New and Complete Preceptor for the Violin, with a Favorite Selection of Airs, Marches, &c*. Philadelphia: G. E. Blake.

———. [1804?]. *Collection of the Most Favorite Cottillions* [sp] *for the Piano Forte, Violin or German Flute, Arranged in Setts, with Figures to Each*. Philadelphia: G. E. Blake.

Bogen-Garrett, Petie, Robert Flippen, Carla Huskey, Mary Prevo, and Robin Sedgwick. 1999. *Farmville, Virginia: Recalling Our Past. An Illustrated History Based on the Exhibit Celebrating Farmville's Bicentennial, 1798–1998 at the Longwood Center for the Visual Arts at Longwood College*. Farmville, VA: Longwood Center for the Visual Arts.

Bradshaw, Herbert Clarence. n.d. *History of Prince Edward County, Virginia: From its Earliest Settlements Through its Establishment in 1754 to its Bicentennial Year.*

———. 1935. "Prince Edward County." In *Today and Yesterday in the Heart of Virginia: A Reprint of the Edition of the Farmville Herald, March 29, 1935.* Farmville, VA: Farmville Herald. 137–62.

Bremner, Robert. 1757. *Scots Reels.* London: Robert Bremner.

Buckley, J[ames] and Sons. 1855. *Buckley's Violin Tunes; A Collection of Beautiful Marches, Waltzes, Quadrilles, Polkas, Schottisches, Operatic Melodies, Hornpipes, Reels, Jigs, etc. etc. and Many Other Melodies Never Before Published, Including Buckley's Celebrated Imitations of the Farm-Yard, and Briggs Power of Music. The Whole Selected, Arranged and Composed for the Violin by J. Buckley and & Sons of Buckley's Serenaders.* New York: Firth, Pond, & Co.

Burke, John S. J., and his students. 1998. *Farmville Architecture: An Illustrated Tour Through 200 Years; A Bicentennial Project by Longwood College Art Students under the Direction of Professor John S. J. Burke. Published in Conjunction with the Exhibit "Farmville 1798–1998: An Illustrated History."* Farmville, VA: Longwood Center for the Visual Arts.

Caruthers, William Alexander. 1845. *The Knights of the Horse-Shoe; A Traditional Tale of the Cocked Hat Gentry in the Old Dominion.* Wetumpka, LA: C. Young.

Cazden, Norman, Herbert Haufrecht, and Norman Studer. 1982. *Folk Songs of the Catskills.* Albany: State University of New York Press.

Cockrell, Dale. 1997. *Demons of Disorder: Early Blackface Minstrels and Their World.* Cambridge: Cambridge University Press.

Coen, Joel and Ethan. 2000. *O Brother, Where Art Thou?* Universal/Touchstone Pictures.

Coes, George H. 1876. *Coes Album of Jigs and Reels. Something New for Professional and Amateur Violinists, Leaders of Orchestras, Quadrille Bands, and Clog, Reel, and Jig Dancers; Consisting of a Grand Collection of Entirely New and Original Clog-Hornpipes, Reels, Jigs, Scotch Reels, Irish Reels and Jigs, Waltzes, Walk-Arounds, Etc., for the Violin.* New York: T. B. Harms & Co.

Cole, M. M. 1940. *1000 Fiddle Tunes.* Chicago: M. M. Cole.

Collinson, Francis. 1966. *The Traditional and National Music of Scotland.* Nashville, TN: Vanderbilt University Press.

Cox, John Harrington. 2013. *Folk-Songs of the South, Collected Under the Auspices of the West Virginia Folk-Lore Society* (1925). Morgantown: West Virginia Humanities Council.

Creighton, Helen. 1932. *Songs and Ballads of Nova Scotia.* Toronto and Vancouver: J. M. Dent and Sons. Dover Rpt. 1966.

Cutchins, John A. 1934. *A Famous Command: The Richmond Light Infantry Blues.* Richmond: Garrett & Massie, Publishers.

Dadman, J. W.; lyrics by John G. Whittier; arranged and with piano accompaniment by Albert S. Allen. 1862. "Song of the Negro Boatman." Boston: Russell and Patee.

Davis, Curtis Carroll. 1949. "The Virginia 'Knights' and Their Golden Horseshoes: Dr. William A. Caruthers and an American Tradition." *Modern Language Quarterly* 10, no. 4: 490–50.

De Kickapoo Whoop, or Pee Wee Songster. 1840. New York: Elton and Harrison.
Downing, Davis L. 1851. "City Blues Quick Step." New York: William Hall and Son.
Dulles, Foster Rhea. 1965. *A History of Recreation.* 2nd edition. New York: Appleton-Century-Crofts.
Ely, Melvin Patrick. 2004. *Israel on the Appomattox: A Southern Experiment in Black Freedom from the 1790s through the Civil War.* New York: Knopf.
Epstein, Dena. 1983. *Sinful Tunes and Spirituals: Black Folk Music to the Civil War.* Urbana: University of Illinois Press.
Farmville Herald. 1935. *Today and Yesterday in the Heart of Virginia: A Reprint of the Edition of the Farmville Herald, March 29, 1935.* Farmville, VA: Farmville Herald.
Farnham, Christie Anne. 1994. *The Education of the Southern Belle: Higher Education and Student Socialization in the Antebellum South.* New York: New York University Press.
Ferrie, Joseph P. 1999. *Yankeys Now: Immigrants in the Antebellum United States, 1840–1860.* New York: Oxford University Press.
Finson, Jon W. 1994. *The Voices That Are Gone: Themes in 19th-Century Popular Song.* New York: Oxford University Press.
Fischer, David Hackett, and James C. Kelly. 2000. *Bound Away: Virginia and the Westward Movement.* Charlottesville: University of Virginia Press.
Flippen, Robert G. 1994. *"Drink and Be Healed": A History of Farmville Lithia Water.* Farmville, VA: R. G. Flippen.
Fuld, James J. 1971. *The Book of World-Famous Music.* New York: Crown Publishers.
Galbraith, Art. 1980. *Dixie Blossoms.* Rounder Records LP 0133.
Gelbart, Matthew. 2011. *The Invention of "Folk Music" and "Art Music": Emerging Categories from Ossian to Wagner.* Cambridge: Cambridge University Press.
Goertzen, Chris. 1982. "Philander Seward's 'Musical Deposit' and the History of American Instrumental Folk Music." *Ethnomusicology* 26(1): 1–10.
———. 1995. "Mrs. Joe Person's *Popular Airs*: Early Blackface Minstrel Tunes in Oral Tradition." *Ethnomusicology* 35(1): 31–53.
———. 2008. *Southern Fiddlers and Fiddle Contests.* Jackson: University Press of Mississippi.
———. 2010. "Texas Contest Fiddling: Moving the Focus or Contrast and Change to Inner Variations." In *Crossing Over: Fiddle and Dance Studies from around the North Atlantic 3*, edited by Ian Russell and Anna Kearney Guigné, 239–49. The Elphinstone Institute, University of Aberdeen, Scotland, in association with the Department of Folklore, MMaP and the School of Music, Memorial University of Newfoundland.
———. 2012. "Texas Contest Fiddling: What Modern Variation Technique Tells Us." In *Routes and Roots: Fiddle and Dance Studies from around the North Atlantic 4*, edited by Ian Russell and Chris Goertzen, 98–111. The Elphinstone Institute, University of Aberdeen, Scotland.
———. 2014. "Southern American Fiddling through the Mid-Nineteenth Century: Three Snapshots." In *Theory and Method in Historical Ethnomusicology*, edited by Jonathan McCollum and David G. Hebert, 257–77. New York: Lexington Books.

Goertzen, Chris, and Alan Jabbour. 1987. "George P. Knauff's *Virginia Reels* and Fiddling in the Antebellum South." *American Music* 5(2): 121–44.

Goodman, H[enry] W[illiam]. [184-?]. "Variations on I'm Afloat, I'm Afloat." n.p.

Gow, Nathaniel. 1809. *Fifth Collection of Strathspey Reels.*

Gow, Niel. [1784]. *A Collection of Strathspey Reels.* Dunkeld: author.

———. [1788]. *A Second Collection of Strathspey Reels.* London and Edinburgh: Dussek.

———. 1801. *First Book of Niel Gow's Reels. 2nd Edition, with Considerable Additions and Valuable Alterations. Dedicated to her Grace the Dutchess of Athole.* Edinburgh: Gow and Shepherd.

Gow, Niel, and Sons. [1799]. *Part First of the Complete Repository of Original Scots Slow Strathspeys and Dances.* Edinburgh: Rob't Purdue.

———. [1802]. *Part Second of the Complete Repository of Original Scots Slow Strathspeys and Dances.* Edinburgh: Gow and Shepherd.

———. [1820?]. *Part Fourth of the Complete Repository of Original Scots Slow Strathspeys and Dances.* Edinburgh: Robertson's, Music Seller to his Majesty.

Green, Steve. 1990. "Title, Text and Tune Interrelationships in American Fiddle Music." Unpublished typescript.

Hamm, Charles. 1983. *Yesterdays: Popular Song in America.* New York: Norton.

Hart, Scott. 1935. "Town of Farmville." In *Today and Yesterday in the Heart of Virginia: A Reprint of the Edition of the Farmville Herald, March 29, 1935.* Farmville, VA: Farmville Herald. 163–66.

Hewitt, John H[ill]. 1837. *The Crow Quadrilles, Consisting of* "Sich a Gittin Up Stairs and Long Time Ago," "Sittin' on a Rail," "Clare de Kitchen," Zip Coon," "Jim Brown," "Gumbo Chaff," and "My Long Tail Blue," *Arranged with Figures for the Piano Forte.* Philadelphia: John F. Nunns.

Holloway, John. 1836. "The Blues Quick Step." Boston: John Ashton & Co.

Howe, Elias, Jr., compiler. 1843. *Instrumental Musician.* 6 vols. Boston: Howe.

———. 1844. *The Musician's Companion.* 1st edition; 4 vols. Boston: Howe.

———. 1850 or so; not the first edition. *First Part of the Musician's Companion: Containing 18 Setts of Cotillions Arranged with Figures, and a Large Number of Popular Marches, Quick-Steps, Waltzes, Hornpipes, Contra Dances, Songs, &c. &c., Several of Which are in Three Parts—First Second, and Bass for the Flute, Violin, Clarionett, Bass-Viol, &c.* ... Boston: Ditson. The *Second Part* ... advertises 36 *Setts of Cotillions.* The *Third Part* ... has 40 sets, and is still published by Howe.

———. 1851. *Howe's School for the Violin: Containing New and Complete Instructions for the Violin, with a Large Collection of Favorite Marches, Quick-Steps, Waltzes, Hornpipes, Contra Dances, Songs, and Six Setts of Cotillions, Arranged with Figures. Containing Over 150 Pieces of Music.* Boston: Ditson.

———. 1863. *Improved Edition of the Musician's Omnibus: Containing the Whole Camp Duty, Calls and Signals used in the Army and Navy, Forty Setts of Quadrilles (Including Waltz Polka and Schottische with Calls*[)]; *and an Immense Collection of Polkas, Schottisches, Waltzes, Marches, Quicksteps, Hornpipes, Contra and Fancy Dances, Songs, &c. Containing Over 700 Pieces of Music.* Boston: Howe.

———. 1869. *Quadruple Musician's Omnibus, Containing 3300 Pieces* . . . Boston: Howe.
Hübner, F. J. 1842. "The Flying Indian, or Daniel Boone, and the New Basket Cotillion, Arranged for the Piano Forte." Philadelphia: Willig.
Hursh, David, and Chris Goertzen. 2009. *Good Medicine and Good Music: A Biography of Mrs. Joe Person, Patent Remedy Entrepreneur and Musician, Including the Complete Text of Her 1903 Autobiography.* Jefferson, NC: McFarland & Company.
Hurt, Adam. 2009. *Perspective.* Ubiquitone CD and MP3.
Irving, Washington. 1842. *Sketchbook of Geoffrey Crayon, Gent.* (1819–20). Philadelphia: Lea and Blanchard.
Jabbour, Alan. *Fiddle Tunes of the Old Frontier: The Henry Reed Collection.* Recordings from 1966 to 1967, and transcriptions of these. http://www.loc.gov/collections/henry-reed-fiddle-tunes/.
"Jim Brown. A Favorite Comic Song." 1835. New York: J. L. Hewitt.
Johnson, David. 1972. *Music and Society in Lowland Scotland in the Eighteenth Century.* London: Oxford University Press.
———. 1984. *Scottish Fiddle Music in the Eighteenth Century.* Edinburgh: John Donald Publishers Ltd.
Kendall, John. 1999. *About Suzuki: The Suzuki Violin Method and American Education.* Los Angeles: Alfred Music Publishing.
Knaebel, S[imon]. 1843. "The Indians, Consisting of King Phillips Quick Step, Song of the Red Man, On-ka-hye Waltz, Osceola Quick Step, Keocuck Quick Step, Black Hawk Quick Step, Nahmeokee Waltz." Boston: Henry Prentiss.
Knauff, George P. 1839. *Virginia Reels.* 4 Vols. Baltimore: Willig. (His complete known works are listed in chapter 1 of the present volume.)
Koczwara, Franticek. 1788. "The Battle of Prague, Sonata in F Major with [optional] accompaniments for Violin, Cello, and Drum." Boston: Graupner.
Kuntz, Andrew. 2012. *The Fiddler's Companion, 1996–2009.* http://www.ibiblio.org/fiddlers/RI_RJ.htm.
Levin, Simon A., ed. 2012. *Princeton Guide to Ecology* (electronic resource). Princeton, NJ: Princeton University Press.
Lincecum, Dr. Gideon. 1874–75. *Personal Reminiscences of an Octogenarian.* Published serially in *The American Sportsman;* quotes used from the episode printed in the November 21, 1874, issue, 10–13.
Lott, Eric. 1993. *Love and Theft: Blackface Minstrelsy and the American Working Class.* New York: Oxford University Press.
Luebke, Frederick C. 1990. "Patterns of German Settlement in the United States and Brazil, 1830–1930." In his *Germans in the New World: Essays in the History of Immigration.* Urbana: University of Illinois Press. 93–109.
Marshall, Howard Wight. 2012. *Play Me Something Quick and Devilish: Old-Time Fiddlers in Missouri.* Columbia: University of Missouri Press.
Marshall, William. [1822]. *Marshall's Scottish Airs.* Edinburgh: Marshall.
Martin, Joseph. 1835. *A New and Comprehensive Gazetteer of Virginia and the District of Columbia, by Joseph Martin. To which is Added a History of Virginia from its First*

Settlement to the Year 1754; with an Abstract of the Principal Events from that Period to the Independence of Virginia. Charlottesville, VA: J. Martin.

Martin, Julien Dwight. 1935. "First Citizens." In *Today and Yesterday in the Heart of Virginia: A Reprint of the Edition of the Farmville Herald, March 29, 1935.* Farmville, VA: Farmville Herald. 135–36.

Martin, Susan F. 2011. *A Nation of Immigrants.* New York: Cambridge University Press.

McArthur, Arthur. [181-?]. Untitled manuscript music commonplace on deposit at the New York Public Library.

McCollum, Jonathan, and David G. Hebert, eds. 2014. *Theory and Method in Historical Ethnomusicology.* New York: Lexington Books.

McFarlane, Thomas. [181-?]. Untitled manuscript music commonplace on deposit at the New York Public Library.

McHardy, Stuart. 2004. *MacPherson's Rant and Other Tales of the Scottish Fiddle.* Edinburgh: Birlinn Ltd.

Meignan, L. 1832. "Love from the Heart, Arranged for the [voice and] Spanish Guitar." Philadelphia: Willig.

Miller, Rodney, and Randy Miller. 2007. *New England Chestnuts: New England Contra Music, Great Meadows Collection* (2001). Great Meadows Music. 2 CD set.

Ming, Hoyt, and His Pep Steppers. 1928. "Indian War Whoop." VICTOR 21294.

Morris, Terry. 2000. *Pure Texas Fiddling.* Proprietary recording; original copyright date 1987.

Mount, William Sidney. [1850s–1860s]. Manuscript music collection, on deposit at the Long Island Museum of American Art, History and Carriages.

Noles, Randy. 2002. *Orange Blossom Boys: The Untold Story of Ervin T. Rouse, Chubby Wise and the World's Most Famous Fiddle Tune.* Anaheim Hills, CA: Centerstream Publishing.

Nolcini, [Charles]. 1839. "The Grasshopper's Waltz, Composed by Nolcini. The Subject of this Composition Was Derived from the Motion of the Insects Whose Name It Bears." Boston: Prentiss.

Oakey, Henry. [184-?]. *The Ethiopian Quadrilles.* London: Publisher unknown.

O'Connor, Mark. 2009. *O'Connor Violin Method, Book One.* New York: O'Connor Musik International.

Odell, John "Digger." 1997. *Indian Bottles and Brands.* Lebanon, OH: Digger Odell Publications.

"The Old Maid, or When I Was a Girl of Eighteen Years Old." [n.d.]. Philadelphia: Willig.

Onyqjva, A. Najerj [probably a fictional name]. 1843. *Ethiopian Quadrilles.* New York: Firth and Hall, 1843.

———. 1848. *Ethiopian Quadrilles.* 12th edition. New York, Wm Hall and Son.

Pappas, Nikos. 2012. "'Eck' Robertson's 'Sallie Goodin' and the Cultivation of the American Old-time Division Style." Paper read at the annual meeting of the Society for Ethnomusicology.

Riley, Edward. Volumes from 1814, 1817, 1820, and 1827. *Riley's Flute Melodies.* 4 Vols. New York: Riley.

Robertson, Eck. 1991. "Lost Indian." *Famous Cowboy Fiddler, Talking Machine and Radio Artist. 1963 Recordings by John Cohen, Mike Seeger, and Tracy Schwarz*. County 202, Side A, cut 3.

Rouse, Ervin T. 1938; not immediately published, but recorded 1939. 78 rpm disc by "The Rouse Brothers" (Ervin and Gordon): "My Family Circle" ("Will the Circle be Unbroken" with flip side "Orange Blossom Special." Bluebird 8218.

Russell, Henry. Lyrics by Eliza Cook. 1861. "I'm Afloat, I'm Afloat." Boston: Geo. P. Reed.

Sacks, Howard, and Judith Rose Sacks. 1993. *Way Up North in Dixie: A Black Family's Claim to the Confederate Anthem*. Washington, DC: Smithsonian Institution Press.

Scott, Martin C. 1999. "Interpreting 'Metamora': Nationalism, Theater, and Jacksonian Indian Policy." *Journal of the Early Republic* 2: 73–101.

Scott, Sir Walter. 1820. *Ivanhoe; A Romance*. Edinburgh: Archibald Constable and Co.

———. 2008 (1810). *The Lady of the Lake*. Champaign, IL: Book Jungle.

Seward, Philander. [1807 or soon thereafter]. "Philander Seward's 'Musical Deposit.'" Manuscript music commonplace book largely for unspecified treble instrument (probably violin) compiled in Fishkill, New York, on deposit in the Music Library of the University of Illinois.

Shepard, William. 1935. "Buckingham County." In *Today and Yesterday in the Heart of Virginia: A Reprint of the Edition of the Farmville Herald, March 29, 1935*. Farmville, VA: Farmville Herald. 199–205.

———. 1940. "Buckingham Female Collegiate Institute." *The William and Mary Quarterly*. Second Series 20, no. 2 (April): 167–93. Concluded in 20, no. 3 (July): 345–66.

Slate Mountain Ramblers. 2006. *A Pile of Fiddle Tunes*. Proprietary recording.

Smith, Christopher J. 2013. *The Creolization of American Culture: William Sidney Mount and the Roots of Blackface Minstrelsy*. Urbana: University of Illinois Press.

Smith, William B. 1838. "The Persimmon Tree and the Beer Dance." *Farmer's Register: A Monthly Publication* (1833–1843), (April 1): 6, 1.

Sonneck, Oscar, and William Treat Upton. 1945. *A Bibliography of Early American Music*. Washington, DC: Library of Congress. Rpt. Da Capo, 1964.

Stone, John Augustus. 1941. *Metamora, or the Last of the Wampanoags: An Indian Tragedy in Five Acts* (1829). Princeton, NJ: Princeton University Press, 1941.

Suzuki, Shinichi. 2007 (1978). Suzuki Violin School, Vol. 1. Violin Part. Rev. edition. Summy-Birchard, Inc.

Taylor, James B. 1833. "Sambo's 'Dress to the Bred'rin. As Sung with the most Enormous Applause, Mr. Davis' Musical Parties, on Friday Evenings, Broadway House, by Mr. Brower, the Celebrated Comic Singer. Respectfully Dedicated to all his Friends. Arranged with Symphonies and Accompaniments by James B. Taylor." New York: Thos. Birch.

Thomasson, Benny. 2005. *Legendary Texas Fiddler: Recordings from 1966–1969*. County Records CO-CD-2737.

Thomasson, Lewis. 2009. "Indian Whoop." *Old Texas Tunes Played the Old Way*. Old Blue Records CD 501, cut 13.

Thompson, Samuel. 1773. *Thompson's Compleat Collection of 200 Favorite Country Dances, Vol. 3*. London: Samuel, Ann and Peter Thompson.

Totten, Christine M. 1983. *Roots in the Rhineland: America's German Heritage in Three Hundred Years of Immigration 1683–1983*. New York: German Information Center.

Twain, Mark. 1917. *Life on the Mississippi* (1874). New York: P. F. Collier & Son Company.

Waldon, Carolynn Knauff. [n.d.]. "Timeline of George P. Knauff's Life." Unpublished typescript.

Watkins, Samuel. 1815. Unpublished manuscript music commonplace book, on deposit at the University of Colorado Library.

Wells, Paul F. 1978. "New England Traditional Fiddling." Liner Notes to *New England Traditional Fiddling: An Anthology of Recordings 1926–1975*. One LP. Los Angeles: John Edwards Memorial Foundation JEMF-105.

———. 2003. "Fiddling as an Avenue of Black-White Musical Interchange." *Black Music Research Review* 23, nos. 1–2: 135–47.

———. 2010. "Elias Howe, William Bradbury Ryan, and Irish Music in Nineteenth-Century Boston." *Journal of the Society for American Music* 4, no. 4: 401–20.

West, Sue Roberson. 1990. *Buckingham Female Collegiate Institute: First Chartered College for Women in Virginia, 1837–1843; 1848–1863*. Charlotte, NC: Delmar Printing.

"Whar Did You Cum From? Knock a Nigger Down. The Celebrated Banjo Song, as Sung with Great Applause at the Broadway Circus by Mr. J.W. Sweeny." n.d. New York: Firth and Hall.

Winans, Robert B. 1976. "The Folk, the Stage, and the Five-String Banjo in the Nineteenth Century." *Journal of American Folklore* 89, no. 354: 407–37.

———. 1984. "Early Minstrel Show Music, 1843–1852." In Glenn Loney, ed., *Musical Theater in America: Papers and Proceedings of the Conference on Musical Theater in America*. Westport, CT: Greenwood Press. 71–97.

———. 1990. Black Instrumental Music Traditions in the Ex-Slave Narratives." *Black Music Research Journal* 10, no. 1: 43–53.

Winner, Septimus. 1861. *Winner's Perfect Guide for the Fife*. New York: Ditson.

Winner, Septimus (under the pseudonym of Alice Hawthorne), lyrics, and Richard Milburn, music. 1855. "Listen to the Mockingbird, Sentimental Ethiopian Ballad." Philadelphia: Winner & Shuster.

Wolfe, Richard J. 1964. *Secular Music in America: 1801–1825*. 3 vols. New York: New York Public Library.

Index

Page numbers in **bold** indicate that the melodies cited appear in music notation on those pages.

"22nd of February, The," 20, 76–77, 90
"93rd Psalm," 42

"Afton Grove Waltz" (Knauff) 17, 67, 69
Aitken, John, 88
"Alabama Gals," 92
"Allegheny Waltz" (Knauff), 17, 67, 85
Allen, Albert S., 112
"All the Blue Bonnets Over the Border," **88**
Amelia Springs (recreational establishment), 66–67, 69, 155
"Amelia Springs Cottillion" (Knauff), 17, 66 67, 69
Andal, Tyler, 132–34
Anderson, Alex[ande]r, 205ch4n3
Anderson, Paul Christopher, 156
"Angeline the Baker"/"Angelina Baker" (Foster), 76–77
Appalachian String Band Music Festival. See Clifftop
Appomattox River, 6–7; navigable, 7, 60
"Arkansas Traveller," 75
"Awake My Love and Come With Me" (Knauff), 17, 69

Backus, Zeke, 146–47
Bahin, Louis Joseph, 56, 65
Baillie, Pate, 103
Baltimore, Maryland, 4, 8, 11, 16, 201ch1n1

Banjo, 67, 94, 99, 107, 113–15, 117–25, 150
Barlow, Milton, 45
"Battle of Prague" (Kocswara), 14, 201n4
Bayard, Samuel P., 104–5
"Beaus of Albany, The," **106**
"Beautiful Waltz by Beethoven" (arr. Knauff), 18, 67
"Belle of America, The" (Knauff), 19, 66
Benteen, F. D. (publisher), 15, 17–22, 160, 204n1
Bigelow, Ms. O. A., 12
"Bile Them Cabbage Down," 75–76, 170, 172
"Billy in the Low Grounds," xi, 21, 55, 70–71, 75, 90, 104–5, **106**, 128, 167, **192**
"Billy in the Lowlands," 105
"Billy in the Woods," 22
Binder's volumes of sheet music, 13, 22
"Black-Eyed Susie," 75–76
Blackface minstrelsy, 14, 20, 32, 67, 69, 73, 99, 111–43, 146
"Black Hawk Quick Step" (Knaebel), 136
Blackwell, Dr., 26–27
Blake, George E., 35, 37, 39, 82, 89, 170, 203n4
Blake's New and Complete Preceptor for the Violin. With a Favorite Selection of Airs, Marches &c. Fourth Edition, 35–39
Bland, James, 59, 77

215

Blood Image: Turner Ashby in the Civil War and the Southern Mind, 157
"Blue-Bonneted Scotts," 17, 66, 85, **88**, 105
Bluegrass music, 168, 171–72
"Blues" and "Greys" as parts of names of military units, 204n4
"Boatman Dance" (Emmett), 55, 65, 73, 75, 111–12, 126, 128–29, **131**, **132–33**, 134, 141–42
Bolick, Harry, xiii, 168
"Bonaparte Crossing the Rhine," 76
"Bonaparte's Quick Step," 18, 68
"Bonaparte's Retreat," 170
Bond, Eddie, 121, 124–26, 150
Bondurant, Ann S. C. *See* Knauff, Ann S. C. Bondurant
Bondurant, James, 6, 10
Booker, George, 65–67, 139
Booker, "Marse Tom," 67
Bowman, Richard, 150–51
"Braes of Auchtertyre, The," 105–6, **106**
"Braes of Baluquhither, The," 97
"Bragg's Retreat," 154
"Breaking Up Christmas," 76
Bryan, James, 141, 143
Buckingham County, 24, 59, 61–62
Buckingham Female Collegiate Institute, 2, 10–17, 23–27, 29, 59, 61, 67, 69, 79, 118, 201n2
"Buckingham Grand March" (Préot), 2, 16
Buckingham High School for Young Ladies, 12
Buckley, James, 135, 140
Buckley's Serenaders, 140
"Buffalo Gals," 55, 73, 92, 134, 137, 141, 151, 167, 170
"Bumblebee in a Jug," 172
Burke, Mary S., 17, 67

C., Mrs. J. E., 17
"Camp Chase," 75
"Camptown Hornpipe," 115
"Camptown Races" (Foster), 115
Caruthers, William, 156

Census records: related to immigration, 4; value of, 6
Chaff, Gumbo, 161
Child ballads, 104
"Chinky Pin Hunting," 75
Chivalry, 155–57
Christy's Minstrels, 146
Civil War, 4, 26, 63, 83, 112, 154–57
"Clare de Kitchen," 115–16
Clifftop (Appalachian String Band Music Festival), 74–76, 99, 120–21, 123, 135, 168–69, 205ch5n3
"Cluck Old Hen," 172
Cockrell, Dale, 115, 206n9
Coes, George H., 146, 161
"College Hornpipe," 37
"Colonel Crocket," 21–22, 65, 76, 90, **191**
"Colonel Hubard's March and Quick Step" (Knauff), 17, 68
"Come and Kiss Me" (Coes?), 155
Contest style fiddling. *See* Texas contest style fiddling
Contradancing, 47, 49
Cook, Eliza, 14
Cotillion, 203n4
"Cotton-Eyed Joe," 76, 205ch5n2
Crawford, Roy, 172
Crocket, David, 65, 79
Cross-tuning. *See* Scordatura
Crow Quadrilles, The (arr. Hewitt), 115–16
"Cumberland Gap," 75

Dadman, J. W., 112
"Darling Child," 120, **124–25**, 126, 150
"Devil's Dream," 40
Dinwiddie County, 24
"Dixie's Land" (Emmett?), 128
Donley, Tim, 109
Donna del Lago, La (Rossini), 203n6
Dow, Daniel, 48, 50
Dr. Morse's Indian Root Pills, 137
Drone, 119–21
Dubois and Stodart (piano manufacturers), 8

"Ducks on a Pond," 54, 92–94, **95**, 157, 165
"Duke of Gordon's Rant, 70–71
"Duke of Holstein's March," 43
"Durang's Hornpipe," 37, 76

Edge effect, as applied to fiddling, 145, 166–69
Educational Amusement Company (EACO) Theater, 25–27
"Eighth of January," 76
Ely, Melvin, 116–17, 127
Emmett, Daniel Decatur, 128
Epstein, Dena, 113
Ethiopian music, 19, 22. *See also* Blackface minstrelsy
Ethiopian Quadrilles (arr. Onyqjva[!]), 129–30, 205ch5n2
Ethiopian Quadrilles, The (Oakey), 129
Evans, Frank, 121–23, 125

Fairchild family (of teachers), 12
Farmville, Virginia, xi, 2, 54, 60, 69, 201n1; history of, 6–7, 47, 116, 126, 204n8; Knauff's home in, 5, 25–26, 118, 127
Farmville Herald, 25–26
Farmville Music and Fancy Store, 7–9
Farnham, Christine, 12–13, 16
Female seminaries and the education of young women, 5–6, 8, 11–16, 20, 24
Fiddle contests, xii, 50, 158, 160, 170–72
Fiddle music arriving in the colonies and young US, 33–34, 82
Fiddle tunes: preferred keys, 89–91; ranges, 91, 96; rhythms, 97, 99; structures, 44–46
Fiddle tune titles, 55–77, 154–58; titles' meanings as reflected in musical sound, 138–43
Fiddling: African-American/black, 83, 113–19, 165; for dancing, 79–80, 89–92; formation of repertoires, 92–93; imitating animals, 135; motives for, 79–84; pedagogy, 169–72; regional styles, 160–62; spread in US, 127–28; variation, 103, 126, 134, 163
"Fire in the Mountain," 75
"Fisher's Hornpipe," 37, 40, 115
"Fisher's Waltz," 18, 67
Fishkill, New York, 38, 42
Flippen, Robert G., 204n8
"Floating Scow of Old Virginia" (Christy), 59
"Flowers of Edinburgh," 29, 32–33, 37, 40, 43–44, 70–71, 73, 94, 107, **108**, 139, 141
"Fly Around, My Pretty Little Miss," 76
"Flying Indian, The," 21, 76, 90, 137, **200**
"Flying Indian, The" (Hübner), 206n10
Folk music overlapping with pop music, 33–54
"Forkedair Jig," 146–47
"Forked Deer," 20, 32–33, 55, 58, 75, 90, 104, 139, 141, 144–67, **148–49**, **152–53**, 158–59, 161, 163, 165, 167, **180**
Fort Monroe, 62
Fort Wool, 62, 69
"Fox Hunt, The," 22
Francisco, Peter, 61, 74
Friedrich, Caspar David, 66
Fryeburg Academy, 48

Galax (Old Fiddlers Convention), 74–76, 99, 109, 125, 135, 169, 205ch5n2
Galbraith, Art, 107–8
"Gary Owen," 40
"Gaston," 21, 64, 75–76, 90, **196**
Gatherings (Knauff), 18, 67–68, 84
"Geary Owen." *See* "Gary Owen"
"Geminiani's Minuet," 42
"General Green's March," 40
"General Harrison's March," 84
"General Pierce's Presidential Inauguration March and Quick Step"(Knauff), 18, 68
Germany, 4; contributions to American culture, 5; immigration from, 4–5

"George Booker," 21, 54, 65, 70–71, 76, 78, 90, 94, 96, **98**, 99, **100–101**, 104, 139, 141, 163, 165, 167, **190**
"Getting Up Stairs." See "Sich a Gittin Up Stairs"
Glen Lyn, Virginia, 54
"Golden Slippers" (Bland), 76–77
Goochland County, 65
Gow, Nathaniel, 105–6, 108–9
Gow, Neil, 48, 106, 108
"Grand Trial between Nance Holmes and Suse Bryant, on Long Wharf, Boston," 115
"Grapevine," 115
"Grasshopper's Waltz, The" (Nolcini), 140
Green, Steve, xiii, 56–57
"Grey Eagle," 75
Grim, Brian, 52–53
"Guest March in Ye Battle of Orleans," 43
"Gumbo Chaff," 115–16

Hague, Michael, 79
"Hail Columbia" (Phile, lyrics Hopkinson), 40, 84
Halifax County, 23
Hallettsville, Texas, 50, 101–2
Hamm, Charles, 34
Haney, Aubrey, 172
"Hangman's Reel," 76
Hart, Scott, 25
Hartford, John, 142, 171
Hawkins, John P., 6
"Hell Broke Loose in Georgia," 75
"Hero, The," 20, 23, 61, 73–74, 76, 90, 92, 165, **186**
Heterophony, 119–21
Heustis, Miss Sarah A., 15, 202n5
Hewitt, John Hill, 115–16
"Hillbilly" recordings, 47
Hollow Rock String Band, 93
Home construction in antebellum Virginia, 6
Hopkins, Bubba, 164
Hopkins, Carl, 151, 164

Howe, Elias, Jr., 23, 46–47, 49, 52, 85, 106, 108, 140, 146, 161, 202ch2n3; *Quadruple Musician's Omnibus*, 140; *School for the Fife*, 43, 72–73, 88
"How Imperfect Is Expression," 43
Hubard, Col. Edmund W., 17, 68
Hurt, Adam, 107

"I'm Afloat, I'm Afloat" (Russell), 14, 201n3
Independence, Virginia, 52
Indian Removal Act, 136–37
Indians: in Farmville, 6; and homeopathic medicine, 137; and minstrelsy, 137; variety of pop culture images, 135–36
"Indians, Consisting of King Phillips Quick Step, Song of the Red Man, On-ka-hye Waltz, Osceola Quick Step, Keocuck Quick Step, Black Hawk Quick Step, Nahmeokee Waltz The" (Knaebel), 136–37
"Indian Squaw," 76
"Indian Whoop," 21, 58, 75–76, 90, 111, 135, 137–38, 141–42, **143**, 171, **197**
"Irene Waltz" (Knauff), 18, 67
"Irish Washerwoman," 37, 40
Irving, Washington, 136
"Island," 20, 62–63, 69, 75, 90, 128, **187**
Ivanhoe (Scott), 155, 159

Jabbour, Alan, xii–xiii, 54, 93–94
"Jack of Diamonds," 37
"Jackson's Cotillion" (Knauff), 18, 66
James River, 60
"James River Reel," 22
Janissary Music, 68
Jarrell, Tommy, 162
"Jenny Get Your Hoecake Done," 115
Jeter, Ms. M. J., 8
"Jim Brown," 115–16
"Jim Brown, A Favorite Comic Song" (Hewitt), 114–15
"Joe Sweeney's Jig" (Sweeney?), **147**
"John Brown's Dream," 76
John Brown's Raid, 64

"John Henry," 76
"Johnny in the Nether Mains," 40, 70–71, 105
Jordan, Dr. James, 25–26
"Julie Ann Johnson," 76
"Juniper Hall," 22

"Keocuck Quick Step" (Knaebel), 136
"Killie Krankie," 20, 33, 40, 43, 47, 58, 65, 70–71, 73, 75, 90, 104, **176**
Killie Krankie, battle of, 65
King Philip, 136
"King Phillips Quick Step" (Knaebel), 136
Knabe, William, 11, 37
Knaebel, Simon, 136
Knauff, Ann S. C. Bondurant, 5; death, 10; home, 6; marriage, 5–6
Knauff, George P., xi, xii, 37; advertising techniques, 8; arranging vs. composing, 18–19, 66; birth, 4; business activities, 7–11, 29; business reverses, 10–11, 23–24; death, 24; drinking, 25; education, 5; employment, 2; immigrant, 5; marriage, 5; parents of, 6; piano construction and sales, 10, 25; piano teacher, 5–6, 8, 11–15; sheet music publishing, 17, 24; social station, 28; store owner, 7, 30; training, 5
Knauff, Johann Conrad, 4
Knauff, Johann Friedrich, 4
Knauff, John Wellington, 10, 24
Knauff, S. A. Irene, 10, 17, 24, 66, 69
Knights of the Golden Horseshoe, 156
Koczwara, Franticek, 14, 201n4
Krack, Jake, 99–102, 104, 167

"Ladies Quick Step" (Knauff), 18, 68
"Ladies Waltz," 18
"Lady of the Lake, The," 21, 54, 65, 76–78, 90, 92–94, **95**, 128, 156, 157, **193**, 204n6
Lady of the Lake, The (Scott), 155, 157–59; as a widely used title, 204n6, 206n1
Lafayette, Marie-Joseph Paul Yves Roch Gilbert du Motier, Marquis de, 61

Ländler, 28
"Largo's Fairy Dance," 108, **109**, 110
"Leather Britches," 23, 37, 58
Life on the Mississippi (Twain), 127
Lincecum, Gideon, 83, 113
Lincecum, Jerry, 83
"Listen to the Mockingbird" (Milburn, lyrics Winner), 135, 142
Lithia Water, 205n8
"Lockwell," 21, 65, 75–76, 90, 104, **192**
"Long Time Ago," 115–16
Longwood University, 2, 12, 16, 25–26
"Lord McDonald's Reel," 23, 37
"Lost Girl," 76
"Lost Indian," 75–76, 141, **143**
"Louisa Waltz" (Knauff), 18, 68–69
"Love from the Heart," 21, 55, 76, 90, 108, **109**, **198–99**
"Love from the Heart" (Meignen), 202ch3n1
"Love and Pastry" (Knauff), 18, 69
"Love in the Village," 20, 76, 90, 141, **181**
Loving, Robert G., 15, 202n5
"Lucy Long," 115, 134

"Madam Parisott's Hornpipe," 37, 70–71
Mahr, Mr., 27
"Major Minor," 39
Malloy, Mary Katherine, 15–16
Malloy, Sarah Knight, 14, 201n3
Marburg, Germany, 4
"Marquis of Huntley's Farewell," 70–71, 94, 96–97, **98**, 99, 104, 139, 141, 205ch4n3
"Mason's Apron," 37
Mayo, W. T., 18–19
McArthur, Arthur, 48–49, 51
McFarlane, Thomas, 45
McPherson, Lieutenant William, 203n4
"McPherson's Blues," 203n4
Medicinal Springs, 66–67
"Metamora Waltz, The" (Knauff), 18, 68
"Midnight Serenade," 21, 73, 76, 90, 92, 137, 141, 151, **201**

Miller, Rodney, 53
Miller and Beachem, (publishers), 16, 18
Ming, Hoyt, 142, 171
Minstrelsy. *See* Blackface minstrelsy
"Minuet in Samson" (Handel?) 42
"Miss Brown's Reel," 23, 73
"Miss Clark's Hornpipe," 22
"Miss Farquharson's Reel," 71, 120, **122**, 126
Mississippi fiddling, 41–43, 154
"Mississippi Sawyer," 20, 33, 55, 58, 74–75, 90, 104, 108, **109**, 110, 128, 165, **198–99**
"Mississippi Sawyer" (title attached to unrelated tune by Knauff), **179**
Missouri fiddling, 50
"Mohegan Waltz" (Knauff), 18, 67–68
"Money Musk," 23, 28, 33, 37, 40, 43–44, 47–49, **50, 51, 52, 53,** 54, 65, 70–71, 73, 104, 134, 163, **176**, 204n6
Montague, W. L., 17
Morris, Terry, 163
Morris Museum of Art, 56
Mount, William Sidney, 108–9, 127, 140, 205ch4n3
"Mount Elba Waltz" (Knauff), 18, 67, 69
"Mrs. Brown's Reel," 92
"Mrs. McLeod's Reel," 21
Music commonplace books, 38–43, 160
"My Dog Dies" (Backus?), **147**
"My Long Tail Blue," 115–16
"My Love She's But a Lassie Yet," 63, 71, 73, 119–20, **122**, 123, 126, 139, 141

"Nahmeokee Waltz" (Knaebel), 136
"Nancy Anderson," 21, 64, 76, 90, **200**
"Napolean's Grand March," 18, 68
Nash, E. P., 11
Natchez, Mississippi, 128, 204n7
"Natchez on the Hill," 20, 33, 35, 55, 58, 65, 73, 75, 90, 107, 139, 141, **177**
"Natchez under the Hill," 55, 65; painting, 56, 65, 141
"National" Fiddle Contest in Weiser, Idaho, 162–64
New Ballard's Branch Bogtrotters, 150

New England Fiddling, 40, 43, 47, 49, 52
"New Haven Green," 40, 43, 105, **106**
New Store, Virginia, 61, 69
Nolcini, Charles, 140
North Atlantic Fiddle Convention, 29
Nostalgia, 59, 77, 135, 145, 155–60, 164–66, 168–74

"O Dear Mother, What Shall I Do?," 85, **88**, 105
Oakey, Henry, 129
O'Connor, Mark, 170
O'Connor violin method, 170–73
"Ohio River," 21, 55, 65, 73–75, 90, 111, 128, **132**, 134, 141–42, **199**
"Oh Where Did You Come From," 21, 76, 90, **190**
"Old Dominion Reel," 22
"Oldenplace" (Knauff), 19, 24, 66, 69
Oldenplace Female Seminary, 18, 24, 66, 68, 69
Old Fiddlers Convention. *See* Galax
"Old Joe Clark," 170
"Old Maid, or When I Was a Girl of Eighteen Years Old, The," 31
"Old Molly Hare," 108, **109**, 110, 140
"Old Virginia," 20, 32–33, 40, 43, 58–59, 67, 70–71, 73, 75, 77, 89–90, 94, 96, 104, 107, **108**, 139, 141, **183**
"Old Zip Coon," 33, 35, 73, 107, 115–16
Old-Time music of the Upper South, 32, 50, 52, 74–76, 89, 92, 99, 111–43, 150, 164–65, 168–69
"On-ka-hye Waltz" (Knaebel), 136, 170–72
Onygqjva, A. Nagerj, 129–30
Oral tradition, xii–xiii, 32, 78–110, 128
"Orange Blossom Special" (Rouse), 135, 142, 172
"Osceola Quick Step" (Knaebel), 136
Ozarks fiddling, 47, 49–50, 107–8

Padilla, Juan, 16
Panic of 1837, 16
Pappas, Nikos, 103

"Persimmon Dance," 117, 119
"Perthshire Hunt," 70–71
"Peter Francisco," 20, 55, 58, 61, 69, 73, 76–77, 90, **186**
Petersburg, Virginia, 7, 60, 69, 128
Petersburg Greys, 63
"Petersburg Ladies," 20, 59–60, 69, 75, 90, **185**
"Philadelphia March," 40
"Philander Seward's Musical Deposit," 37–40, 42
Poe, Samuel, 117
"Polecat Blues," 75, 77
"Polonaise," 18
Popular music, as defined by Charles Hamm, 34
"Port Gordon," 43
Powhatan Confederacy, 6
Powhatan County, 65
Préot, Arnaud, 2, 15–16
"President's March" (Phile), 40, 43
"Priest in His Boots," 37
Prince Edward County: demography of, 8, 126–27; economy of, 9–10, 24; history of, 6–7, 9–10, 65, 116–17
Prince George County Poor House, 61
Prouty, Scott, 120–21, 123, 125

Quadrilles, 134
"Quick Step by G. P. Knauff," 18

"Ragtime Annie," 75–77
"Railroad Overture," 134
Reed, Henry, 54, 93–94, 105
Reed Island Rounders, 93
"Republican Spirit," 20, 76, 90, **176**
Revolutionary War, 61–63, 65, 72
Richmond, Ham, and Petersham Open Spaces Act of 1902, 60
Richmond, Virginia, 4–5, 7–8, 59, 69, 128
"Richmond Blues," 20, 55, 60, 62–64, 69, 71, 73, 75, 77, 90, **122**, 123, 125–26, 139, 141, 143, 151, 155, **188**
Richmond Enquirer, 6–8, 10–11, 23, 60

"Richmond Hill," 60, 69–71, 75, 90, **183**
"Richmond Ladies, The," 19, 66
Richmond Light Infantry Blues, 63–64, 125
"Rickett's Hornpipe," 37, 40
"Ridge, The," 21
Riley, Edward, 36–37, 72, 82, 89, 170
Riley's Flute Melodies, 36–37, 72–73
"Roberta," 19, 66
Robertson, Alexander Camel "Eck," 103, 141–43, 146, 163
Robertson, Dr. William Henry, 25
"Rose on the Mountain," 21, 58, 75, 90, **191**
"Rose Tree," 35, 37, 73
Rosenkranz, Ernest, 16, 25
"Roslin Castle," 43, 91
Russell, Henry, 14
Ryan, William Bradbury, 203ch2n3

Sacks, Howard and Judith Rose, 128, 206n4
"Sail Away Ladies," 76
"Sailor's Hornpipe," 37
"Sally Goodin," 103, 146
"Sambo's 'Dress to the Bredrin" (Brower), 113–14
Saponi Indians, 6
Scordatura, 121, 142
Scots-Irish as colonists and fiddlers, 6, 80–82, 118–19
Scottish fiddling, 37, 43, 48–49, 70–72, 80–82, 89, 92, 96–97, 103, 119, 126
Scott, General Charles, 65, 69
Scott, Martin, 137
Scott, Sir Walter, 65, 77, 155–59, 203n6, 206n1
"Scotts Favorite," 21, 65, 69–71, 76, 90, 156, **193**
Seay, Dr. Junius, 67
Seward, Philander, 38–40, 42–43, 49, 51, 106, 160
Seward, William, 40
"Shelvin' Rock," 75
Shepard, William, 14, 16, 25–26

Shields, Miss Virginia A. B., 18, 67
"Sich a Gittin Up Stairs," 21, 55, 57, 73, 75–76, 90, 92, 96, 103, 115–16, 135, 137–38, 141–42, 151, **195–96**, 205ch5n1
"Sir Archibald Grant of Moniemusk's Reel," 70
"Sittin' on a Rail," 115–16
Slate Mountain Ramblers, 150–51
"Slighted Jenny," 20, 58, 64, 76, 90, **179**
Smith, Christopher, 127
Smith, William B., 117
"Smith's Reel," 58
Snowden family, 128
"Soldier's Joy," 37, 75, 77, 170
"Song of the Negro Boatmen" (poem by Whittier, and song Dadman/Allen), 112
"Song of the Red Man" (Knaebel) 136
"Sourwood Mountain," 75
"Speed the Plough," 20, 23, 28, 33, 35, 37, 43–47, **45**, 55 , 58, 71, 73, 75, 77, 90, 104, 139, 141, **178**, 204n6
Spottswood, Alexander, 156
Spraggins, Captain Thomas, 23
"Star-Spangled Banner" (Smith, lyrics Key), 172
State Theatre. *See* Educational Amusement Company (EACO) Theater
Stone, John Augustus, 136
Stoneking, Fred, 102
"St. Patrick's Day in the Morning," 37
Strathspey, 97–99
Sustainability, 145
Suzuki violin method, 170–73
Sweeney, Joel, 117–18, 141, 146–47
"Sweet Sally," 19, 66
"Sweet Sixteen," 120

Taylor, Bobby, 99, 148–50
Tennessee Valley Old Time Fiddlers Convention, 132, 134, 167, 170–72
"Tennessee Wagoner," 92
"Tennessee Waltz" (King, lyrics Stewart), 58

Texas contest style fiddling, 32, 49, 51–52, 91–92, 102–3, 140–41, 150–51, 162–65, 168–72
Thomasson, Benny, 162–64, 171
Thomasson, Lewis, 141, 143
"Three Farmers Went a Hunting," 18, 69, 84–85, **86–87**
"Three Huntsmen," 85
"Three Men Went a Hunting," 85
Tobacco trade, 7, 60
Todd, Marsha Bowman, 150
"Toothache or the Quilting, The" (Knauff), 18, 69, 118
"Too Young to Marry," 120, **123**
"Trumpet March" ("partly" composed by Knauff) 19, 68
Tucker, Stephen B., 154
Tune families, 104–5
"Turkish March" (Knauff), 19, 24, 68
Tuscarora Rice, 137
Twain, Mark, 127–28, 155–56, 203n5, 204n7
"Twenty-Second of February," 20, 58, 62, 64, **187**
"Twinkle, Twinkle, Little Star"(lyrics Taylor), 172
"Two Sisters, The," 20, 58, 64, 76, 90, 128, **178**, 203n5, 204n6

Urban revivalist fiddlers, 164–65, 168–69

Variation as an ingredient of performing fiddle tunes, 32, 39–40, 150–51; in piano sheet music, 137–38
"Villalave," 20, 60–61, 76, 90, 141, **184**, 202ch3n1
Villalave, M., 202ch3n1
Violin vs. fiddle, 36, 42, 48, 80–83, 103–4, 161–62, 164, 168, 172–73
"Virginia," 19, 66
"Virginia Breakdown,"115
"Virginia Cotillion" (Knauff), 19, 66
Virginia Cotillions (Knauff), 19, 24, 66
Virginia Historical Society, 8

Virginia Minstrels, 113, 128, 130
"Virginia Quick March" (Knauff), 19, 68
"Virginia Reel," 21, 23
Virginia Reels, xi; comparisons of individual members with other versions of them, 45; dating, 111; genre of dance, 22–23, 27–28; as pop music of its time, 31–54; publishing of, 3, 17, 19–23, 28; tune titles from in or near Knauff's Virginia, 31
Vornbrock, Betty, 93, 95, 169

"Wagoner," 92, 165
"Wait for the Wagon," 19, 22, 24, 68–69, 84, 204n1
Waldon, Carolynn Knauff, xii, 4, 10
"Walkin' in the Parlor," 76
War of 1812, 62, 72
Washington, George, 61–62, 77
"Washington's Grand March," 83
"Washington's March," 42
"Washington's Ode," 40
Watkins, Samuel W., and his commonplace book, 41–43, 49, 51, 160
Weisgerber, Alita Stoneking, 50, 99–104, 163
Weisgerber, Tom, 50–53, 102, 163
Wells, Paul F., xii–xiii
West, Sue Roberson, 14–15
Westmoreland, Wes, III, 150–52, 163–64
West Virginia fiddling, 99–101, 120–21, 148–50
"Whar Did You Cum From?," 118, 205ch5n2
"Whiskey Barrel," 20, 37, 70–71, 75, 90, **180**
"Whistle O'er the Lave O't," 40
"Whistler's Waltz," 172
"White Cockade," 35, 37
Whittier, John Greenleaf, 112
Wilbur, Mrs. Mary C., 15
Wilbur, Reverend Perlee B., 15
Willig, George, Jr., 17–22, 31, 97, 160
Willig, George, Sr., 37

Winans, Robert, 119, 128, 134
Wine, Melvin, 99
Winner, Seth, 120, 126
Winston, Judge, 61
Wright's Indian Vegetable Pills, 137

"Yew Piney Mountain," 76

"Zion's Hill," 42